Whitman · An Official W

INSIDE THE
RARE COIN
MARKETPLACE

SECRETS TO BEING
A SMART BUYER

Q. DAVID BOWERS

FOREWORD BY KENNETH BRESSETT

INSIDE THE RARE COIN MARKETPLACE
SECRETS TO BEING A SMART BUYER

© 2017 Whitman Publishing, LLC
1974 Chandalar Drive · Suite D · Pelham, AL 35124
ISBN: 0794845258
Printed in China

You can join the American Numismatic Association (ANA), the nation's largest hobby group for coin collectors. The ANA Young Numismatists program is for collectors 5 to 17 years old. Collect coins, learn about numismatic collectibles, participate in auctions, and make friends with the YN program. Learn more at www.Whitman.com/ANA.

OCG™ COLLECTING GUIDE   WCG™   WHITMAN®

CONTENTS

FOREWORD

You might not associate baseball legend Yogi Berra with numismatics. I really don't know if he ever participated in the hobby, but he did offer a piece of advice that all serious collectors should heed. "You've got to be very careful if you don't know where you're going, because you might not get there."

Sadly, all too many people begin their entry into coin collecting without any set plan or purpose. A compelling magazine advertisement, an offer on eBay, or something seen on television may trigger the impulse purchase of a "rare Morgan dollar," or a modern United States $5 gold piece "directly from our vault" (complete with a picture of uniformed officials guarding this treasure). Such ads are ubiquitous and invariably the source of over-priced or over-graded items that only tend to sour any taste for continuing to collect. Even worse, those who do continue to buy ultimately discover their investment losses only at some future time when they decide to sell their prized collection.

People are drawn to collecting coins or similar items for a number of reasons and objectives. Some do so strictly as an investment in the hope of making a profit. Others find it a relaxing hobby and take their rewards from exploring a new field of interest and exposure to art, history, and diverse cultures. A well-informed and dedicated collector can have a lifetime of enjoyment with a hobby that is both entertaining and profitable. The key to success is first learning the fundamentals, caveats, and sage advice that can make it all possible. Then find your own passion and pursue it.

This book, by Q. David Bowers, one of the world's leading authorities on the subject, presents a factual, down-to-earth approach to becoming a successful coin collector, investor, or student, through his entertaining stories and accounts of personal experiences over the course of more than six decades. It tells a story of how to succeed by carefully avoiding pitfalls and making the right moves at the right time in order to get the most out of the hobby.

Scientists say people who have hobbies are not just filling time; they may also be extending their life span, increasing their energy level, and living a more rewarding life.

There is no question about this in my mind. Those who actively participate in some absorbing activity nearly all live longer, happier lives. And it is never too late for anyone to begin enjoying hobby benefits. Clarence S. Bement, who formed one of the finest collections in American numismatics, did not start until he was past 70 years of age.

This is not to suggest that simply adding a hobby to your daily routine will insure you live to a ripe old age. Genetics and a healthy lifestyle play a major role in how long we live. We all have the potential to live longer if we do the right things and get a bit lucky. Adding an enjoyable hobby to the mix has been shown to minimize stress and increase creativity. Coin collecting can also foster a sense of achievement and mental development.

So, will having a hobby help you make it to your 100th birthday? Almost certainly it will help, but other factors are also important. Numismatic stalwart Ursula Kampmann expressed it best when she wrote "Numismatics is the ideal fountain of youth. It keeps our brain active and constantly provides us with new challenges. It offers us the chance of social contacts with other numismatists from all over the world. Numismatists are lucky people because they know what they can dedicate their life to. It comes as no surprise, then, that many numismatists die only at a great age."

One of the most important pieces of advice that Bowers espouses in this book is building a library of information on your chosen topic. Whatever your reason may be for acquiring coins, learning as much as possible about them before investing in them is essential for lasting success. *Saber es poder*, and fortunately there are many avenues to numismatic knowledge leading to power in terms of success. Books are essential, and they are plentiful and readily available through purchase, or even on loan to all members of the American Numismatic Association. The Internet is another rich source for instant information on nearly any conceivable numismatic question.

Yes, there are secrets to becoming a smart coin buyer, and to enjoying a great coin collection—secrets in the sense that few beginners take time to explore and study them. But within the following chapters you will learn and benefit from them all. As a bonus you will be treated to stories and legends that have made the study of numismatics so enjoyable for millions of people perhaps since the first coins fell from their dies.

Kenneth Bressett

PUBLISHER'S PREFACE

"Buy the book before the coin" is good, solid, often-quoted advice for newcomers to the hobby. Frankly, it's guidance for a *lifetime* of collecting; we should all heed it well beyond the beginner stage. And fortunately for today's hobbyist, this advice has never been easier to follow—thanks in large part to one incredibly productive author, Q. David Bowers.

Numismatic publishing has experienced a renaissance, an exciting boom, over the past two decades. In chapter 6 of this book, Dave Bowers relates how he joined forces with Whitman Publishing in 2003 as the company's numismatic director and as research editor of the *Guide Book of United States Coins* (the hobby's best-selling annual price guide and reference, known everywhere as the "Red Book"). Dave had been a Red Book contributor for years before that, and had helped with other Whitman projects. But it was in 2003 that the relationship was formalized—if a handshake agreement can be called "formal"—and things really took off.

I joined Whitman Publishing the following year as the company's publisher. I've been a coin collector since around age seven, and like any good collector I owned a number of well-read Bowers books, most of them bought directly from his company (at the time, Bowers and Merena Galleries) when I was in my teens and early twenties. Among the Bowers books that traveled with me from my little hometown of Phoenix, New York, to college in Rochester, and later to Atlanta, were his 1987 monograph *The Strange Career of Dr. Wilkins: A Numismatic Inquiry*; the 1988 reprint of his 1964 classic, *Coins and Collectors*; and the 13th (!) edition of *High Profits From Rare Coin Investment* (1991).

By the time I started working for Whitman Publishing, Dave Bowers was a world-famous numismatist with decades of experience. Several hugely successful companies had his good name attached to them as a founder and officer. He had served as president of the Professional Numismatists Guild and the American Numismatic Association. His track record as a dealer and auctioneer included selling many of the finest, most valuable, and most historic coin collections ever assembled. For years I (and many other fans) had read his *Coin World* column, "The Joys of Collecting." He'd been named as one of only six living people in a roster of eighteen "Numismatists of the Century" in a 1999 poll conducted by *COINage* magazine. And as a book author he had a long shelf of numismatic titles to his credit, many of them best sellers.

I remember my first conversation with "Mr. Bowers" (as I addressed him a couple times), made by phone because he was in New Hampshire and I was in Georgia. Finally he said, "If you keep calling me 'Mr. Bowers,' I'll have to call you 'Mr. Tucker.'" From that point on it was "Dave," as he prefers it, as relaxed and down-to-earth as can be.

Since then I've emailed Dave or spoken with him on the phone nearly every day, and we've published dozens of new "QDB" books ranging from 96-page monographs to 900-page encyclopedias (plus several editions of the 1,504-page *Mega Red*, for which he serves as research editor). Here are some thoughts on the development of the book you're now reading, *Inside the Rare Coin Market*, and where it stands in his oeuvre.

In 1999 Whitman Publishing had released an excellent new book by Kenneth Bressett, longtime editor of the Red Book. His *Whitman Guide to Coin Collecting* quickly established itself as a popular and best-selling introduction to the world of numismatics. In my first year at Whitman, one of my big projects with Dave Bowers was another new book that might be placed on the other end of the spectrum. Its title is *The Expert's Guide to Collecting and Investing in Rare Coins*. Because of its sheer size (688 pages) it's tempting to characterize the *Expert's Guide* as a book reserved for advanced collectors. In reality, this was (and is) a volume for everyone with a serious interest in the hobby, whether new or old. As Dave wrote in his introduction, "It is never too early or too late to discover coins and the other delights that make up the world of collecting. If you are a preteen, welcome! Similarly, if you are in retirement, welcome! Numismatics knows no restrictions of age, race, religion, politics, or anything else."

The *Expert's Guide* was a monumental undertaking, compiling Dave's 50-plus years of hobby/industry experience in 34 chapters of engaging prose with more than 1,300 illustrations. We released it in October of 2005 with much fanfare, including mainstream publicity in the *Wall Street Journal*. Collectors immediately fell in love with the book, and it earned strong reviews. "Dave Bowers is uniquely qualified to write this book," said Clifford Mishler, retired chairman of Krause Publications. "He brings proper balance to the interplay of collecting and investing in our hobby community." Ken Bressett, who wrote its foreword, asked rhetorically, "Are there really 'secrets' to successful coin buying? You bet! And Dave Bowers reveals them. His style is entertaining, informative, and motivating. The profits you will accrue from reading this book extend far beyond the monetary." Bill Fivaz, coauthor of the *Cherrypickers' Guide to Rare Die Varieties of United States Coins*, said, "If there's a single person who could write this book, it's Dave Bowers"—and he jokingly opined that the prolific author's next book would be *The History of the World*!

Dave tells me that of all his books, the *Expert's Guide* is the one that generates the most enthusiastic letters and emails from readers. He likens reading it and absorbing its lessons to getting a master's degree in numismatics. Sales numbers confirm its popularity: Whitman has sold tens of thousands of copies since 2005.

About 10 years later we were planning on updating Ken Bressett's *Whitman Guide to Coin Collecting*, by then well established and popularly known as the "Yellow Book." It had been reprinted several times over the years and was ready for a new edition. As I studied our publishing list and talked with our sales team (who interact every day with collectors nationwide), I noted that we have the Yellow Book as a beginner's introduction to coin collecting, and the 688-page *Expert's Guide* for more advanced students of numismatics. Was there an opportunity for a companion to these two titles—specifically, a book for intermediate collectors who have devoured the Yellow Book and the Red Book, and want to continue expanding their knowledge? Knowing the hobby community and the needs and interests of collectors, I strongly believed the answer was "yes."

So in 2017 we released two new books (among others): for hobby newcomers, a freshly revised, updated, and expanded new edition of the *Whitman Guide to Coin Collecting*; and for continuing students of the art and science of numismatics, *Inside the Rare Coin Marketplace: Secrets to Being a Smart Buyer*. With each book you get more and more information to add to your storehouse of numismatic knowledge.

In Bressett's *Whitman Guide to Coin Collecting*, the newcomer learns about coin collecting as a hobby; reasons people collect coins; coins as historical documents; how coins are made; where to find them; what factors affect their value; and the basics of grading coins, studying them, storage and display, maintaining a collection, and other points of interest. Bowers's *Inside the Rare Coin Marketplace* tells you how to successfully navigate the numismatic marketplace and find high-quality coins; how to build a great collection; and ways to explore new highways and byways of the hobby. Dave shares wit and wisdom from his experiences as a professional coin dealer, today adding up to 60-plus years in numismatics.

Bressett's Yellow Book offers, among other resources, an illustrated catalog of all U.S. coins by type. Chapter 3 of Bowers's *Inside the Rare Coin Market* does as well, but with a more in-depth approach, and many more photographs. The information is compiled with the goal of making you a smarter buyer of high-quality coins, no matter which series you collect.

In chapter 4 Dave shares stories about colonial and early American coins and tokens, treasure-ship coins, commemoratives, private and territorial gold pieces, numismatic books, historical medals, counterstamps, and other specialties. Many of these subjects are introduced on a basic level in the Yellow Book; here they're given more analysis, with case studies; and in the *Expert's Guide* most of them get even deeper coverage in their own individual full-length chapters.

Chapter 5 introduces dozens of numismatic personalities from yesterday and today, many of whom Dave knew personally, and gives a history of the rare-coin market and its historical cycles. Chapter 6 offers a guided tour down memory lane, with the author sharing his recollections of the marketplace in a "personal scrapbook."

My hope for this book is that, whether you're a fresh face in the hobby or have been around a while, you'll learn something new, you'll pick up a few good "coin stories" to share with friends and family, you'll discover ways to sharpen and hone your collecting habits and strategies, and—of course, because this is a Dave Bowers book—you'll be thoroughly entertained along the way.

Dennis Tucker
Publisher, Whitman Publishing

AUTHOR'S PREFACE

I would like you to become an expert collector of your choice of specialties: coins, tokens, and/or medals (I will save paper money for another book). In the pages to follow I share my knowledge, based on my own journey, starting from scratch when I first discovered numismatics as a young teenager in 1952, and continuing to the present day. I am continually learning. While I could close my eyes and give an hour-long talk on Morgan silver dollars from 1878 to 1921, or Vermont copper coins from 1785 to 1788, or even the coinage of Queen Victoria, I would be at a loss to say anything useful about coinage of the Vatican, Japan, China, or Turkey.

My thesis is that to collect coins successfully (and hopefully to build a collection that will be a store of value over the years) you need to know about them. By this I do not mean only the grade and market price of a coin—both of which are subject to change while you are not watching—but also how coins were minted, how within a given series the quality can differ vastly from one example to another, and how for a certain variety in a certain grade you should eagerly buy one kind of example at full retail value and ignore another at half the price.

Also, and of equal importance, I want you to enjoy your numismatic experience. In today's market and in years past (as I will discuss) there are many uncertainties about grading, pricing, and other matters. In context I will try to make these understandable to you. If you enjoy numismatics you will become a collector for life.

An outstandingly successful investor in securities is someone who knows about market trends, changing preferences, interest rates, the importance of management, the position of a company within its industry, and more. Such an investor probably reads the *Wall Street Journal* for starters, and possibly the *Financial Times* (published in England and giving worldwide commentary), *The Economist* (also published in England, but with much focused coverage of America), quarterly reports, and news releases of key companies of interest, and otherwise keeps abreast of what is going on. In the field of art, knowledge is similarly necessary to insure success. Walking into a gallery and buying something that looks nice or is recommended by a salesperson may provide enjoyment, but not likely a permanent store of value. If a person had a winning lottery ticket or inherited, say, $100,000 and heard that buying real estate can lead to great profits, it might be disastrous to walk into a real estate office and say, "Sell me something that is a good investment." You might be successful, but chances are good that you would lose money if you tried to flip most properties for profit.

Despite such seeming common sense, all bets are off when it comes to people buying coins. In the marketplace there are no rules or regulations to be a professional coin dealer. All one needs to do is to have business cards printed. Television and print promotions trumpeting the desirability of getting in on the ground floor on a new issue, "vault releases," and the like usually offer coins that can be purchased for much less if from a really established professional numismatist who has been knowledgeable and in the trade for many years. Even something as basic as checking prices on the Internet can be worthwhile. Amazingly, many people show no caution at all.

Over a long period of years I have studied the coin market carefully, back to the first boom-and-bust cycle in 1859 and 1860. The first cycle was small in terms of variation in value, but it was a precursor of things to come.

On July 15, 1980, while teaching my "All About Coins" class at the American Numismatic Association Summer Seminar in Colorado Springs, I was interviewed by Jim Lyons, who later published this in *Coinwatch*. This excerpt is relevant:

Coinwatch:	Dave, what has taken place the fast few months in the coin market?
Bowers:	Certain prices have dropped—have adjusted—that went up fast earlier in the year. Other coins have increased in value, such as scarce colonials and the like, so it's been a rather mixed market.
Coinwatch:	You issued several warnings of an impending market crash in 1964, and you were right. What do you think is coming in the U.S. market?
Bowers:	There have been three crashes that I have correctly predicted so far, but when the market crashes, only part of the market crashes. For example, when Proof sets crashed in 1957, type coins were as good as ever, large copper cents were as good as ever. In 1964 when the roll, bag, and Proof set market crashed, early coins that were basically rare were as strong as ever and kept going up in price. In 1975 and 1976 when gold coins crashed, type coins were as strong as ever. . . .
Coinwatch:	Where do you see most investors making mistakes?
Bowers:	By not building a numismatic library, by not joining the American Numismatic Association, by not coming to a Summer Seminar such as this—not reading, but instead just throwing their money at the nearest coin seller.
Coinwatch:	Blindly so to speak.
Bowers:	Right.

For 18 years, starting in the 1990s I was a guest lecturer at Harvard University. The title my program was "Collections and Curation: Collecting in the Marketplace." My audience was comprised of graduate and other students who hoped to go into historical research, museum curatorship, and related fields. As part of my program I discussed market cycles and fads in many categories—from fine art to coins, and from stamps to autographs. All such categories that attract moneyed buyers who seek to make extensive purchases have gone through similar cycles!

I do not pretend to predict cycles for modern art or autographs or restorable Victorian houses, but I have had a lifetime of experience with rare coins, enabling me to predict (so far) various sea changes in that market.

For you to be a successful buyer of rare coins will require some work on your part. Reading this book may take an evening or two to do. Among other things I believe you will gain an appreciation for coin-market cycles and will be able to see them as they occur. Building a basic working library of useful books is essential and will cost several hundred dollars for starters. The passage of time is needed to gain experience. The reward may well be the addition of a new element of challenge and enjoyment to your life, the making of many new friends, and the reward of investment success.

When I began in the rare coin business in the 1950s, one of my correspondents and suppliers of coins for my inventory was Robert K. Botsford, of Nescopeck, Pennsylvania. Bob gave me much advice and was very helpful. He was also a philosopher, as evidenced by this commentary he contributed to *The Numismatist* in July 1933 (excerpted):

> It is absolutely necessary for a well-balanced individual to have both a vocation and an avocation. The vocation feeds the body. The avocation feeds the soul. There is a distinct place for both of these activities, and it is not wise to go to extremes with either one. The border line of each blends into the other with a nicety. Yet each individual must maintain a physical and a mental poise in order that he may escape the ravages that beset the fanatic.
>
> Mr. Average Citizen is a coin collector and is generally interested in odd or unusual dates, designs or figures. He wants to know the whys and wherefores. . . . If one is desirous of traveling on the numismatic path he must depend on what he can pick up from dealers' catalogues and other odds and ends of numismatic literature that he is able to secure. Coins—gold, silver, nickel, copper—of this age and of the ages long since gone by are a medium of exchange recognized for their bullion value at any period and any time. They speak the universal language of values known and recognized by mankind. History is written upon their faces. Great events are recorded on the coins used by man. The likenesses and images of the world's famous personages are handed down to posterity on the coins of the various nations. . . .
>
> The great numismatists of the United States are the kindliest of men, ever ready and ever willing to be of service. They take great pride in their collections and are always ready to show their choice specimens to those who will appreciate the rarity and handle properly. Just go to visit some well-versed numismatist and find out what a real man he is. Call on him and let him see and know how much you are interested. Why, my friend, you have a treat in store for you that will live for years as one of the happiest, most pleasant memories of a lifetime. Words cannot give you the revelation that you will receive of what a brother really is until you spend some hours with such a man. That is, providing you are a numismatist at heart and long to learn the vast facts of the world's coins and how this kindred spirit has acquired and taken care of the specimens that have come into his possession.

Part of the above is enjoying and appreciating the lore and lure of coins. I have always said that if owning a coin is worth 1 point and the art, history, and romance concerning it is worth another point, if you have both, 1 + 1 can equal not just 2, but 3 or 4. Coins are meant to be enjoyed.

Dealing in coins has been a part of my life since 1953, a year after I started collecting. I have mostly learned by doing—including making my share of mistakes, but trying to benefit from them. I have personally known and met with most of the "greats" in numismatics, a long list that included by 1960 such names as B. Max Mehl, Morton and Joseph Stack, John J. Ford Jr., Oscar G. Schilke, Stephen K. Nagy, Lewis M. Reagan, Kenneth E. Bressett, Eric P. Newman, Norman Shultz, Sol Kaplan, Ambassador and Mrs. R. Henry Norweb, Chet Krause, Lee F. Hewitt, Abe Kosoff, J. Hewitt Judd, John J. Pittman, Aubrey and Adeline Bebee, James Randall, Abner Kreisberg, Richard S. Yeoman, James O. Sloss, Louis E. Eliasberg, Charles Foster, William T. Anton Sr., Art and Paul Kagin, Jacob Shapiro (a.k.a. Jake Bell), and many others. From the outset I enjoyed sitting at the feet of such people and taking mental notes.

Although the book you are now reading is primarily devoted to American coins, medals, and tokens, it is important to note that the hobby of paper money has been important and dynamic over the years and a major aspect of my business. In other books I have written extensively about it. In 1953 Robert Friedberg issued a book that would become a standard reference, *Paper Money of the United States*, which gave "Friedberg numbers" to a confusing (to many) array of currency from many series. In the mid-1950s I met and talked with Bob Friedberg. He operated leased coin boutiques in over a dozen different department stores. This was a very stressful business, he told me, as keeping track of what the managers bought over the counter was very difficult to do. In our first conversation he was struggling with such a problem.

Another paper money expert, Matt Rothert, became a fine friend. He was responsible in 1957 for having Congress add IN GOD WE TRUST to paper money. It had been used on coins since 1864. Matt lived in Camden, Arkansas, and operated a furniture factory there. One day while driving a rented car to see him I saw a box turtle cross the road, picked it up, and took it home as a pet. Years later my company showcased his magnificent collection at auction.

In the early 1950s I was the new kid on the block. Today as you read these words I am an old timer—but am still as enthusiastic as ever. As far as I know, of the 45 dealers who set up at the 1955 American Numismatic Association convention in Omaha, I am the only one still living today. My youth helped—I was only 16 years old at the time.

Writing this book has brought back many wonderful memories. The front part of my narrative is devoted to basics—my advice on how to buy coins in an advantageous manner so as to build a collection that will be stimulating to assemble, will be of high quality no matter what your budget is, and will be a fine store of value.

Speaking of budgets, while it is a challenging pursuit to assemble a specialized collection of early copper cents, Capped Bust half dollars, or other traditional series, some of which involve large expense, there are many alternatives. I enjoy my own collections of State and other quarters from 1999 to date—each with its own story. A complete collection of gem Mint State and Proof coins can be assembled for less than a thousand dollars. My collection of Sacagawea dollars from 2000 to 2008 is a prized possession as well. The curious and rare "Cheerios" dollar of 2000-P cost me a strong four-figure price, and the interesting special Glenna Goodacre dollar of the same year, struck from burnished dies, ran into the hundreds of dollars. However, these are the exceptions. Most coins cost just a few dollars each. The 2005 Jefferson nickel with its "Ocean in View" altered spelling is another favorite. A gem costs less than a dollar, but what an interesting story!

Just as long ago I enjoyed having B. Max Mehl, Abe Kosoff, Abner Kreisberg, John Ford, and others tell me about auctions they held and people they knew, much of the last chapter shares my fond memories of presentations of the collections formed over a long period of years by T. Harrison and John Work Garrett, Ambassador R. Henry Norweb and his wife Emery May, Harry W. Bass Jr., Robert Galiette, Brent and Mack Pogue, and others—among the finest ever formed.

To be a successful collector today, or a successful investor, or a nice combination of both, the lessons of history are well worth knowing. After you have read this book you will know what has happened in the past and should easily understand new developments in the market as they unfold. Thus equipped, I hope that you will become a sophisticated collector.

Enjoy the experience!

Q. David Bowers

CHAPTER 1

COINS, THE MARKETPLACE, AND YOU

This chapter begins with some basic information about the minting processes that create coins and often determine the sharpness and beauty of a coin. Then I discuss how you can effectively navigate the numismatic marketplace and find quality.

MINTING AND DISTRIBUTION

The Minting Process

Coins are struck from two dies, obverse and reverse, placed in a coining press. A blank disc or planchet is centered over the bottom or "anvil" die, as it is called. The top or "hammer" die comes down with great force and squeezes the metal of the planchet into the recesses of the dies, sometimes into an edge die or collar with reeding or lettering.

The Philadelphia Mint in the early 1900s. This, the third Mint building, was in operation from 1901 to 1967. There have been four mints in Philadelphia, the current structure having opened in 1967.

In America the minting processes have evolved over a long period of years. The first coins struck in what is now the United States were the New England (NE) silver threepence, sixpence, and shilling coins of 1652. These were made by cutting a circle from a sheet of silver, stamping one side with a punch

For many early American coins, such as this 1787 Connecticut copper, crude and irregular striking is normal and is expected by collectors, including advanced specialists. For some varieties of early American coins the finest-known example may be well-worn, in a grade such as Very Good-8.

In contrast to early times, perfection in minting quality is the rule for modern U.S. Mint coins sold at a premium to collectors. Virtually all are sharply struck and without problems. Mint State and Proof grades of 68 to 70 are the rule, not the exception.

engraved NE, flipping over the coin by hand, and stamping the other side (at the opposite end so as to avoid harming the NE impression) with the denomination of III, VI, or XII. Next came the Willow Tree silver coins of Massachusetts, made from two dies, one fixed on an anvil or solid surface, and the other loosely placed above it, with a blank planchet in between. A sledge hammer or related implement struck the assembly to produce coins. A roller press was later used, with obverse and reverse designs engraved on circular rolls. When a blank planchet was placed and the rolls turned by a crank or wheel, a coin came out the other side.

The first steam-powered coining press delivered to the Philadelphia Mint in early 1836. A special ceremony inaugurating it was held on March 23 of that year. Small copper medals from dies engraved by Christian Gobrecht were struck at that time.

The screw press came later and was used throughout the 1700s and early 1800s. A man would turn a long lever attached to a screw that would drive the top die downward to strike a planchet resting on the bottom die. In one version or another, such screw presses were used at the Philadelphia Mint from the first year of its operation, 1792, to the transition to mechanical force in 1836. On March 23 of the latter year a special ceremony inaugurated the first steam-operated press.

American coinage technology lagged behind that of Great Britain. In the 1790s the private mint of Boulton & Watt in Birmingham, England, offered a steam-driven press that automatically fed blank planchets between the dies and kept count of how many pieces were struck. The mechanism was so well constructed that a boy could tend four such presses at the same time.

After steam presses were put in use in Philadelphia and, later, at all of the branch mints, there were still many variations in quality. If the collar had ridges, it imparted a reeded edge. Some collars had lettering or devices, such as Saint-Gaudens $10 and $20 coins from 1907 to 1933, called lettered edges. As a general rule most *minor coins*, referring to denominations made in copper or nickel alloy, had and still have plain edges. Reeded edges have been used on silver and gold coins and, presently, on clad coins of denominations of 10 cents or higher, with some exceptions. Electricity replaced steam to power presses, starting in the 1890s.

A row of electrically driven presses in use in the Coining Room at the Philadelphia Mint in the early 1900s.

Planchet Quality

Adjustment marks are common among silver and gold coins of the 1790s, less so for those moving into the early 1800s. The adjustment marks on this 1795 half dollar are extreme.

Detail of the center obverse of a high-grade 1795 Flowing Hair silver dollar with light adjustment marks visible. This area is weakly struck. If it had been sharply struck the marks would have been eliminated.

Planchets for silver and gold coins were often made slightly overweight, then placed on scales and hand-filed to remove metal so that each would be of the authorized weight. Adjustment marks are very common on silver and gold coins of the 1790s. They are less common on later pieces, but can be found well into dates of the first two decades of the 1800s century. Mention of adjustment marks is usually absent on certified holder labels and in other descriptions, but they can be detected easily by observation. It is best to avoid a coin with prominent adjustment marks unless it is of a variety that is so rare that another cannot be found.

Planchet defects are common and to be expected on certain early Vermont coins, especially the die varieties struck in the town of Pawlet, as here. Reuben Harmon Jr., who held the coining contract, used copper made from regionally mined ore. The minting processes were primitive. The same can be said for most other mints that were operated privately or under contract in the 18th century.

In many instances, especially among colonial and early American coins, planchets were crudely made. Coins struck from these planchets have pits, fissures, and other problems. Coins struck at the private mint in Pawlet, Vermont, which had a contract to make coppers for the Republic of Vermont, were made on crude planchets. Problems are the rule for such coins of 1785 and 1786 and so these kinds of flaws are generally ignored by advanced collectors. On the other hand, copper half cents and cents struck by the State of Massachusetts in 1787 and 1788 were carefully struck and on planchets of high quality. Accordingly, Massachusetts coppers with defects are not desirable. From series to series among early issues there are often widely different characteristics of planchet and striking quality, so some research into the general quality of each series is recommended before making any serious investments.

Sharpness of Details

If the dies are spaced very close together in a coining press, there is extra metal that is forced up and/or down at the edge of the collar, causing a wire rim. At the Mint this feature is called a *fin*. This is often the effect when slightly overweight planchets are used. At the same time with close die spacing the metal fills the deepest recesses of each die, resulting in a sharply struck coin. For these the term Full Details can be used. Such coins are often very special. However, close spacing results in the dies wearing more quickly and sometimes cracking, shortening their useful life. It is more economical and efficient to space the dies slightly farther apart than to create Full Details coins. In that way the occasional overweight planchet does not cause problems, and die wear is less.

The sharpness of details has numismatic importance. For some coins—Washington quarters are an example—the deepest parts of the die do not have intricate details. Accordingly, nearly all coins have an attractive appearance. For some others, a lot of attention is paid to the sharpness of details.

A coin with Full Details is more desirable than one that has certain features weakly struck. In nearly all instances *you* need to determine whether a coin has Full Details, or whether it is attractive without Full Details, by visual inspection. For some series there are definitions, as outlined below. However, these definitions are not precise.

Mercury dimes minted from 1916 to 1945 often have the horizontal bands on the reverse fused together. Exceptions are called Full Bands, abbreviated FB, but some of these, including some of 1921, have weak dates or indistinct rims. It is always best to check *every* detail of an offered coin.

For Standing Liberty quarters 1916 to 1930, the obverse areas with intricate details include the head of Liberty and the rivets in her shield. Those with *above average* head details are often certified as Full Head, or FH, even though some head details are missing and, further, some shield rivets may be weak or missing.

My advice: When paying a premium for a coin certified as being "full" bands, or head, or some other aspect, use your eyes to see if *all features* are full. If not, you will save a lot of money by buying coins without such notations, but you will need to cherrypick for quality when doing so.

Most series have no individualized terminology to designate sharpness. This pays rewards for careful buyers. Among Buffalo nickels 1913 to 1938 many coins, particularly branchmint issues of the 1920s, lack Full Details. The fur on the head and shoulder of the bison often lacks hair strands and appears as a blob, and on the obverse there is weakness at the center. The most notable issue is the 1926-D, for which most coins are weak on both sides, with fewer than 10% appearing with Full Details. If you are patient you can find one of these for no extra cost. If perchance Full Details became a popular term and was used by the certification services, an FD 1926-D nickel would be priced for a great multiple.

This 1917-D Variety 1 Standing Liberty quarter has been certified as FH (Full Head). The head is indeed full, and the shield rivets are bold. Only a tiny percentage of certified FH quarters are even nearly this sharp.

This 1926-D quarter was certified as Full Head. In actuality part of Liberty's hair is weak, some shield rivets are missing, and the center of the shield is weak (as outlined in red). This is typical of coins called FH. For a sophisticated buyer such a coin should be passed over, and the search continued for a sharper example. Very few buyers are aware of this.

The reverse of a sharply struck 1926-D Buffalo nickel, a *rarity* as such. And yet in the marketplace a sharp coin of this or any other Buffalo nickel varieties costs no more than a weakly struck coin, as most people do not known what to look for.

Nearly all 1926-D Buffalo nickels are weakly struck on both sides. This is most noticeable on the fur on the head which on this coin is a blob without details. Certification services take no notice of such weakness.

One would think that Proof coins, sold to collectors at premium prices, would all be sharply struck. In reality some 19th-century Proofs are weak on certain areas, such as the star centers. Others have lint marks impressed into the field—from threads left over from oily rags used to wipe the dies.

In contrast to the situation of years ago, most modern Proofs, commemoratives, and other coins sold to collectors at a premium by the U.S. Mint are of excellent quality, exceptions being circulation-issue coins sold in bulk in roll or bag quantities. The fact that superb gems among collector coins sold at a premium are the rule is not widely known to the general public, and some advertisements in popular media give the impression that such pieces are rare. For example, in 2016 the West Point Mint struck special gold coins with the designs of the 1916 Mercury dime, Standing Liberty quarter, and Walking Liberty half dollar: every one I have seen in its original packaging is absolute perfection.

Into Circulation

All early colonial coins were made for circulation. There is no record of any contemporary collector, college, museum, or other entity saving Massachusetts silver coins when they were issued beginning in 1652, or for any other pre-Revolutionary issues that have gained numismatic interest. Although there were a few numismatists here and there in the late 1700s, again there is no record of the copper coins of Vermont, Connecticut, New Jersey, Massachusetts, or other issues being set aside for cabinet purposes. Accordingly, the survival of Mint State and other high-grade coins is a matter of rare chance. There are many varieties for which the best known coin shows extreme wear.

Federal coins from 1792 onward were nearly all placed into circulation as well. As the art and science of coin collecting became popular, especially beginning in the late 1850s, those who desired current coinage usually acquired Proofs. Branchmint coins were ignored. The earliest records I have found of a collector systematically seeking mintmarked examples of all denominations and mints up to the double eagle is that of John M. Clapp, a Pennsylvania oilman, who ordered one of each available coin in 1893 from the Carson City, New Orleans, and San Francisco mints.[1]

Accordingly, for most colonial and federal issues from the early days, continuing through the late 1800s, the survival of Mint State coins is a matter of chance. As a general rule, for coins with high mintages the chances of examples being saved are greater than for low-mintage pieces. Another general rule is that more Mint State coins survive of later years than of earlier years. Many coins of the 1890s are readily available in Mint State, but all Mint State coins of a century earlier in the 1790s are rarities.

Effects upon Circulating Coins

Copper, nickel, and silver coins typically began to acquire patina or toning (the word "tarnish" is a numismatic no-no) after being placed into circulation, less so if put into storage. Copper (and bronze) naturally tone to an attractive brown hue. Nickel becomes light gray or slightly iridescent. Silver tones through various shades. Nickel and silver coins that circulate to an extent are usually light gray. Gold remains fairly brilliant.

A circulated 1851 silver three-cent piece with natural light-gray toning. This
denomination, sometimes called a trime, was minted from 1851 to 1873.

Over the years copper and nickel coins have seen the greatest use in circulation,
followed by silver. Many early coins are worn down to the point at which design
details are lost. Gold coins in their time circulated to a much lesser extent, except in
the American West. Most late 1800s and early 1900s gold coins are in higher grades,
often AU or Mint State.

While normal wear does not affect the desirability of a coin within a given grade,
some other effects such as scratches, holes, initials, quality of strike, and corrosion
are negative, and pieces with such problems should be avoided. The key is that within
a specific grade you should seek the finest quality possible.

Coins for Collectors

Ever since the early 19th century the Philadelphia Mint has provided Proof coins,
patterns, and other issues for collectors. The earliest known full Proof set is in the
National Numismatic Collection; it is dated 1821, and contains all of the denominations of that year: cent, dime, quarter, half dollar, quarter eagle, and half eagle.

From then onward, the Mint obliged collectors by supplying coins as requested.
In some instances, such as in 1834, Proof sets were made for presentation to foreign
diplomats, these being the Sultan of Muscat and the King of Siam. In 1860 the Japanese embassy visited the Philadelphia Mint and received a cased Proof set complete
from the cent to the double eagle.

An 1858 Proof Liberty Seated silver dollar from the first year that Proof coins were widely sold to
collectors. It is thought that 210 pieces were struck.

Proof coins were openly sold to collectors beginning in 1858, when 210 silver
sets were made, plus a larger number of copper-nickel cents and a very few gold
coins. Early Proofs were made with deeply mirrored fields that contrasted with frosty

letters and devices. From 1909 to 1916 Matte Proof Lincoln cents were made, and from 1913 to 1916 Matte Proof nickels were struck. These have satiny rather than mirrorlike fields. From 1908 to 1915 Satin Finish and Sand Blast surfaces were given to Proof coins. After 1916 the issuance of Proofs to collectors stopped, although a few were made for special occasions.

A Proof dime of 1936, the first year since 1915 that silver Proofs were available to collectors.

Coinage of mirror-surface Proofs resumed in 1936 and continued until 1942. Coinage of Proofs was then suspended due to World War II. In 1950 Proofs were again made, now available only in sets, which were sold for $2.10. These sets were made through 1964, then suspended. In 1968 Mirror Proofs were again made, but now at the San Francisco Mint, with S mintmarks on the coins, instead of Philadelphia. Recently a number of innovative Proof or special finishes have been used as a sales incentive for various issues made for collectors.

In addition to Proofs, the various mints and the Treasury Department have provided circulation-strike coins to dealers and collectors for many years. These have included packaged sets with one of each denomination as well as rolls and bags for dealers. The cost has been face value plus transportation or, in recent times, face value, plus a small premium, plus transportation.

The *Guide Book of United States Coins*, regular edition, and the *Deluxe* or *Mega Red* edition give mintage figures and current values for circulation strikes and Proof coins.

Cleaning and its Effects

In many ways, coins in the hands of collectors suffered more problems than equivalent coins hidden away in dresser drawers or kept in hoards. This is little understood and thus merits some detail here.

"Brilliant is best" was the catch phrase from the late 1800s into the late 1900s. To be salable to 90% or more buyers, an Uncirculated or Proof silver or gold coin needed to be bright. Such coins were called BU for Brilliant Uncirculated. If a coin was toned, nearly all collectors and dealers dipped it to make it brilliant. In itself this was harmless enough, but silver

Court Coin Company advertisement in the *Numismatist*, November 1967. Unless silver coins were brilliant and bright, few collectors would buy them.

tended to re-tone (again, "tarnish" was a word not used then or now), and dipping was needed again. And again. Eventually, this caused a dullness or cloudiness of the surface.

Rather than dip coins, many collectors and dealers used silver paste or polish. These involved friction and imparted microscopic hairlines to the surfaces of Proof coins and dulled the luster of Mint State coins. It is probably the case that over 95% of the silver Proofs in existence today were cleaned with a polishing at one time, and they have microscopic hairlines as evidence. Otherwise, all Proofs could be graded as being perfect, as high as Proof-70 to use today's system. Fortunately, today many Mint State and Proof silver coins are once again toned, often artificially, which hides hairlines and dullness and gives some a very pleasing appearance.[2]

In August 1903 this comment by Farran Zerbe was published in *The Numismatist*. He had recently visited the Philadelphia Mint to see the collection on display:

> I found many of the silver Proof coins of late years partially covered with a white coating. On inquiry I learned that an overzealous attendant during the last vacation months when the numismatic room was closed took it on himself to clean the tarnished coins, purchase some metal polish at a department store, and proceeded with his cleaning operation. Later a coating of white appeared on the wcoins, which was now slowly disappearing. I expressed my displeasure at this improper treatment of Proof coins, and the custodian explained, "That is nothing. I have been here eight years and they have been cleaned three or four times in my time."

To the official magazine of the American Numismatic Association, *The Numismatist*, January 1949, G.R.L. Potter contributed an article, "Let's Keep It Clean!" Potter stated that the advice "don't clean your coins" is sound, especially to the general public, but not necessarily so for numismatists.

> Of the desirability of "clean" coins there can, I think, be no doubt. The most casual scrutiny of catalogues or dealers' lists shows that 'brilliant Uncirculated' is the condition commanding the highest price, and it must follow that anything that will maintain or restore such a condition is desirable. It is my contention that such restoration and maintenance is often a very simple matter, and that the procedure is well within the capacity of any collector of average intelligence—which, of course, means all of us!

The writer told of taking a Canadian cent of 1911:

> [This coin] had obviously never been in circulation, but whose brilliance was dimmed by a film of cuprous oxide unevenly distributed over the whole coin. Taking it by the edge with a pair of forceps, I dipped it into the solution. In a flash—literally in a flash, it was as brilliant as the day it had come from the press. A similar experiment with a slightly tarnished

silver coin yielded like results. Since that day I have treated hundreds of coins, of various metals, and in various conditions, with almost unvarying success.

From that point, Potter went into deep water and recommended that numismatists use potassium cyanide. To be sure, he noted that it is a deadly poison, but then he went on to say:

If the procedure . . . is carefully followed, no contact with the cyanide solution will occur. But accidents will happen, and if you do happen to get any cyanide solution on your skin wash it off immediately in running water until the greasy feel at point of contact has entirely disappeared. Cyanide is like a great many other things in life—fire, electricity, motor cars, or what have you—very dangerous if not properly used, but both safe and useful in careful hands.

Concerning coins in circulated grades he added:

Now, despite all the pretty talk about "toning," this is definitely not a desirable condition. Silver has been used from earliest times, not merely because of its relative scarcity, but also because of its beauty of color and surface. Tell any collector of antique silver—numismatists apart— that he must on no account disturb the tarnish and grime that disfigures the metal, and he will probably tell you to go and have your head examined. As suggested above, the general objection to cleaning, as a means of preventing irreparable injury by the unskilled, was to that extent sound. Also, even skillful cleaning, in the absence of subsequent protection, might have to be repeated at intervals, and the ultimate result would be as bad. But, with the lacquering process, the coin is preserved indefinitely, and I therefore consider it wisdom to make my worn silver as presentable as possible before lacquering. First cyanide, then a good silver polish, applied with an old tooth-brush and, if necessary, a final rub with chamois leather and rouge.

Anyone following Potter's advice ran the definite risk of injury or death to himself or members of his family, and of seriously damaging his coins' value. In each and every instance the use of "a good silver polish" has caused hairlines and other irreparable damage.

Proof coins when minted had no hairlines, even under high magnification. Dipping coins to make them bright might make the surfaces cloudy over a period of time, but no hairlines would be added. The use of silver polish and other abrasives caused hairlines. Today, as noted earlier, more than 95% of the older Proofs in the marketplace have hairlines. Those with a lot of hairlines are graded Proof–60 to 62 or so, with fewer, 64 or 65, and with fewer still, perhaps 66 or higher. With no other

A Proof-62 1839, No Drapery, Liberty Seated half dollar. This coin, a beautiful rarity worthy of the finest collection, was certified in the grade noted. Microscopic hairlines from a long-ago cleaning defined the grade. If the holder had been marked "Proof-62 cleaned," buyers would have been few. Without this adjective, intense competition resulted when it crossed the auction block.

choices, Proof coins in these grades are collectible today and are widely sought. However, it is desirable to know of past numismatic preferences and traditions. Certified coin labels give few clues as to past cleaning, even if it was harsh. If they did, *every* Proof coin below, say, Proof-68 would be called cleaned, as "Proof-65 cleaned." Under the mindset prevalent in numismatics, such accurate descriptions would unfairly reduce the value of such coins. On the bright side, there are many Proof–63, 65, and other-grade coins with hairlines that are very attractive. Just keep your high-powered magnifying glass in your pocket. As it is, some such coins are labeled as cleaned, vastly decreasing their value, and others are not. There is little consistency among third-party commercial grading services.

As you can see by now the more information you have, the easier the intricacies of numismatics are to understand!

In the course of looking over the manuscript of this book, Kenneth Bressett suggested this:

> Add a comment that approximately 98% or all ancient coins, and probably 85% of all colonial coins have been cleaned at one time or another. Collectors must accept this as a fact of life and overlook the effect on any but those that have been seriously defaced.

How true this is. And how true it is that the word "cleaned," which can properly apply to a huge number of coins, cannot be discussed openly without fear of harming a coin's value. To use a classic comment, the emperor has no clothes, but his subjects dare not to mention it.

The late Harry W. Bass, Jr. was a specialist in United States gold coins and patterns. Among the patterns he acquired were copper strikings that had been in the collection of King Farouk of Egypt. The "Playboy King," as he was called, collected coins, watches, jewelry, pornography, and other things. After he was deposed by a military junta in 1953 his holdings were sold at auction in Cairo under the title of The Palace Collections. Among his coins were copper patterns that he had had polished to make them bright. Pieces that were acquired by American buyers were

11

brought back to the United States. When offered to Harry Bass and others they were usually described as "cleaned" or "polished." After Harry Bass's passing his ex-Farouk coins were auctioned and described as such. Lo and behold! Most of those were put in the hands of conservators, and today they are on the market in holders certified as Proof-63 to 65 with no mention that they were once polished.

At first read you probably will think that the restoration of the Farouk coins was a caper, something that should not have been done. There are two sides to the story. Today, the coins are more attractive than they were when Farouk owned them and are prized additions to several collections. In other fields of collecting such as art, autographs, classic automobiles, and the like, restoration is standard and is accepted.

A brilliant Gem 1874-S Liberty Seated dime. The coin was dipped at one time, perhaps multiple times, as countless thousands of other Liberty Seated dimes, quarters, and related pieces have been. Otherwise it would be toned.

A 1921 dime certified as MS-66+, one of the highest grades known. The irregular toning did not appeal to any buyer when offered at auction, and this coin did not sell. (Although the reserve price may have been another factor.) If it was carefully dipped and emerged without hidden problems being revealed, bidders would come in from all directions. Such a conservation procedure would seem to be common sense.

This very attractive and desirable 1866 quarter has been graded Proof-63 by a third-party service. There is a lot to like in this coin, as brilliant as when it was first minted.

In the meantime the nomenclature regarding coin conservation, dipping, and cleaning—three different activities—is erratic, undefined, and confusing. It remains a challenge for the numismatic hobby as a whole to consider terminology and perhaps make revisions. What you have read so far in this chapter has given you knowledge that few other coin buyers have!

Keep a smile on your face. Coins are delightful to own, just as are conserved antiques and paintings. The difference is that, per the emperor analogy, coin conservation cannot be discussed aloud.

The Effects of Atmosphere

In the past some have suggested that those who live near the sea not collect copper coins. Tiny salt particles in the air will create microscopic black or green specks on the surface of coins. Today, with many coins encased in plastic holders this is less of a threat, although many holders have spacers so that the edges can be seen—which at the same time allow air into the sealed area.

Furnaces that use coal, oil, or gas often give off fumes containing sulfur. These vapors cause coins to tone, often in attractive colors on silver coins if exposed for a relatively short period of time. Industrial fumes and those caused by traffic can be harmful if they reach the surface of a coin.

In New York City the Cleopatra's Needle stone obelisk on the grounds of the Metropolitan Museum of Art on Fifth Avenue has had most of its inscriptions etched away by acid particles in the air. Years ago the New York Public Library, also on Fifth Avenue, consigned its coin collection to us for auction. Many coins had been stored on trays in wooden cabinets. Most silver issues were deep gray or black on the obverse, the side exposed to the air, and mostly brilliant on the reverse. On the other hand the fine collection kept for years by the American Numismatic Society in its museum at 155th Street and Broadway was not seriously affected by the atmosphere, although some pieces toned slightly over a period of time.

In summary, do not expose the surface of your coins to fumes or contaminants.

THE ELEMENTS OF A COIN'S VALUE

There are several elements that combine to determine the value or market price of a coin. Of these, one of the most important is the *grade* of a coin. More than just a few people consider grade to be the most important. All other factors being equal, a coin in MS-65 or Gem Mint State grade is more valuable than one at the AU-55 or About Uncirculated level.

In actuality, other factors beyond grade are vital as well. *Eye appeal* is essential to sophisticated buyers. A coin graded MS-65 that is stained, dark, or as ugly as a toad is not as desirable in my opinion as an AU-55 coin that is beautiful to behold.

As illustrated here, *demand* or market popularity is essential as well. The 1794 copper cent variety known as Sheldon-48, the Starred Reverse, exists to the extent of nearly 100 examples in various grades, the finest of which is about EF-40, as shown. A high-grade coin such as this will bring hundreds of thousands of dollars at auction. If it were a large copper cent without the stars, and of comparable rarity, it would be worth only a fraction as much.

A high-grade 1794 Sheldon-48 cent. For some unknown reason the Mint engraver inserted 94 tiny five-pointed stars around the reverse border. Nearly 100 examples are known, thus it is hardly a rarity. Because of this curious feature, however, a Very Fine example will cross the hundred-thousand dollar mark. The finest grade known is Extremely Fine. The illustrated coin has natural brown toning acquired over a long period of time.

There are many varieties of Civil War tokens of which fewer than a dozen are known that in Mint State can be purchased for well below $1,000, sometimes below $300, as specialists for such tokens are far fewer than for large copper cents. Widespread popularity is not there.

Whenever a beautiful Mint State 1909-S V.D.B. cent is offered there is a lot of bidder and buyer interest. In the 1950s I had a rule in my advertisements and catalogs: do not offer 1909-S V.D.B. cents as they would soon sell out and I would have many disappointed customers.

This Gem 1909-S V.D.B. cent is worth $5,000 or more, although thousands are known.

A Mint State example of one of several varieties of Civil War tokens depicting the USS *Monitor* ironclad. Several hundred are known in this grade. The token bespeaks history. The market price is less than $200, however, as the number of specialists in the series is a few thousand at most. Again, there is no widespread demand, but it is greater than the earlier-mentioned streetcar token.

Today a superb Gem 1909-S V.D.B. cent is worth $5,000 or more, although at least several thousand exist at this level. If there are many in existence at this level, why is it so valuable? The answer is *demand*. Everyone who collects Lincoln cents would love to have one of this quality. A Gem streetcar token of Scranton, Pennsylvania, of which fewer than 10 are known would likely sell for below $50, as there are not many collectors within this specialty.

Grade as an Element of Value

The grade of a coin reflects the amount of wear and handling a coin has had. That's it. Seems simple enough. In brief, a Mint State or Uncirculated coin has seen no wear from circulation at all. None. It may have some nicks and marks from being ejected from the coining press, run through a counting machine, and being tossed into a canvas bag on the way to a bank, merchant, or other entity placing it into circulation.

This Gem Mint State 1881-S Morgan silver dollar is from a hoard,
has never circulated, and therefore shows no wear.

Once a coin entered commerce it was handled, rubbed, slid across counters, dropped, and otherwise subjected to the conditions of use. A slightly worn coin is graded About Uncirculated, from AU-50 to AU-58. A coin that has seen decades of use may be worn down to have many details lost and can be Fair-2, About Good-3, Good-4, or Very Good-8.

A 1793 Wreath cent, well worn, graded VG-8. Coins such as this,
worth several thousand dollars today and are eagerly sought.

Typical coins in pocket change today, if several decades old, are usually in Very Fine or Extremely Fine grade.

The Evolution of Grading Standards

When numismatics became popular in the United States in the late 1850s, and continuing for decades afterward, there were no grading standards at all, not even informal ones. One person's "Proof" might be another's Uncirculated or nearly Uncirculated, but polished. Notations such as "Was Proof, now Uncirculated" were seen in auction catalogs, along with such things as, "Very Fine, or perhaps Uncirculated." Nevertheless, time dealers dealt and collectors collected, and the hobby was widely enjoyed.

This 1879 quarter eagle may be equal to an Uncirculated III on the 1892 scale,
a system than never gained much notice.

The first technical discussion I have encountered on the subject appeared in *The Numismatist* in the February 1892 issue and was by Joseph Hooper. "Coins are graded as to condition, and the following terms thereto apply," noted the writer, who then gave a list ordered by Roman numerals:

I.   Mint Brilliant Proofs, or first strikes on planchets, especially prepared for numismatic purposes.

II. Mint Proofs, on ordinary prepared planchets. Brushing Proofs produces what is termed 'hay marks' and should never be adopted, the sale value being lowered. [Later collectors were to refer to these as "hairlines."]

III. Uncirculated, showing no abrasion or wearing of the reliefs, scratches, nicks or indentations. A coin may be Uncirculated and yet not have the sharp impression of the first strike as the dies tire, widen in sinkages, and lose their sharpness, gradually, in so much that the later impressions have often been mistaken for die varieties, more especially where the same dies have done long service for a large issue.

IV. Extremely Fine.

V.   Very Fine.

VI. Fine. Below this condition, unless in extreme rarities, we would not recommend the bidding on at auction sales.

VII. Very Good.

VIII. Good. The latter conditions as described in the sales are often disappointing, the terms applied misleading, until understood, being used by dealers to describe a certain state of preservation.

IX. Very Fair.

X.   Fair.

XI. Poor.

XII. Very Poor.

While specimens in the lower order of conditions are better than none at all, still the aim of the collector should never be below VI or Fine. On account of distance, the large majority of collectors cannot attend sales, and have to be guided by descriptions as given in the sale catalogues, and for this reason, if no other, extreme care should be exercised by the cataloguer in making it a true description of the coins to be sold.

There we have it— numerical grading, albeit in Roman numerals, as early as 1892! Into the 20th century as coins increased in value and more information about them appeared in print, the call for grading standards grew. In September 1910 in *The Numismatist* there was a report of the Committee on a Uniform Standard for Classifying the Condition of Coins. Chairman Henry Chapman stated:

I made a report at the Montreal convention to the effect that we found it absolutely impracticable to arrive at any standard to which the dealers would adhere.[3] It would be an excellent thing to fix a uniform standard, but it is utterly impossible. It is, of course, a very serious matter and I wish that something could be done to compel people to give truthful descriptions. I know, however, that this is very difficult when there is a defect in a coin. It is very hard to be truthful when a slight defect would take off half the value of a coin or medal offered for sale.

In 1934 Wayte Raymond introduced *The Standard Catalogue of United States Coins*. This was the first text to be updated regularly, to give coin values in multiple grades, and to list mintage figures. It pioneered a grading system than within the next few years was adopted by many collectors and dealers:

Proof: Specially struck coins with a mirrorlike surface.
Uncirculated: A new coin never in circulation.
Very Fine: From circulation, but no signs of wear.
Fine: Slightest sign of wear, but still an attractive piece.
Very Good: Somewhat worn, but still desirable.
Good: Worn, but type all clear.
Fair: Considerably worn and type does not all show.

This was simple enough, and served well for a time. Notice that Very Fine, Extremely Fine, and About Uncirculated are not in the Raymond system, although Very Fine and Extremely Fine were widely used anyway. In auction listings the above grades were often supplemented with adjectival descriptions, particularly in the case of valuable coins. Raymond did include modifiers that today in modern grading are not official, such as "an attractive piece" and "desirable."

The coin market was expanding and prices were rising. Collectors and dealers took shortcuts. "Very Fine" was no longer desired as a description of a coin that was nearly but not quite Uncirculated. In the December 1943 issue of *The Numismatist* ANA member Michael A. Molony addressed the issue:

"UNCIRCULATED WITH PRACTICALLY
NO SIGNS OF CIRCULATION"

The present boom market in numismatic buying and selling has served to accentuate the long standing need for more nearly exact standards in the classification of coin condition. . . . This article is concerned with the slow but steady relaxation in the rules of general classification which has been evident, even among the most reputable of dealers, for the past several years.

This slowly progressing relaxation of the condition rules doesn't make for a healthy state of numismatics. It is setting up a false system of values which will someday work to the disadvantage of both collectors and dealers.

The relaxation in observance of time-honored coin classification principles can probably be most readily noted in the case of early American specimens currently being offered in catalogues. In most instances one of these coins now has to be listed as "strictly Very Fine" before a bidder or buyer can assume that it is at all Very Fine. The "Extremely Fine" coins today aren't often as fine as the "Very Fine" ones of 15 years ago. . . . Coins in very superior, but nevertheless circulated, condition are frequently offered as Uncirculated. . . .

I wish to point out that dealers who sell by catalogue would be doing themselves a favor if they at this time would subscribe to a strict code of condition classification, and would then stick to it. If the rules of such classification keep on relaxing as they have been in the past, the coin market will finally become so confused that many collectors will finally retire in disgust. . . .

The definitions of coin conditions in the Wayte Raymond catalogue are good, but they could stand at least a slight degree of elaboration. Even these Raymond definitions would serve, however, if they were actually observed by most cataloguers—but they are not. Raymond's "Very Fine" is "Extremely Fine" as far as most dealers are concerned; the Raymond "Fine" fits what most sellers claim is "Very Fine,'" and so on.

It would be to the advantage of both buyers and sellers of coins if the ANA would sponsor an official, highly detailed and exact code of definition of coin conditions, formulated by responsible authorities of the Association. Cataloguing dealers would be under no obligation to accept such a code, but they would attract more customers and higher prices if they did. Dealers who appreciated the advantages of following such a code could either print it in its entirety as a foreword to their catalogues, or could advise of their acceptance of it by simply running such a line as "Classification of coins listed in this catalogue made according to the ANA specifications of condition."

Such a code of classification might go well beyond the mere description of wear or non-wear evident on a coin. Some dealers classify the evidence of wear precisely enough, but fail to present information on pertinent details of patina, stains, edge dents, or boldness of strike. This I have found to be particularly true in the case of early American silver coins. It would not be at all impossible to set up a series of abbreviations to convey data on such facts to a prospective buyer, just as the degree of wear of a coin is more or less conveyed by such abbreviations today. . . .

My motives in writing this article are altogether altruistic. I am not furthering my own economic interests by writing it. As a matter of fact, the contrary is true. During the past 20 years I have acquired a good many of the coins in which I am particularly interested, the U.S. silver dollars from 1794 to 1803. Many of those which I purchased as "Fine" could be sold as "Very Fine" or "Extremely Fine" today. If I didn't have the interests of the coin collecting fraternity at heart I would sit tight, keep my mouth shut about standards of classification, and patiently wait for the day when my Fine duplicate dollars miraculously became "Uncirculated"—which is exactly what they would do, if today's trend in classification continued unchecked.

What Molony wrote in 1943 in many instances is still applicable today as you read these words, despite endless effort to formulate grading standards that all would adhere to! The more things change, the more they remain the same, it has been said. That may not be true of everything in life, but it would seem to apply to coin grading.

The Sheldon System

Dr. William H. Sheldon, a long-time numismatist, liked to classify things. Apart from numismatics he is infamous for creating the field of somatotype and constitutional psychology—a widely discredited attempt to correlate body types with behavior, intelligence, and social hierarchy, which relied heavily on a series of nude portraits he created for the purpose.

He also devised a hokey system for determining the market value of coins, indeed the one we use today. Unlike his medical work, now reviewed by many as ridiculous, his numismatic work was and is worshiped. I need not go into the documentation that he provably stole coins from collectors (including ANA president T. James Clarke) and from the American Numismatic Society (if interested in the sordid details, poke around the Internet).

In his 1949 book, *Early American Cents*, Sheldon, then riding high as a well-respected figure in medicine as well as numismatics, attempted to devise a *market formula* in which a particular die variety of copper cent dated from 1793 through 1814 (he considered no other coins) could be reduced to numbers, enabling a numismatist to quickly calculate the market value.

As die varieties vary considerably in their value, and such issues as the 1793, Chain AMERI.; 1793 Liberty Cap; and 1799 are more valuable than, say, a common variety of 1803, different *basal values* were set up. For purposes of illustration here, a variety that was not particularly rare may have been given a basal value of $1 in 1949, while a scarce or rare piece might have been assigned $5.

Sheldon's idea was to then determine a pricing scale by numbers, so that if the grading number was multiplied by the basal value of the variety a market value could be obtained. Back then the emphasis on Uncirculated coins was not as strong as it is today. While, of course, collectors would rather have a coin in Uncirculated grade than one in, say, Extremely Fine, most specialists in the field of copper cents 1793 to 1814 were content to have a "nice" example in a grade they could afford. It was often the case that an Uncirculated piece would sell for just slightly more than one in EF or AU grade. This seems amazing to consider today.

The *American Journal of Numismatics* published this pictorial plate of 1793 cent varieties in 1868. The Chain AMERI. is at the upper left.

All of this changed, and dramatically so, in later years when Uncirculated coins, which Sheldon called Mint State, were avidly collected for this category alone, and prices broke away sharply from circulated grades.[4] Back in 1949 there was not a tremendous premium for a typical early cent in Mint State.

Sheldon's scale from 1 to 70, later adapted and revised as the Official ANA Grading Standards, was simple enough at first glance. Per his logic, a rare cent with a basal value of $5, if in VF-30 grade, would be worth $5 times 30, or $150. A coin in Mint State-60 would be worth twice as much, or $300. On the other hand, a coin with a basal value of $2, if in EF-40 grade, would be worth $80. And so it went.

The grading numbers from 1 to 70 were created in 1949 *to fit the prices then in effect*. It may have worked for a very short while. At the time the coin market was in a slump, licking its wounds from a postwar boom, and just beginning to revive. In the early 1950s, a new surge of interest emerged, prices rose sharply across the board, and more emphasis was placed upon Mint State coins. By 1953 the Sheldon market formula (for that is what it really was) was essentially useless.[5] It bore absolutely no relation to the pricing of high-grade cents.

To collectors, however, the numerical system was heaven sent. Now, grading was mathematical, or so it seemed, and, by extension, scientific. It did away with approximation. A stock price of $131 per share is precise. If 873 people were said to have attended a high school graduation in Shrewsbury, Massachusetts that is precise as well, as is the gold content of an ingot stamped as .875 fine. Now, Mint State-65 seemed precise, while the somewhat fuzzy term *Brilliant Uncirculated* was not.

The *Official American Numismatic Association Grading Standards for United States Coins*, first published in 1977, used the Sheldon numbers to cover all coins from half cents to double eagles.[6] Mint State categories included 60, 65, and 70, leaving just two usable grades as few coins were MS-70 (perfect). Later the ANA added 63 and 67 and still later all grades 60 to 70. Not content with this, certain third-party grading services in the 21st century added plus marks, giving this as the Mint State range:

MS-60, MS-60+, MS-61, MS-61+, MS-62, MS-62+, MS-63, MS-63+, MS-64,
MS-64+, MS-65, MS-65+, MS-66, MS-66+, MS-67, MS-67+, MS-68, MS-68+,
MS-69, MS-69+, and MS-70.

I give a nod to humorist Wolcott Gibbs who said, "Backward ran sentences until reeled the mind" in his parody of the complicated writing style of *Time* magazine. Likewise my mind reels when I consider 21 different grades. I have never met anyone who could even consistently grade with the 11 points earlier in play. The same coin sent to the same grading service can be given different grades.

Grading is Not Scientific

If you were an experienced real-estate broker and were asked to grade a vacation cottage on a scale of 1 to 70, you would scratch your head in bewilderment. If you were on the Library of Congress staff and asked to grade a copy of *Uncle Tom's Cabin* on a scale of 1 to 70 you would be rewarded with similar disbelief.[7]

In rare coins, directly attributed to the Sheldon scale and expanded by the realization that if coins could be given numbers they would be easily understood by newcomers, the system of 11 "official" Mint State grades plus 10 unofficial ones used by third-party grading services, has resulted in untold millions of dollars of coins being sold to investors who find security in these 21 numbers. But this sense of security has no foundation in reality.

At an American Numismatic Association convention the Professional Numismatists Guild (PNG) and the Industry Council for Tangible Assets (ICTA) held a symposium on grading. Barry Cutler, an attorney with the Federal Trade Commission, had a "raw" (not in a holder) 1908 Saint-Gaudens double eagle. He showed it to an assembled group of people who earned their living grading coins for the third-party services. One by one they gave their expert grades, which ranged from AU-58 to MS-64.[8]

Today if a group of two-dozen Mint State examples of a given coin, say a common one-cent piece of 1851 with much frost or luster, was given to a third-party service on Monday, graded, removed from the holders and sent back on Tuesday, many of the grades would be different.

Moreover, as is well known, many coins have graduated up the Mint State scale. Coins that were once unknown or rare in such grades as 67 or 68 are now very common in those grades. Back in the early 1990s certain commemorative half dollars such as the Arkansas, Booker T. Washington, and Carver-Washington half dollars were rarely certified above MS-65. Today MS-66 examples of these coins are as common as fleas on a stray dog. The coins themselves have not changed. The grades have. Thousands of gold coins that used to be called About Uncirculated-58, which is defined as having light wear, are now in holders marked Mint State—which defies the definition that such coins show no wear at all.

For a system to be scientific it must be defined in text or in images. With a copy of the grading standards in hand a dealer or collector viewing a coin in Tacoma, Washington; Snowville, New Hampshire; and Bug Tussle, Alabama, would find it to be the same grade as would an owner of the guide in Cincinnati, Ohio; Wildwood Crest, New Jersey; or Bellefonte, Pennsylvania—but that is a near impossibility under the current system. This consistency has never happened. However, the situation is rarely discussed in print—once again the emperor is without clothes.

Unlike in the Mint State and Proof categories, for circulated coins the situation was fairly stable in the 1970s. *Photograde*, written and sold by James F. Ruddy, quickly sold out the first several printings in 1970 and went on to become a best seller. It used pictures to define such circulated grades as Good, Very Good, Fine, Extremely Fine, and About Uncirculated. It was well accepted, as was the ANA guide. Today, many of these grading-standard interpretations have been inflated as well. Whereas full LIBERTY letters on the obverse of a Fine-12 coin was once necessary to meet the standard, today there are certified VF-20 coins that have some letters missing! Keep it up and these VF coins will someday be graded as Uncirculated, to use Mr. Molony's 1943 example. It will be, as Yogi Berra famously said, déjà vu all over again.

Regardless of any numbers assigned, in any given market, a coin *truly* in a higher grade will have more value than a lower grade coin if there are no impairments.

In the meantime, to make you comfortable I will state that in the fields of collecting books, mechanical banks, prints, autographs, antiques, clocks, postcards, and other specialties that are dynamic and have no numerical grading at all, most people are quite happy and are having a good time! In my postcard collection I have the "Waverly Cycles" card by Alphonse Mucha, the great classic rarity in that specialty. It is very nice, has never been used, and has bright colors. I am not sure, however, if it is MS-62+ or MS-65, and I don't care either.

I go to the next element of a coin's value and will return in the next chapter to share thoughts on how grading numbers may not be as important to you as they are to most others. In a phrase, *not to worry*. Everything will be just fine for you (I can't vouch for others, however).

Eye Appeal as an Element of Value

The Beauty of a Coin

Although beauty is in the eye of the beholder, just about any group of collectors viewing coins on exhibit can pick out the ones that are attractive, pretty, nice to view, or whatever terms you want to use. In a phrase, all other things being equal, a beautiful coin is more valuable than an ugly one (except for buyers who purchase by labels on holders and do not look at the coins).

As instructor Bill Fivaz has pointed out in his classes at American Numismatic Association Summer Seminars, if one takes 10 coins in the same numerical grade, most students, even beginners, can arrange them in order of beauty—from the least attractive to the most.

Many early copper cents have surfaces that are very attractive,
such as the Sheldon-24 1794 cent shown here.

For an appreciation of early copper cents it is hard to improve on what Dr. William H. Sheldon had to say about this in his book, *Early American Cents*, published by Harper in 1949:

> Old copper, like beauty, appears to possess a certain intrinsic quality or charm which for many people is irresistible. An experienced dealer in American numismatic materials recently wrote as follows: "Sooner or later, if a collector stays at the business long enough, it is three to one his interest in all the other series will flag and he will focus his attention on the early cents."
>
> Gold, silver, and even bronze appear to be very much the same wherever you see them. Coins made of these metals become "old money" and "interesting," like the stuff seen in museums, but copper seems to possess an almost living warmth and a personality not encountered in any other metal. The big cent is something more than old money. Look at a handful of the cents dated before 1815, when they contained relatively pure copper. You see rich shades of green, red, brown, yellow, and even deep ebony; together with blending of these not elsewhere matched in nature save perhaps in autumn leaves. If the light is good (direct sunlight is preferable) you will possibly observe that no two of the coins are of quite the same color.

Copper coins can be very attractive in almost any grade, an interesting aspect to contemplate.

Nickel coins can be attractive in ranges from light iridescent or gray toning to brilliant. Most that have been in circulation for many years are a light gray color which is quite satisfactory.

Most advanced collectors will agree that early silver coins if naturally toned lightly, sometimes with iridescent hues, have very nice eye appeal. Brilliant silver coins can be very appealing as well, especially if, for Mint State coins, they have rich luster and for Proofs, deep mirror surfaces.

Most observers will probably agree that this MCMVII (1907)
High Relief double eagle has very nice eye appeal.

For Mint State gold coins, brilliant, lustrous surfaces are preferred. For worn gold, as most early issues are, especially those minted from 1795 to 1834, light and reasonably bright surfaces are preferred, and if with traces of luster, so much the better.

While well-worn copper, nickel, and silver coins in such grades as Fine and Very Fine can be attractive, even beautiful, as a rule gold coins in these low grades are *not*—this situation is quite different from the situation with copper.

While preferences will vary, a lot can be learned about the eye appeal of coins by examining images. An easy way is to go on the Internet or to an illustrated catalog and look at various depictions. Sometimes coins in lower grades can be more appealing than those in higher grades. Often a lower-grade coin will offer a lot of beauty. While there is great pride in owning a coin that is among the finest known of its variety from a numerical viewpoint, this is usually not necessary to obtain a coin in a lower grade that is cheaper and equally attractive. Cherrypicking pays!

Below are some examples in different grades and the prices they recently sold for at auction.

1853 Half Dollar with Arrows and Rays

MS-64 $3,290

MS-64 $8,225

MS-65 $13,225

MS-65+ $94,000

1921 Peace Silver Dollar

MS-62 $243

MS-64 $705

MS-65 $1,400

MS-66 $6,750

1923-S Monroe Doctrine Centennial Commemorative Half Dollar

"Unc. Cleaned." $75   MS-64+ $441

MS-65 $940   MS-66 $3,910

Within nearly all series prior to modern times you will find that some coins are much more attractive than others. It is a secret, sort of, that the most beautiful coins are not necessarily those with the highest grades or those that sell for the highest prices. If you agree with this you have freed your mind from the common belief that the nicest coins are expensive and in high grades. Many high-grade expensive coins are nice, indeed wonderful, but this goal is not necessary to build a great collection.

Using the 1923-S Monroe Doctrine Centennial half dollar as an illustration, to my eyes the "MS cleaned" coin at $75 represents an opportunity for a budget-minded collector to acquire an example for a low price. In comparable grade a full set of 48 different types of commemorative half dollars of the classic era 1892 to 1954 would cost perhaps $5,000. In MS-66 grade a set would run well over $100,000. This poses the question: Do I want *completion* for a low price, or a selection of stray coins, not a complete set, that costs a large sum of money. If money is no object, the question may have no meaning. However, for most buyers lower grades can be very desirable.

To find quality for some coins (but hardly all) it is better to examine 10, 20, or 50 coins before making a purchase. I say more about this in the next chapter. As to "some," I point to San Francisco Mint Peace silver dollars of the 1920s; it takes a lot of looking to find a really beautiful one. On the other hand just about any MS-65 1881-S Morgan dollar, 1928 Saint-Gaudens $20, or 1938 New Rochelle half dollar is beautiful to behold. Not many people are aware that the overall quality of different coins in the same grade can vary widely, sometimes extremely so.

As mentioned earlier, an ugly coin even at a deeply discounted price should be avoided, unless it is of a very rare variety for which a purchase opportunity may not recur for many years. For my money, a lustrous AU-58 light-brown cent of, say, 1839, is a much finer coin to own than an MS-63 that is dull or stained. A sharply struck 1807 Draped Bust half dollar in AU-55 grade is better, in my view, than an MS-63 with a typical flat strike for this date and variety.

As is true in all aspects of building your collection, cherrypicking for quality will pay dividends when the eventual time comes to sell your coins. This point cannot be overemphasized!

Sharpness Adds to Eye Appeal

Coins can vary in sharpness of detail. I have told of the 1926-D Buffalo nickel, a variety of which nearly all are weakly struck, but some exceptions are sharply struck. Therein lies an opportunity—to find a sharply struck or Full Details coin. Such a coin will cost no more than a weakly struck one. This is a secret that can yield many superb coins by paying no more. Most branchmint Buffalo nickels of the 1920s have sharpness problems, but most coin buyers have no knowledge of these at all!

Sharp details, including the all-important hand of Liberty, on a 1936 Proof half dollar.

Over a long period of time I have kept notes, some mental, others in my file, of what varieties among American coins are found sharp and what varieties are sometimes or always weak. In the latter category is the 1923-S Walking Liberty half dollar. In decades of buying and selling such coins I have never seen a circulation strike that has Full Details (full head of Liberty, full details of her hand, well-defined lines in her skirt, etc.). Except for Proof half dollars of the 1936 to 1942 years, very few coins show details of her hand, and even Proofs can have weakness on Liberty's head.

Typical weakness on the higher-relief details of a Liberty Walking half dollar, this being a 1923-S.

In the field of most federal coins from 1792 to date you, as a sophisticated buyer, can cherrypick for quality for no extra cost. This is your secret! Usually sharpness is not mentioned in descriptions. On the other hand, when the desirability of sharpness is emphasized in print, the cost for such quality can be great.

As an example, most Jefferson nickels from 1938 to date depict Monticello on the reverse. This building has six steps leading up to its portico. As this is a high area in the coin design—a deep part in the die—nearly all circulation-strike Jefferson nickels have some of the steps missing. The designation of 6 Full Steps, or 6 FS, can lend value, sometimes extreme. There are some varieties for which neither 5 FS nor 6 FS coins are known.

If the dies are spaced slightly too far apart, nicks and marks from the original planchet will not be eliminated and will be visible on the higher parts of a coin. This 1921 Lincoln cent is a Gem from the standpoint of original color. However, close inspection of the shoulder (see detail) shows a myriad of planchet marks.

The 1945 Mercury dime from the Philadelphia Mint is a very a common date worth about $30 in MS-65 grade. If one is in a holder marked FB, for Full Bands on the reverse, the cost jumps into the thousands of dollars!

Standing Liberty quarters from 1916 to 1930, also discussed earlier, if certified with FH (Full Head) can often sell for multiples of coins not so designated, even though on some the rivets in Liberty's shield can be weak or missing. Another certification-service label that adds value is Full Bell Lines (FBL) for Franklin half dollars 1948 to 1963. The reference is to the nearly horizontal lines in the Liberty Bell.

For *you*, as a sophisticated buyer, it is desirable to be aware of other hidden assets. Here for the first time in any numismatic book, are many things not noticed by certification services, but which can be cherrypicked for no extra cost. In chapter 3 I explain this series by series.

Relative to the above, if someday the third-party services and the general market realize the desirability of sharply struck coins, your coins may have substantial extra value at no additional cost to you. In the 1950s no one ever heard of Full Step Jefferson nickels, Full Bands Mercury dimes, Full Head Standing Liberty quarters, or Full Bell Lines Franklin half dollars. These were popularized and promoted later, to the extent that they have become standard. Never mind that, as stated, some such (particularly Full Head quarters) are in my mind poorly defined and inconsistent.

Sorting out the earlier-mentioned intricacies makes numismatics all the more interesting.

Additional Factors that Determine Value

There are other factors that contribute to the quality and desirability of a coin. Many coins are struck from "tired" dies. After striking hundreds of thousands of coins, as many dies from the 19th century to the present have done, dies can show wear, ridges, and roughness. Coins struck from them can have irregular fields with streaks and graininess instead of rich luster. Coins struck from tired dies are especially common among 20th-century Lincoln cents and Peace silver dollars, but other series can have these problems as well.

Planchet quality is another factor. Although some early coins were made on planchets with

This 1926-S cent struck from *very weak and tired dies* has been certified as MS-63 RD by a leading service. Such a coin will sell readily to, perhaps, 90% of buyers, but a sophisticated buyer would not want it at half the market price.

rifts and irregularities (Connecticut and Vermont copper coins of 1785 and 1786 are classic in this regard, as mentioned earlier), most federal coins can be found on planchets without problems. If a coin is lightly struck in some areas other than the highest parts of the design, this might indicate a fault or a problem that should be investigated.

Some planchet problems create what are called mint errors. These are a separate subject apart from the present study. An otherwise common Lincoln cent with a curved section missing, from improper punching of the planchet from metal strip, or one that is double-struck with the date appearing twice, can have a premium.

The pedigree or past ownership of a coin, also called the provenance, can add value, especially for scarce and rare issues. Coins with proven past ownership to Garrett, Eliasberg, Bass, Norweb, Partrick, Brand, Gardner, Boyd, Bushnell, and other famous collectors are worth more than a similar coin without such a pedigree. If a holder is marked with a past owner that is not familiar, it may have no extra value at all. "Cleveland Bank Hoard," for example, and I am making that name up, may have been requested when someone submitted a coin for certification, but it would be worth just as much without that attribution. If a copper coin is from the Palace Collection of King Farouk, the less said the better!

Coins that can be attributed positively to a treasure recovered from a wreck on the ocean floor, such as the SS *Central America*, SS *Republic*, SS *Brother Jonathan*, SS *New York*, and other ships that are well documented with special third-party grading labels can be worth a significant premium. A subculture of collectors specializes in attributable treasure coins.

IN SUMMARY

As I have pointed out there are challenges for you if you want to form an outstanding collection. Except, perhaps, for modern Mint commemoratives, Proofs, and other coins sold at a premium to collectors—for nearly all are of superb gem quality—purchasing a coin requires study and knowledge. Most advanced numismatists would have it no other way, for learning and exploring add to the thrill of the chase. I hope this will be the case for you.

Today as you read these words there are more opportunities than ever for *you* as a sophisticated buyer!

Again I quote my Robert K. Botsford, whose 1933 wisdom is cited in my Preface. He contributed this to *The Numismatist* in July 1938:

> Coin collecting or numismatics as a hobby or an avocation or diverting pursuit affords the individual more unadulterated pleasure, great interest, and often enhanced values than any other collectible item or items. Of variety there is no end, nor does one ever reach a time or a period in which he can state that his collection is complete. This collecting science is forever new and yet forever old. It offers a cultured pastime from the cradle to the grave.

CHAPTER 2

HOW YOU CAN BUILD A GREAT COLLECTION

As to the definition of "great," this does not mean expensive. Not even close. It means a collection of carefully considered coins, tokens, or medals that are examined and bought one at a time. I have, for example, a complete set of 1971 to 1978 Eisenhower dollars. Completing the set with Full Details coins for several issues and coins with great eye appeal took me several months. In my opinion it is a great collection—lots of history, and it was quite fun to track down needed pieces—but its market value is very modest. If I had not been fussy about getting choice examples I could have completed the set in less than an hour by buying on the Internet.

Forming a set of 1913 to 1938 Buffalo nickels by date
and mintmark is a popular and challenging pursuit.

Some time ago I corresponded with a specialist who spent years collecting and studying Buffalo nickels from 1913 to 1938. This involved finding sharply struck examples of each date and mintmark in Mint State. He did not pay particular attention to numerical grades, but studied the coins themselves. The average grade was MS–63 to 64 in the days before wide gradeflation. Today most of the same coins would be MS–64 to 65. Who knows, some might have previously unknown grades such as MS-65+ (bit of humor here)! His most expensive coin was the 1926-S. Every one of his coins was sharply struck. He looked through old issues of *The Numismatic Scrapbook Magazine* and read *Only Yesterday* by Frederick Lewis Allen to follow the rise of enthusiasm in that era of Buffalo nickels. To be sure, he collected other coin series as well, but Buffalo nickels were his pride and joy. He had complete immersion in his specialty.

In another instance Bob A., a New York City securities broker, had dabbled with various coins but wanted to form a collection that was both challenging and meant something in terms of interest and history. He settled on building a type set of one of each copper, nickel, and silver coin from the 1790s onward—fewer than 100 coins altogether. He carefully chose each item based on some study beforehand. For the Matron Head copper cent type of 1816 to 1839 he selected a gem 1820 from the famous Randall Hoard because he found the story fascinating.

An 1820 copper cent from the Randall Hoard,
a group of cents dated from 1816 to 1820 that came to light in the late 19th century.

For the Jefferson nickel in regular alloy he picked a 1950-D, a so-called "key" coin in many collections, because of its story. The type set took him several years to form. He later consigned to auction, where he realized several times his cost. He decided to not add gold to his type set, although he could have afforded to have done so.

STEP 1: PLANNING

The first step in forming a great collection is to have a plan. If you have been in numismatics for several years, this will be easier to do than if you are a newcomer. Either way, spend some time—at least a week or three—on general ideas. The world of collecting is wide and diverse.

Is there a particular series that interests you? The *Guide Book of United States Coins* is a good place to start. Ideally, if you want to build a set of coins from the 19th century or earlier you will want to select a specialty that will take the best part of a year to assemble, or even longer. This may or may not eliminate certain series. On the other hand, if you would like to build a set of Eisenhower dollars 1971 at 1978 or a set of classic silver commemorative coins from 1892 to 1954, allow a month or two.

As another example, if you want one of each regular-issue Liberty Head nickel from 1883 to 1912, this will not take long to do. Between the Internet and through auction you can probably finish a set, or at least come close, in a grade such as MS-65 or Proof-65 within a week, although the 1885 and 1886 in MS-65 (but not in Proof-65) will be a challenge. Studying the series will be a fascinating experience. For the 1885 1,472,700 were struck for circulation and 3,790 Proofs were made. Few circulation strikes were saved, as collectors ordered Proofs. In contrast, in 1907 39,213,325 circulation strikes were produced and just 1,475 Proofs. For this year Mint State coins are very common today, and Proofs are among the rarest in the series.

The 1885 Liberty Head is the rarest date 1883 to 1912 in Gem Mint State,
but is readily available in Proof format (as shown).

If you want a more difficult challenge, then go after one of each Liberty Head nickel variety 1883 to 1912 in two parallel sets, Mint State and Proof, and insist on coins with Full Details. You will find that if you insist that the obverse of each coin be sharp, with all of the strands in Liberty's hair well defined and with the star centers bold, and all details on the reverse, including the kernels of corn to the left and right of the ribbon bow, be sharp and complete, such a set might take a year or more! For extra credit, so to speak, there are two minutely different reverse styles of 1901, and a few Proof 1903 nickels have the reverse die oriented the same as the obverse, rather than the correct 180 degrees apart.

To be a specialist as above, you will also need to see what you can find in the way of reference books on Liberty Head nickels. While you are at it, read about the life of Chief Engraver Charles E. Barber, the designer of the coins. His interface with Augustus Saint-Gaudens is fascinating. Saint-Gaudens said the work of Barber was "wretched." I won't even mention the World's Columbian Exposition award medal, for which each of the two did a side.

I do not suggest that Liberty Head nickels be your only focus. It is usual to collect other series as well, but not with the passion of the theoretical set described above. I say *theoretical* as I have never heard of anyone completing a set of Mint State and Proof coins with Full Details! You can be the very first!

Your budget is an important consideration when planning. It takes a lot of money to form a significant collection of United States gold coins. Few people have ever put together a set of Liberty Head or Saint-Gaudens double eagles by date and mintmark. Unless you have won the lottery, forming a type set of double eagles is a reasonable alternative. There are six design types from 1850 to 1933.

An 1878-CC Morgan dollar from the first year of issue.
Morgan silver dollars are far and away the most popular
early series of coins in numismatics today.

The most popular of all specialties is Morgan silver dollars from 1878 to 1921, a collection that comprises close to 100 major varieties of dates and mintmarks. Within these is a subset specialty: Carson City dollars 1878 to 1893.

Lincoln cents from 1909 to date probably come in second in popularity. Never before in American history has the same basic design of a coin (in this instance, the portrait of Abraham Lincoln on the obverse) been used for more than a century.

Once you have selected one or several specialties, buy whatever books you can that give information on these. Usually it costs less than $100 to acquire basic titles for a specific series. For Morgan dollars, say less than $300. Some of these books will prove to be useful, while others will prove to be little more than statistical listings of population reports. However, all contribute something that will add to your knowledge. It has always been amazing to me that some collectors will spend $1,000 on a coin instantly, but will be very hesitant to build a basic inexpensive working library of books.

Your budget plays a part in contemplating other series. Beyond the gold coins I already mentioned, if you select U.S. pattern coins, territorial and private gold coins, silver coins of colonial Massachusetts, or Proof coins minted prior to 1858, be prepared to spend hundreds of thousands of dollars to get a good start. Not many people can do this. Even if you can afford such, your interests may lie in a different direction. In chapter 4 I give many ideas for forming great collections that will cost you very little.

A great reason to form a collection in metals other than gold is that most of these coins are relatively inexpensive. A budget of $5,000 to $10,000 per year will permit, in time, for you to collect large copper cents by *Guide Book of United States Coins* varieties 1816–1857, later cents of the Indian Head and Lincoln designs, the aforementioned Full Details double set of Mint State and Proof Liberty Head nickels, Morgan and Peace dollars, modern dollars from 1971 Eisenhower to date, and many other series. Further afield, this would be a very generous budget for collecting Civil War tokens (you would become a leader in that specialty) and would also work for Hard Times tokens.

Many of the above can be acquired in lower grades of condition, but still numismatically attractive and desirable, on a modest budget. The John Reich Collectors Society (https://www.jrcs.org) attracts collectors who enjoy federal silver coins from 1794 through the 1830s. The *John Reich Journal* is filled with interesting articles, news of conventions, and more. The Liberty Seated Collectors Club (http://www. lsccweb.org/) specializes in Liberty Seated silver coins 1836 to 1891 and publishes *The Gobrecht Journal.* It may come as a surprise for you to learn that when lists of members' collections are published in these magazines, nearly all are composed of circulated coins. MS-65 and higher coins are in the minority. In grades from, say, Fine-12 to MS-60, most Capped Bust and Liberty Seated coins are quite affordable, and it is possible to build a nice collection. If MS-65 or higher were to be the goal, only multi-millionaires could assemble a display.

Forming a type set is also a great way to go. Start with coins of the 20th century in the copper, nickel, and silver series, then go to gold types. The only barrier will be the MCMVII (1907) High Relief double eagle, which may cost plus or minus $20,000 for a nice Mint State coin. Quite a few years ago my company had Capital Plastics make up 200 special holders for 20th-century coins from the cent to the dollar, after which Jim Ruddy and I set about finding Gem pieces. The hardest by far was the Barber half dollar. If you can afford gold coins, consider forming a set of the six double eagle types. In Mint State the rarest by far is that minted from 1866 to 1876, With Motto, on reverse and those coins with the denomination as TWENTY D.

Closely related to all of the above is selecting the grades you can afford. For Morgan silver dollars, if you opt for, say, MS-63 for the majority of varieties and then circulated examples of 1879-CC, 1889-CC, 1892-S, and 1893-S, a $10,000 to $20,000 annual budget will do fine, and you can collect all 24 of the 1921–1935 Peace dollars as well.

Keys to Planning

If you do not want to be as specific as the above and would like to learn more before selecting areas of interest, I recommend these Whitman books, available for purchase on the Internet or from your favorite dealer. If you are a member of the American Numismatic Association you can borrow them for free, plus postage, from the Dwight N. Manley Library at ANA Headquarters in Colorado Springs.

A Guide Book of United States Coins, Mega Red, is the regular *Guide Book of United States Coins* on steroids. It is issued annually (the first edition was 2016 with a cover date of 2017), has over 1,500 pages, and is heavy enough that you will want to keep it on a table rather than carry it around. It contains a lot of expanded information. Kenneth Bressett is the editor, Q. David Bowers the research editor, and Jeff Garrett the valuations editor.

100 Greatest U.S. Coins by Jeff Garrett and Ron Guth is a great starting point to pair with *Mega Red*, as it can give you an idea visually as to what you may like and the price point you're looking at.

100 Greatest American Medals and Tokens by Katherine Jaeger and Q. David Bowers contains some of the most visually appealing and sought after medals and tokens. This is a must read before building any type of medal or token collection.

Lost and Found Coin Hoards and Treasures by Q. David Bowers has many interesting stories about coins found in sunken ships and family attics.

Coins and Collectors. Golden Anniversary Edition by Q. David Bowers contains similarly interesting stories.

The Expert's Guide to Collecting and Investing in Rare Coins by Q. David Bowers somewhat parallels the present book, but includes a lot of different information. Of all the books I have done, readers have found this to be among the most useful.

Pleasure and Profit: 100 Lessons for Building a Collection of Rare Coins by Robert W. Shippee was written by a fine client who carefully built a collection, held it, and sold it for a nice profit. It is a great first-hand narrative of building a collection.

When planning, take your time. Read and learn first. Buy coins later. In that way any mistakes you make will be small ones.

STEP 2:
SELECTING QUALITY IN THE MARKETPLACE

Today most coins in the marketplace—in auctions, price lists, or on the Internet—are labeled with grades in the 1 to 70 ANA system (never mind that with gradeflation many no longer adhere to that system).

Such coins will be listed as EF-40, AU-58, MS-63, MS-65+, and the like. Some have Certified Acceptance Corporation (CAC) stickers. The last are found only on coins submitted in recent years, since CAC was founded by John Albanese (who in the 1980s was also a founder of both the Professional Coin Grading Service and the Numismatic Guaranty Corporation). A CAC sticker means that the staff of that company has reviewed a PCGS or NGC coin in a stated grade and has found that within that current grade this is a "nice" or above average example. It does not mean that the coin is graded conservatively by old-fashioned standards.

If a coin has a CAC sticker, much of the work has been done for you. Coins that are just plan ugly are not included. On the other hand, a coin does not have to have Full Details to merit a CAC sticker. To find these sharply struck coins, if such exist for a given variety, you will still have to cherrypick. Using the earlier-mentioned Liberty Head nickels, CAC stickers do not mention that all of the kernels in the ears of corn on the reverse are needed for a coin to have Full Details. In fact, there is no indication of sharpness of any kind.

Coins without CAC stickers constitute the vast majority of pieces offered for sale—for several reasons. First, many millions of coins were certified before the Collectors Acceptance Corporation began business. Second, CAC charges a fee. Third, for some coins such stickers do not add much information—modern Mint commemoratives and other coins sold at a premium being examples. Fourth, many coins simply do not pass muster when examined by CAC.

If you are too busy to cherrypick for quality among early coins, buying coins with CAC stickers is worthwhile to do. Also, when selling coins a CAC sticker often adds value.

Certified coins as well as those not commercially graded can vary widely in eye appeal, as I have mentioned. To verify this without much effort, check out such coins as the 1922 "plain" Lincoln cent and 1923-S Monroe Doctrine commemorative half dollar on the Internet.

More About Modern Grading

No one is a true expert on grading when it comes to assigning 21 numbers in the Mint State category, never mind multiple levels of About Uncirculated and some other grades. However, you are already expert on *the history of grading*, assuming you read chapter 1. You know that grades move around, you know about gradeflation, and you are aware of the positives and negatives.

This beautiful 1892 Barber quarter was certified as Proof-67 a few years ago.
Is it still 67, or perhaps it is 67+, 68, or 68+? No one has been able to define
the 11 (or 21) grades between 60 and 70 and apply them consistently. Therein lies a
challenge for the numismatic community. As David Thoreau said, "Simplify, simplify."

Incentives for Gradeflation

As Arthur A. Molony stated in 1943 and which is still valid today, the loose interpretation of prices increases apparent value. Gradeflation is considered to be win-win by many. Here is why:

If a coin is sent one time to a grading service, just one fee is collected. If it is sent five times, five fees are collected. A leading dealer told me of a rare MS-64 1916-D dime that through himself and friends was sent to the same service 23 times, and then on the 24th try it was upgraded to MS-65, worth thousands of dollars more. He paid hundreds of dollars in grading fees. The grading service benefited and he benefited.

Ask the owner of a certified coin this question: "Your AU-58 coin is worth $1,000. If you can have it "slabbed" as MS-62, and worth $3,000, would you do this?"

The answer is obvious.

The result, however, is confusion. In 2016 Richard Snow, a specialist in Indian Head cents, published a study showing that nearly all of the certified coins he had seen recently were overgraded if compared to *The Official American Numismatic Association Grading Standards for United States Coins.*

In the 1980s an investor who had paid $100,000 for a Proof-68 Morgan dollar did so as it was the only one in the entire world that had received this grade from a leading service. In August 2016 I checked the population reports and learned this:

- **Professional Coin Grading Service (PCGS):** In Proof-68 various grades including Cameo and Deep Cameo, 81 coins. For Proof-69, 9 coins.
- **Numismatic Guaranty Corporation (NGC):** In Proof-68 various grades including Cameo and Ultra Cameo, 260 coins. For Proof-69, 19 coins.

Said another way, today a coin for which a single certified Proof-68 example was known years ago now has 368 other coins in equal or higher grades.

Pricing is all over the map. For quick verification of this check auction records for a given variety of coin certified in a given grade. Sometimes, coins certified the same sell for double or half the prices of ones that have similar descriptions.

As has always been the case, studying the market is worthwhile. Many people feel that in a given grade most coins have more or less standard prices. In reality, especially among coins in ultra-high grades, prices can vary dramatically. A case in point is provided by this sketch by Steve Roach in *Coin World,* monthly issue of December 2016:

AUCTION REOFFERINGS, OR, WHEN A COIN IS TOO FAMILIAR

For some coins, absence may make bidders grow fonder. In looking at recent coin auctions, one can't help but notice the number of coins that return to auction quickly. In reviewing Heritage's recent New York sale held October 31 to November 2, I noticed one coin that crossed the auction block seven times in the past decade before being offered, again, on November 1. An 1896-O Barber quarter dollar graded Mint State 67 by Professional Coin Grading Service, it failed to meet a reserve of $28,000 and was available after the auction for $32,900 (the reserve plus Heritage's 17.5 percent buyer's fee.)

The high consignor expectations were surprising, especially considering that the coin had sold earlier this year at Heritage's May 1 Central States Numismatic Society auction for $29,375 and before that at Heritage's October 2014 sale of the Gene Gardner Collection, Part II, where, then graded by Numismatic Guaranty Corporation, it brought $22,325.

Prior to that, it sold at Bowers and Merena's November 2009 Baltimore Auction for $43,125. Back at the 2009 Florida United Numismatists auction it realized $37,373, and it soared at Heritage's August 2007 American Numismatic Association auction where it sold for $80,500.

What was different in 2007, when it sold for $80,500, and more recently, when it didn't find a bidder at a much more modest level? In 2007 several collectors were putting together sets of high grade Barber quarter dollars and the competition increased prices.

The coin's rarity is unquestioned and it has long been considered among the absolute finest known, tied with one other example also graded MS-67 at PCGS and bested by a lone MS-68 example listed on Numismatic Guaranty Corp.'s census.

Yet, its many trips to auction have had the effect of making the coin appear more common than it actually is. With the 2014 Gardner sale at the $22,325 price level and a reoffering so soon after the last auction at the Central States show, the prior under-bidders would likely not be willing to stretch to a higher price level.

The above scenario is not applicable to high-priced coins, for which there are quite a few in existence at the same level. A good example is the 1889-CC Morgan dollar in grades of MS-63 and MS-64. They are worth tens of thousands of dollars, but trade regularly, and many buyers constantly seek them. Auction prices are not apt to range dramatically.

A typical newcomer to numismatics will have no clue as to the real scenario in the marketplace. He or she will blissfully consider only the grade and the price. For *you* as an incipient connoisseur, there is much to investigate. Doing so will yield a coin of higher—sometimes much higher—quality that might be found by chance. Take your time. Think.

In many ways this is no different from what one of the greatest American collectors, Emery May Holden Norweb, did when she formed her collection. At the time, coins were simply called Uncirculated. She looked at offered coins with a studied eye and bought "high-end" examples. John J. Pittman did the same. Ditto for Harry Bass Jr. in later times. Each of these and also many others formed outstanding collections and had a good time doing so. They were not troubled by grading, any more than I was years ago. With knowledge everything fit nicely into place. I will say more about this in chapters 3 and 4.

For many generations many great collections were formed in an era with few if any grading standards.

My advice is this—In this milieu you can pick out the nicest coins by looking at them carefully. It is best, in my opinion, not to spend a lot of time worrying about grades moving around. Instead, evaluate each coin for traces of wear, for sharpness of strike, and for eye appeal. I reiterate that many lower-grade coins are nicer and are more numismatically worthwhile than some higher-grade ones at much higher prices.

STEP 3:
SELECTING VALUE IN THE MARKETPLACE

In today's market, getting proper value for your money is very tricky. That said, what to do?

I suggest that once you have determined your budget, let's say MS-64 for Morgan silver dollars, you use this as a starting point. Coins graded from MS-62 up to MS-64 can be reviewed by examining their images, a task today that is easier than ever to do. Probably ignore MS-65 as they will be priced at that level, even if they are overgraded or unattractive. Most Internet sellers, auction houses, and others have pictures that are sharper than ever before. To save time disregard 60 and 61 grades as these are unlikely to yield MS-64 coins. The MS-65 coins, although they are not in consideration due to their price, are good reference points. You will take satisfaction that many 64s you are considering are nicer than some 65s!

For all but a handful of Morgan dollars you will have dozens if not hundreds to choose from in any given month. As an example, take the 1891-O. Seek examples that are sharply struck. For 1891-O this will require some looking. Seek examples that are richly lustrous and with good eye appeal. On the other hand, most Carson City dollars are well struck, and less time is needed in the hunt. Do all of the mentioned and you will have a selection of well struck, lustrous coins with excellent eye appeal to consider for purchase.

Next look at each coin in combination with its price. You will find that some MS-63 coins are nicer and have few bagmarks than do some certified MS-64. Some PCGS coins in old green holders (popularly abbreviated OGH) from the early days may be graded MS-62 but be as nice as some recently certified MS-64 coins. You may also find an MS–63 or 64 coin that is as nice as a 65, in which instance you might want to buy it.

Some time ago in my "Joys of Collecting" column in *Coin World* I told the story of my set of 1921 to 1935 Peace silver dollars. I commissioned Melissa Karstedt to build a set for me in certified MS-64 grade. I found that for certain Peace dollars, MS-64 cost multiples of the price of an MS-63. Many of the MS-65 coins were out of the question, this being especially true of San Francisco coins of the 1920s. Melissa has a superb eye for quality. She, in effect, grew up in the rare coin business as her grandfather, the late John Babalis, and her mother, the ever-active Christine Karstedt, were mentors, as was I.

She set about examining countless MS-63 coins. The 1921 was tough to find with the center obverse well struck but mine comes close. Some of the San Francisco dollars had lots of bagmarks on the face and, in particular, the high points of the eagle. By being patient, she found many MS-63 coins that were equal to or finer than MS-64 coins. Two years later my set was complete!

There are some series for which not much attention is paid to numbers at all. Collectors of tokens and medals who seek a high-level piece are nearly always satisfied with a well struck and attractive coin with minimum problems—a "nice" example. Whether it is graded MS-63 or MS-65 is not important in the selection process. The same can be said for many colonial and early American coins.

Important in determining value is to study the availability of a given coin. If you seek the earlier-mentioned 1938 New Rochelle commemorative half dollar in Mint State, nearly all in existence are sharply struck and have good eye appeal. Accordingly, there is no need to pay more than the current market price. On the other hand if you find an MS-65 1926-D nickel, the earlier-mentioned variety that is nearly always found weakly struck, and it is priced 20% over market value, by all means buy it!

As a quick overview, grading numbers are very useful and are a contributor to the relative availability of most coins. However, they are not scientific, and often they vary widely. For you this is an advantage to cherrypick for sharpness of strike and eye appeal while at the same time seeking to find a "high-end" piece within any given category.

The world of numismatics offers you many opportunities to use *knowledge* to great advantage.

You are ready!

You are set!

Now is the time to go!

COINS OF THE
UNITED STATES MINTS

The present chapter gives a synopsis of coins produced by the Mint for circulation from 1792 onward. These coins were produced in mints at Philadelphia (1792 to date), Charlotte (1838–1861), Dahlonega (1838–1861), New Orleans (1838–1909), San Francisco (1854 to date), Carson City (1870–1893), Denver (1906 to date), and West Point (1984 to date). Denominations range from the half cent to the double eagle.

These coins are the focus of interest for most U.S. collectors. *A Guide Book of United States Coins* can be referred to for mintages and current market prices. Other guide books, such as those in the Bowers Series, exist for most individual denominations of federal coinage, and are recommended if you plan to specialize in a given series.

The following denominations are organized from least to greatest denomination, and information is presented to give insights into the manner in which coins from that denomination are most frequently collected, either by type as a denomination, or by date as a type. Some types that have multiple reverse types (such as the Lincoln cent, which has the Lincoln, Wheat Ears Reverse; Lincoln, Memorial Reverse; Lincoln, Bicentennial Reverses; and the Lincoln, Shield Reverse) are represented as a single type.

HALF CENTS, 1793 TO 1857

Half cents, called "the little half sisters" by Roger Cohen in a book he wrote on the series, were minted intermittently over the years and in much smaller quantities than were copper large cents. Accordingly, there are not as many coins to go around in numismatics, and the number of varieties is smaller.

Moreover, quite a few varieties are expensive rarities. Because of these factors, the most popular way to collect them is by acquiring one of each major design or type. Given the budget to do so and several years or more of time, collecting by die varieties is doable. However, in my entire professional life I have only met two collectors who have completed a die-variety collection—Emery May Holden Norweb and Bernard Edison.

The 1796 half cent without a pole to the cap, a die engraving error, is the most famous rarity in the half cent series. All known examples show a horizontal die crack, evidence that the obverse die failed soon after it was first used. This is the variety known as Cohen-1.

Liberty Cap half cents were made from 1793 to 1797 and vary widely in sharpness of strike and quality of planchets. For example, most 1795 half cents are on smooth planchets, while many 1797 coins are porous or have other problems. Supplies of copper were of varying quality during the era.

Half cents of 1793 are of a separate type with Liberty facing to the left. Beginning in 1794 she faces to the right. Coins dated 1794 have a large head or portrait, while those of 1795, 1796, and 1797 have a small head with a large, open field surrounding it—creating a very pleasing cameo-like design.

Half cents of 1802 are nearly always seen in lower grades (as is also true of 1797, of an earlier design). Most are on dark planchets, the illustrated coin being an exception.

Half cents of 1804 exist in many die varieties and are popularly collected as such.

Draped Bust coins were made from 1800 to 1808. Those of 1802 are nearly always found on dark planchets and in low grades. Half cents of 1804 are common and are often collected by die varieties. Coins grading from EF-40 to Mint State are easily found for some of the varieties, pieces in the latter category originating from old-time hoards.

This popular half cent variety of 1828 is from an error die with 12 stars instead of the standard 13. These are fairly common, especially in grades of Very Fine to About Uncirculated.

Classic Head half cents were made over a long range of years, intermittently from 1809 to 1836. The 1809 is the most common date in circulated grades. Mint State coins from hoards can be found for some of the dates in the 1820s and 1830s. Half cents of 1831 and 1836 are prime rarities.

A Proof 1841 half cent.

Braided Hair half cents were made from 1840 to 1857. Those of 1840 to 1848; the 1849, Small Date; and the 1852 were struck only in Proof format. The Proofs of the 1840s come with three reverses: Large Berries, or originals, and two styles of Small Berries, or restrikes. Of the latter category, the First Restrikes have the wreath ribbon slightly doubled, and the Second Restrikes have diagonal raised die lines over the RICA of AMERICA. As mentioned, I have only met two specialists who endeavored to get one of each date with each of the three reverses. Mrs. Norweb in the 1950s was the only collector in the marketplace for these, but she was later joined by Mr. Edison.

Mint State half cents of 1850 and 1853 to 1855 often come from old-time hoards and are nice additions to any collection. If you enjoy learning about things buy or borrow a copy of my book, *Lost and Found Coin Hoards and Treasures: Illustrated Stories of the Greatest American Troves and Their Discoveries*. Whitman Publishing has issued many of my books on specialized series. If you belong to the American Numismatic Association (https://www.money.org/) you can borrow them from the Dwight N. Manley Library there, paying just the round-trip postage. The ANA has all of my books, including some that are out-of-print.

LARGE CENTS, 1793 TO 1857

The very first American cent—1793 Sheldon-1 with a chain
on the reverse and with the legend abbreviated as AMERI.

Large copper cents, first made in 1793, were made each year except for 1815 when there was no supply of blank planchets on hand. Large copper cents have a special appeal, and have for a long time. In the preceding chapter I quoted the paean that Dr. Sheldon gave on these.

For many series, especially those of the mid-19th century onward, well-worn coins are not widely collected by specialists. The typical person assembling a set of 1892 to 1916 Barber quarter dollars or Standing Liberty quarters from 1916 to 1930 would not aspire to coins in Good-4, Very Good-8, or Fine-12 grade except, perhaps, for rarities. In contrast, specialists in the field of early coppers dearly love well-worn coins, and for many varieties they are the only alternative. In 1958 I and my coin-dealing young friend Ken Rendell toured the State of California, from the Gold Country in the north to the Mexican border south of San Diego. We were the overnight guests of Dr. Charles Ruby, of Fullerton, who was a university professor. He dearly loved the cents of 1793 and had dozens of duplicates. That evening we all enjoyed looking at them one-by-one, and we discovered that they were mostly in grades from Good to Fine.

The first large copper cents were released in March 1793. The reverse displayed a chain motif, which some said was not representative of the land of liberty. The first reverse die, Sheldon-1, had the inscription UNITED STATES OF AMERI. This was soon changed to a full spelling.

A Mint State 1793 Wreath cent, S-9. This type is in high relief and from dies with exquisite detail.

A wreath motif was soon adopted along with a portrait of Liberty in very high, almost sculptured relief. These have a special artistry, obverse and reverse, and are enjoyable to study with the aid of a magnifying glass. This type was minted for a relatively short time and was discontinued in the autumn of 1793.

Strawberry Leaf 1¢ sets record
$414,000 highest ever for U.S. copper coin

The finest one of four known 1793 Flowing Hair, Strawberry Leaf cents has sold for $414,000, breaking the record for a U.S. copper coin.
Telephone bidders competed with about half a dozen floor bidders in Baltimore, where American Numismatic Rarities LLC put the rare large cent die variety on the auction block Nov. 30.

The coin now resides in the collection of an East Coast collector. John Gervasoni, a coin buying agent who placed the winning bid, said he sold it within hours of placing the winning bid. He did not disclose the winning bid. He did not disclose his sale price to the collector.

The piece was authenticated and graded Fine 12 by Numismatic Guaranty Corporation of America.

The price, which includes the 15 percent buyer's fee, surpassed the previous record for a U.S. large cent in a public auction, set just months ago in a sale by the same firm. A 1793 Flowing Hair, Chain, AMERICA, With Periods cent, Sheldon variety 4 (William H. Sheldon, *Penny Whimsy*),

See **1793 CENT** Page 8

Images courtesy of American Numismatic Rarities LLC
A RECORD PRICE of $414,000 was paid for this 1793 Flowing Hair, Strawberry Leaf cent, sold at auction in Baltimore Nov. 30. The coin broke the old record for a U.S. copper coin.

CLOSE-UP IMAGE depicts the trefoil leaves that lead to some calling the cent the Strawberry Leaf variety.

In 2004 a long-hidden 1793, Strawberry Leaf, cent surfaced, was consigned to American Numismatic Rarities, and sold for $414,000—the highest price that had been recorded for a copper coin up to that point. Among classic coins, records are made to be broken, and this figure has been surpassed since.
(*Coin World*)

One of the more curious, interesting, and rare 1793 cent varieties is the Strawberry Leaf variety with a spring of that fruit above the date.

1794 Liberty Cap cent, S-31. This style was used from late 1793 into 1796.
All are from hand-cut dies that vary in characteristics and style.

Liberty Cap cents were introduced in late 1793, from dies engraved by Joseph Wright. An artist of high talents, he was expected to add beauty to all of the designs as they were introduced by the young Philadelphia Mint. Unfortunately, he died of yellow fever in September in the year he was hired, and the hope was never fulfilled. The Liberty Cap design was used through part of 1796. The year 1794 in particular has attracted much attention due to the dozens of die varieties, some such as the Starred Reverse and Missing Fraction Bar being particularly important. At one time Al Boka, important in the Early American Coppers club (http://eacs.org), organized the "Boys of 1794," who specialized in collecting this particular year.

The rarest date in the large cent series is the 1799. The finest-known example,
popularly known as the Hines specimen, later found in the D. Brent Pogue Collection, is shown here.

The Draped Bust type introduced in 1796 was continued through 1808. Key
among the dates is the rare 1799 and the overdate 1799, 9 Over 8. For some reason
nearly all 1799 cents are well worn.

The notable exception to this rule is the Hines specimen, as it is called, graded
MS-61 by PCGS and MS-62 by NGC. It is popular practice for a pedigree or provenance—a list of former owners—to be kept with particularly rare or important early
cents. Representative of this I give the pedigree for the Hines coin:

> ***Provenance:*** From A.H. Baldwin & Sons, Ltd. (London); Frank H. Shum-
> way; Elmer S. Sears; Wayte Raymond; Henry C. Hines; William H. Shel-
> don; Harold E. Whiteneck; Numismatic Gallery's (Abe Kosoff and Abner
> Kreisberg) ANA Sale, August 1947, lot 851; Harold E. Whiteneck; Abe
> Kosoff's sale of the James O. Sloss Collection, October 1959, lot 50; W.M.
> "Jack" Wadlington; Ira and Larry Goldberg's sale of the Dan Holmes Col-
> lection, September 2009, lot 352, graded AU-55 by Chris Victor McCawley
> and MS-62 by NGC; D. Brent Pogue Collection, Stack's Bowers Galleries,
> March 2017, MS-61 (PCGS).

Beyond the above, the Hines cent has generated many paragraphs of print over
the years.

1801 Draped Bust cent with error reverse. The fraction was first made as the mathematically
meaningless 1/000 and then corrected by punching a 1 over the erroneous 0. Sheldon-221 variety.

Among Draped Bust cents there are many interesting die varieties. Some of
the more notable ones are listed in the *Guide Book of United States Coins*. Most are
very affordable.

Classic Head cent of the 1808 to 1814 type. Most cents of
1814 are rather dark in appearance, similar to this one.

Classic Head cents, from dies by assistant engraver John Reich, were struck from 1808 to 1814. The scarcest date, but hardly a rarity, is 1809. Cents of 1814 were made on dark and sometimes porous planchets.

Matron Head cents were coined from 1816 to 1839 in many die varieties and several different portrait types classified under the general name of Matron Head, one of the terms devised years ago by Kenneth Bressett, editor of *A Guide Book of United States Coins*. Collectors often call these Middle Date cents.

Cents of the 1816 to 1857 years are attributed by the numbers created by Howard R. Newcomb in *United States Copper Cents 1816–1857*, first published by Stack's in 1944 and later updated. Newcomb, born in 1877, lived in Detroit, joined the American Numismatic Association in the early 1890s. He loved numismatic research and was one of the first to describe the die varieties among Morgan silver dollars of 1878, to take notice of the rarity in the marketplace of certain Carson City Mint dimes, and to explore many other byways of collecting. Perhaps anticipating what Sheldon would write years later, Newcomb finally turned his attention to copper cents. He spent his life as a numismatist and was richer in many ways from the experience.

Certain die varieties of 1816 to 1820 are often available in Mint State from the Randall Hoard, a group of thousands of cents of uncertain origin, although one story has it that they were found beneath a railway platform in Georgia shortly before the Civil War.

Detail of the 1823, 3 Over 2, overdate cent.

The rarest date is 1823, which also exists as an overdate, 1823, 3 Over 2. In the early years of collecting, someone assigned fanciful names to certain varieties such as the Silly Head and Booby Head of 1839. It may have been Jeremiah Colburn, an early scholar who often wrote popular articles on coins that were published in the *Evening Transcript* of Boston and *Historical Magazine*.

1839, 9 Over 6, overdate cent, Newcomb 1, with plain hair cords. This was made by overpunching the date on an 1836 die. This is a variation of the Matron Head obverse style used from 1816 to 1839.

The 1839, 9 Over 6, overdate, Newcomb 1, is rare in all grades and is especially so if Extremely Fine or higher. Unlike all other 1839 cents, which have beaded hair cords, the overdate has plain hair cords.[1]

1841 Proof cent. All are of the Newcomb-1 variety, a combination used only for Proofs. While hardly common overall, this date is the most available Proof cent of this era, until the mid-1850s. The reason is not known, although it was an inaugural year (for William Henry Harrison, who caught cold at the swearing-in event and died within the month), and there may have been some ceremony.

Detail of the date on an 1844 N-2 cent with an error date. The first two digits, 18, were first punched in upside down, after which the 1844 date was added in the correct position.

In 1839 the Braided Hair design made its appearance and was used continuously through 1857. Cents in this range are often called Late Dates. All years from 1816 to 1837 are classified by Newcomb numbers. Certain die varieties of the 1850 to 1856 years can be found in Mint State with original color and trace their origin to old-time hoards.

A Mint State 1855 N-4 cent from an old-time hoard.
Cents of this year divide themselves into two categories:
with upright 5s in the date as here and with slanting 5s.

Now, some general information that may be useful when buying large cents:

When coin collecting became widely popular in America beginning in the late 1850s, copper cents were the first specialty to attract a large number of numismatists. Continuing to the present day, these have been the most extensively documented federal series. Those who have formed extensive collections have been remembered in many instances by extensive biographies. The extensive correspondence by John W. Adams in his search for such coins occupied many pages when edited and reprinted in *Penny-Wise*, the journal of Early American Coppers, run by editor Dr. Harry Salyards.

For early cents of the Chain and Liberty Cap types, check all features. For Draped Bust cents 1796 to 1807 check the high points of the hair on the obverse and leaf details on the reverse, ditto for the Classic Head cents of 1808 to 1814. Cents of 1814 are often porous. For cents of 1816 to 1857 check the high points of the hair, the star centers, and the denticles. On the reverse examine the high points of the leaves.

Two 1809 Sheldon-280 cents from the same die pair. The one on the left is from an earlier stage of the obverse die. Beyond that the stars are fairly sharp. The one on the right is from a later or "tired" state with stress lines in the field. The stars on the left are flatly struck. What to expect from a given variety can be ascertained by studying illustrations in reference books, of which there are many specialized texts for cents. Some varieties are not known with Full Details. Others are regularly seen with sharp features. Die spacing also plays a part.

There are more fine studies, books, and commentaries on large cents than on any other early series. Review or borrow these and see which ones you would like to own. Early American Coppers is worth joining if you make such coins a specialty. You will enter a dynamic subculture in numismatics.

A Case Study of a Copper Cent Variety

Before leaving copper cents behind I give a scenario, quite typical, for examples of a popular cent in high grades. While at first glance it may seem complicated, upon reflection it makes sense in that it confirms that opinions vary concerning grade, appearance, and rank.

Members of Early American Coppers have developed standards for copper coins. These are outlined in a book, *Grading Guide for Early American Copper Coins*, by William R. Eckberg, Robert L. Fagaly, Dennis E. Fuoss, and Raymond J. Williams. As a collector of these coins I feel that the grading standards therein (in comparison to the ANA Standards) are conservative, and for many certified coins they are *very* conservative. Ideally, it would be nice to buy at EAC standards and sell at currently inflated grades!

Actually, this scenario has not caused any problems. Auction catalogs issued by leading firms such as Ira and Larry Goldberg, Heritage Auctions, and Stack's Bowers Galleries often list the EAC grade as well as the (usually higher) grade on a certified holder. Further, coins for sale are illustrated with sharp photographs, which allow buyers to make their own determinations of desirability. Some of the finest collections such as those of John W. Adams, R.E. ("Ted") Naftzger Jr., Daniel Holmes, Walter Husak, Tom Reynolds, Twin Leaf, and others have been presented with detailed descriptions, often a page in length for a single piece. The appeal and importance of pedigrees—past owners—is also a part of the lore and lure of early cents.

Across the entire numismatic spectrum pricing is indeed flexible for coins whose value is based purely on collector demand. Coin prices based on silver or gold bullion values are much more consistent in a given time, but vary with metal prices. A scenario involving one of my favorite varieties illustrates this. The coin is an 1817 copper cent with 15 stars on the obverse instead of the usual 13. The die cutter made an error, creating an issue that has been popular for a long time. This variety is listed in the *Guide Book of United States Coins* and is sufficiently plentiful that examples are very affordable in lower grades. Perhaps 1,000 or so exist.

SELECTED PRICES

- ***Guide Book of United States Coins*, 2017 edition:**[2] G-4: $30 • VG-8 $40 • F-12 $50 • VF-20 $150 • EF-40 $600 • AU-50 $900 • MS-60 $2,800 • MS-63 BN $3,600
- **NGC On-line Price Guide:** G-4: $55 • VG-8 $65 • F-12 $120 • VF-20 $275 • EF-40 $600 • AU-50 $1,600 • MS-60 $4,750 • MS-61 $6,500 • MS62 $8,250 • MS-63 $13,000
- **PCGS CoinFacts with Two Auction Sales of PCGS-Graded Coins:** MS-60 $6,750 • MS-64 $58,750

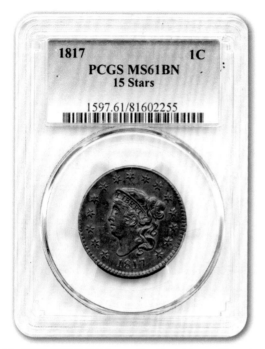

Steven Ellsworth's notes on this particular coin as written on a paper envelope.

NGC insert saved from a previous certification of this coin.

The 1817 N-16 MS-61 (PCGS) cent offered by Col. Steven Ellsworth.

A clearer view of the coin—a well-struck cent with nice color and eye appeal.

At a convention of the New England Numismatic Association I stopped to visit with Col. Steven Ellsworth, who conducts Butternut, a rare-coin dealership in Virginia. Steve is a member of the ANA Board of Governors, has been in coins for a long time, and is recognized as a leading expert in early copper coins. In his bourse case he had a beautiful example of the 1817, 15 Stars, cent graded by PCGS as MS-61. Earlier it was in an NGC holder as MS-63, but Steve "crossed it over" to PCGS and kept the NGC tag. Graded by EAC standards the coin is AU-58+, as he noted on a paper envelope he kept with the holder.

What grade is this coin? AU-58+? MS-61? MS-63? If gradeflation continues, at some future date will it be MS-65 or higher?

How does one go about buying such a coin?

The answer is to study prices to get an approximate idea of value. Then carefully study images of the coins offered. Some have prominent nicks and cuts. Others have dark or unappealing surfaces. Others, such as this one, are very nice overall.

The 1817 N-16 cent from the Twin Leaf Collection. Certified as MS-64 RB, this seems to have more original color than any other known example. It sold for $58,500 at auction in 2016.

Another coin, possibly the finest known or certainly close, and likely the one with the most original color, was cataloged by John Pack and offered in the Twin Leaf Collection by Bowers and Merena Galleries in August 2016 and sold for a record $58,750. The description (excerpted):

1817 N-16. 15 Stars. MS-64 RB PCGS.) CAC. Rarity-1. 15 Stars. Noyes Die State A/A. Fabulous Condition Census 1817 15-Star Highly lustrous and eye-catching surfaces. Pale steel overtones are seen on the obverse, which is otherwise almost perfectly blended faded mint red and medium brown. A small carbon spot at Liberty's nose is the one useful identifier worthy of mention. The reverse exhibits much more original color, with a bit of faint violet iridescence in places. A couple of small spots are noted on this side as well, but all such marks are quickly forgiven on this lovely coin, one of the finest 15-Star examples. Struck from an early state of the dies, with the obverse in particular being quite sharp as it was a new die. All star centers show and the radial lines of each are well defined.

The reverse is a second appearance of the 1817 N-1 die, and shows a little more wear but it is still in the "perfect" state for this variety. The reverse is aligned a little to the right, typical of the variety, and the left-most denticles are consequentially broad. This is the third time we have had the pleasure of cataloguing this fine specimen over the years. We sold it for Herman Halpern in 1988, and more recently for Mr. Naftzger in 2001. The line of past owners contains several illustrious figures, known for their excellent taste where choice large cents and other coins are concerned.

In 2001, this coin was in the Noyes Census as tied for finest known. Today, it is ranked as tied for CC#4, although it seems to have more generous mint color than some of those ranked equal to or above it. It was called MS-63 by us in 1988, called the same by Naftzger and once again the same by us in 2001. It was the cent selected as the plate for Noyes' own book, and remains so in the most recent edition. As a word of caution, the coin is quite a bit more red than seen in the Noyes plate where it appears largely tan.

The 1817 15-Star cent is unique among large cents for its star arrangement and has long been a popular variety. Though the date 1817 may be easily acquired in Mint State due to Randall Hoard coins, this variety is not known to have been found among them. The best 15-Star to sell at auction since our 2001 sale of this piece was Goldberg's February 2009 sale of the Ted Naftzger coin (ex Homer Downing). That example was graded MS-65BN by PCGS and remains the only piece graded finer than this one. It sold for an incredible $50,600 and is ranked as CC#2 in the Noyes Census.

Again, we call attention to the generous original color of the present piece. In this respect it is much finer than the former Downing coin, and we suspect that the list of connoisseurs whose collections have contained it will increase by one more name destined for numismatic greatness. EAC grade: MS63.

Pedigree: Ex George Woodside; New York Coin and Stamp Co., April 1892; Benjamin H. Collins; B. Max Mehl (personal collection); Emanuel Taylor, Roy E. Naftzger, Jr.; T. James Clarke; Abe Kosoff, April 1956: 157; Oliver E. Futter; Louis Helfenstein; C. Douglas Smith; Herman Halpern, Stack's, March 1988: 351; Anthony Terranova; Roy E. Naftzger, Jr.; Bowers and Merena, August 2001: 22.

The preceding narrative reveals several things. Although the general market for high-grade federal coins was "quiet" in the summer of 2016, and many prices for coins were depressed (especially for high-grade silver and gold coins advertised of "investment quality"), this classic copper coin sold for a record price. It also illustrates a slight diversity of opinion as to its ranking among the finest known. The narrative is typical for many classic coins—going far beyond a simple statement of numerical grade. Further, the pedigree or list of former owners contains some of the most famous names in numismatics. I personally knew them all, from Mehl forward. All told, this coin will forever echo in the halls of numismatics.

But see below for an economical alternative—not with fame, not necessarily owned by illustrious predecessors, but a nice coin to own:

An 1817 N-16 cent graded as EF-45.

Plan B: Buy a hand-picked EF-40 to 45 coin for $600 to $800 or so!

SMALL CENTS, 1856 TO DATE

Flying Eagle Cents, 1856 to 1858

The Flying Eagle cent struck in copper-nickel was struck for circulation for only two years.

The Coinage Act of February 21, 1857, discontinued the copper half cent completely and provided that coins of the cent denomination be of a reduced diameter, lighter weight, and of copper-nickel alloy. Patterns dated 1856 were minted to the extent of nearly 1,000 pieces for distribution to congressmen, newspaper editors, and others of influence to acquaint them with the new design. These patterns have been adopted into the regular series by numismatists and are eagerly sought today.

The obverse design by engraver James B. Longacre copied Christian Gobrecht's eagle from the silver dollar of 1836. The agricultural wreath on the reverse was copied from that created by Longacre himself for use on the gold $1 and $3 of 1854. So, what we have here is not an original-design coin, but one that is popular and attractive.

Flying Eagle cents for circulation were distributed beginning in May 1857. The design is such that the head and tail of the eagle on the obverse die were directly opposite in the coining press from the high-relief wreath in the reverse die. This caused the details of the eagle to be weak on many coins. The design was discontinued following the coinage of 1858.

Although the sharpness of most coins in the marketplace is fairly good (but should be checked), eye appeal can vary widely. To find one that is just right often involves examining multiple pieces.

Indian Head Cents, 1859 to 1909

An 1898 Indian Head cent, one of the more common dates,
in Mint State, retaining most of its original red-orange color.

In 1859 the Indian Head cent was introduced. Designed by Longacre, the obverse featured a fancifully stylized Native American woman wearing a chief's bonnet. The reverse of the 1859 cents showed a laurel wreath. From 1860 onward the reverse displayed an oak wreath and shield. Cents from 1859 through the spring of 1864 were made in copper-nickel alloy on 72-grain planchets. Later cents through 1909 were made on 48-grain bronze planchets.

Indian Head cents are one of America's most popular series. The key rarity is the 1877 cent. The 1908-S cent was the first minor (copper or nickel) coin struck at a branch mint.

The tips of the headdress feathers are shown here on two 1863 Indian Head cents, both Gem Mint State. The tips on the left are sharply struck. Those on the right are weak. As holders as well as printed descriptions make no note of sharpness, it is up to you to find coins with Full Details if they are available.

Striking quality varies. Check all areas, especially the tips of the feathers in the headdress. On copper-nickel cents in particular these can be weak. Eye appeal varies all over the place. Coins certified as Mint State RB can have varying amounts of red color—sometimes nicely blended, other times splotchy. Coins certified as RD will have some light toning unless they have been dipped. Cherrypicking for quality is absolutely essential, especially for Mint State and Proof coins. You may have to consider a dozen coins before you find a nice one. The advantage is that, as usual, cherrypicking for quality costs no more than forming a lower-quality set of the same pieces. Richard Snow (you can find him on the Internet) has specialized in Indian Head cents, and his books and catalogs may be a good place to start your search for high-quality cents. Snow is also important in the Fly-In Club (Flying Eagle and Indian—get it?), which can be found at http://www.fly-inclub.org/.

In my opinion Mint State and Proof coins certified as BN (brown) can be very attractive at a cost far less than RB and RD coins. You might want to check these out. Similar to large copper cents, Indian Head cents can be very attractive in circulated grades. A nice set in VF or EF grade is quite affordable.

Lincoln Cents, 1909 to Date

1909 V.D.B. Lincoln cent.

Lincoln cents made their debut in circulation in August 1909, and with several variations to the reverse, have been struck every year since then. Those distributed in August 1909 had the initials of the designer, Victor David Brenner, at the bottom of the reverse. Following complaints that Brenner had been paid for his work and there was no need to "advertise" him on the coins, the initials were discontinued. This was illogical as on most other coins the initial or initials of the engraver were in place (such as the monogram of Augustus Saint-Gaudens prominently on the obverse of current $20 coins), and anti-Semitism may have played a role in the outcry against Brenner. In 1918 the V.D.B. letters were put back—in tiny letters on Lincoln's shoulder.

The sharpness of detail varies considerably among Lincoln cents. As a general rule those of the first several years are usually sharp. From about 1916 through the 1920s many were struck from overused dies or with the dies spaced too widely. This was particularly true of Denver and San Francisco issues. Cherrypicking is essential for quality if you are seeking high-grade coins.

Lincoln cents have a multitude of complexities that require time and patience to analyze if you seek the best quality coins. For starters, check Lincoln's shoulder. Even on high-grade Mint State coins magnification may show tiny nicks and marks. These are marks on the original planchet that were not flattened out during striking, as the shoulder is one of the deepest areas of the die. The shoulder of a 1921 cent with such marks is shown in chapter 1. Tired dies can be a problem from the early years onward, particularly with branchmint coins of the 1920s. In contrast, as a general rule cents from 1930 onward, particularly 1934 onward, are so plentiful that finding one that is just right will be no problem.

1943-S zinc-coated steel Lincoln cent.

In 1943 the Mint produced cents of steel with a coating of zinc, so that copper could be used in the war effort. These proved to be unsatisfactory as they were often mistaken for dimes and, as if this was not enough, they became stained and spotted after being in circulation for just a short time. In 1944 bronze metal was resumed.

To observe the 200th anniversary of Lincoln's birth the mints in 2009 produced four different reverse designs for this year only. Unfortunately, the country was in an economic recession that had started in 2008. The Federal Reserve had a reduced call for new coins from member banks. As a result the distribution of these unique designs was very erratic, and the opportunity to publicize them as a boon to coin collecting was lost.

These coins were followed by the Lincoln, Shield Reverse, cent in 2010, which is the design used to date. Due to the high standards of the modern Mint, high quality is universal for these issues.

While owning a rare 1909-S V.D.B. cent is nice, don't overlook that the zinc-coated steel cents of 1943 have a special story and appeal as do the cents of 2009, each of which is very inexpensive. Sometimes in numismatics common coins are overlooked.

TWO-CENT PIECES, 1864 TO 1873

A high-quality Proof two-cent piece of 1871.

Bronze two-cent pieces were introduced in 1864 at a time when, due to uncertainties as to the outcome of the Civil War, citizens had been hoarding coins. At the time the only other federal coins in circulation were cents. The two-cent piece was the first circulating coin to bear the motto IN GOD WE TRUST. One variety of that year has Small Motto letters and is somewhat scarce. In 1865 the nickel three-cent piece made its debut, after which the popularity of two-cent pieces declined. They were last struck for circulation in 1872, in limited numbers. In the last year, 1873, only Proofs were made.

As a general rule most two-cent pieces are well struck. Check all features including the leaves on both sides and the horizontal lines in the shield. Eye appeal can vary widely, especially among Mint State and Proof coins. I have never seen a full set of RD coins of original mint color for which every coin was of high quality.

There are so few two-cent pieces that collecting them is usually not a specialty itself, but is done in connection with other series. Only one coin is needed if you are forming a type set.

THREE-CENT PIECES, 1851 TO 1889

Nickel Three-Cent Pieces, 1865 to 1889

A beautiful Proof 1880 nickel three-cent piece. As is the case for many Proofs of this era, the fields are a combination of mirror surface and a tinge of frosty luster. The same is true of many Proof Shield nickels of this era. Proofs of both denominations of the year 1878 are often nearly completely frosty with few mirror characteristics. It is interesting to study the characteristics of 19th-century Proofs year by year.

Nickel three-cent pieces were struck continuously from 1865 through 1889. They were made of an alloy of 75% copper and 25% nickel, the latter being enough to give the coins a silvery appearance. A complete set consists of one of each year plus the 1887, 7 Over 6, overdate. Assembling a quality set of Proofs is easy enough to do, but you must pay attention. I don't think anyone has ever completed a set of circulation strikes with Full Details. When found, such sharp coins cost no more than weak ones. The trick is in finding them. While forming a specialized collection of this denomination is hardly a long-term pursuit, such a set can be a nice adjunct to other specialties.

Most Proofs are sharply struck. However, among circulation strikes weakness is sometimes seen on the wreath leaves and, especially, with some lightness in the tiny vertical lines that make up the III Roman numerals. The eye appeal of most coins is usually quite good.

Silver Three-Cent Pieces, 1851 to 1873

Silver three-cent pieces, sometimes called trimes, can be an interesting specialty in combination with other collections formed at the same time. There are three basic types: I from 1851 to 1853, II from 1854 to 1858, and III from 1859 to 1873. All were struck at the Philadelphia Mint except for the 1851-O from New Orleans. There are no rarities. These coins did not circulate after hoarding of all silver coins began in 1862. Most later issues are Proofs made for collectors.

THE THREE CENT COIN, FOR POST OFFICE USE.

This coin is somewhat thinner and smaller than a half dime, and while new has the appearance of silver, with rather a slippery feeling; 3333⅓ of these pieces make a hundred dollars, and contain $83,33 of silver, leaving a profit in the hands of the Mint of $16,67 on every $83,33.

In its issue of May 10, 1851, Gleason's Pictorial Drawing Room Companion announced the new three-cent piece. It was stated as being especially useful for buying three-cent stamps at the Post Office.

The 1851-O silver three-cent piece is the only coin of this denomination struck at a branch mint.

A typical 1856 silver three-cent piece. On the obverse the tops of all the letters are weak, as are the bottoms of the date numerals. The three-line frame around the star is missing in some sections and weak in others. The horizontal lines in the shield are wavy and irregular. On the reverse the stars, which should have sharp centers, are as flat as a pancake. The leaves and arrow details are weak.

Type I coins are often weak at the tiny shield at the center of the obverse star and on the stars and leaves on the reverse. Cherrypicking is needed to find a nice one, which will cost no more than a low-quality one of the same grade.

The Type II coins may well be the single worst strikes in 19th-century numismatics. While rare Proofs are somewhat sharp (but nearly always appear with some stars weak), nearly all circulation strikes of 1854 to 1858 have parts of the three frame lines surrounding the star weak or incomplete, and the shield is weak as well. Elements of the reverse are also weak. I have never seen a set of these five years with all pieces being sharply struck. In fact, even a single Full Details coin is a rarity. If you have the time and inclination, try building a set of circulation strikes with Full Details. You will be the first person in numismatic history to do this, if you are successful! Only a tiny percentage of coin buyers are aware of this—or of many similar situations involving strike (see my comments about Liberty Head nickels later, as another "secret").

Type III nickel three-cent pieces are usually well struck, but normal care should be taken to inspect all details.

NICKEL FIVE-CENT PIECES, 1866 TO DATE

Shield Nickels, 1866 to 1883

An 1866 nickel five-cent piece, the first year of the denomination.
The rays between the stars were discontinued in early 1867.

Nickel five-cent pieces were first struck in 1866. The alloy was 75% copper and 25% nickel. The new coins of the Shield design became popular and in time reduced the demand for nickel three-cent pieces. Shield nickels were made continuously through early 1883. In 1877 and 1878 the mintage consisted only of Proofs for collectors. Most of 1878 have a lot of mint frost or luster instead of deep mirror surfaces.

As is true of most series of coins of this era, circulation strikes can vary in sharpness, while Proofs usually have all features well defined. Circulation-strike Shield nickels of 1866 and 1867 with rays on the reverse often have weakness at the top of the shield on the obverse and the centers of the stars on the reverse. Later issues of 1867 through 1883 are usually fairly sharp.

The eye appeal is usually quite good. Circulated coins are typically light gray. Mint State and Proof coins are brilliant or appear with light toning. As always, avoid spotty or unattractive coins. For most series and specialties of this era a good way to go is to look at a lot of MS-64 and MS-65 coins and cherrypick the nice ones.

Liberty Head Nickels, 1883 to 1913

The Liberty Head nickel was launched in early 1883, following the production of Shield nickels of that date. Designed by Charles E. Barber, the obverse featured a classic head of Liberty, possibly a representation of Diana the huntress of ancient mythology, surrounded with 13 stars and with the date below. The reverse depicted an agricultural wreath enclosing the letter V for the denomination and an inscription around the outside border. The Roman numeral V for FIVE or 5 followed in concept the III used on the reverse of three-cent pieces. Sharpers took the new nickels, which were the diameter of a $5 gold coin, gold plated them, and passed them out as half eagles—a twice-told tale reprinted many times in narratives about numismatic history. Within a short time the word CENTS was added in prominent letters to prevent such fraud.

The first Liberty Head nickel design of 1883 lacked the word CENTS on the reverse.

Liberty Head nickels were made continuously through 1912. In 1912 nickels were struck for the first time at the Denver and San Francisco mints. In 1913 a Philadelphia Mint employee, Samuel Brown, secretly and illegally made five coins with the date 1913.

A detail of an 1886 nickel showing kernels on the corn ears. Most circulation strikes have some or most kernels missing, and some Proofs are weak in this area as well.

Circulation-strike Liberty Head nickels sometimes show weakness at the highest point of the hair on the obverse and at the star centers. On the reverse the kernels of corn are *usually* weak. Cherrypicking is needed to find coins with Full Details. Hardly anyone knows about these points of weakness, and such issues are not reflected in most catalog descriptions. Accordingly, when you find sharp coins the cost will be no more than for weak coins. Most Proofs are very sharp, but on quite a few the corn kernels are weak.

Eye appeal is usually quite good across the board. Liberty Head nickels form a beautiful collection—with the two types of 1883 and one of each later date through 1912, plus the 1912-D and 1912-S. Gradeflation has resulted in many MS-65 coins being called 66 or 67. Once again the key is to look through a number of coins to find one that is just right in terms of eye appeal and price. Many 65 coins are just as nice as those certified in higher grades in recent years.

Buffalo Nickels, 1913 to 1938

In 1913 the nickel was redesigned by James Earle Fraser, a nationally famous sculptor. The obverse featured an Indian (Native American) as taken from life (in contrast to the fanciful portrait used on Indian Head cents and 1907 $10 gold coins). The reverse depicted an American bison, popularly called a buffalo. The first issues of 1913 had the bison on raised ground. This was changed part way through 1913 to flat ground. Buffalo nickels, as they are universally nicknamed, were minted through 1938 with the exception of 1922, 1932, and 1933.

The first Buffalo nickel—1913 with the
buffalo (bison) standing on raised ground.

As a general rule, Philadelphia Mint coins are more sharply struck than are those of the branch mints. In the 1920s many Denver and San Francisco coins were struck with the dies too far apart in the press, resulting in weakness. The points to check are the center of the obverse above the braid and, on the reverse, the shoulder and fur of the bison. On coins with Full Details these should be sharp, including all of the hair on the bison's head. As discussed earlier, in the marketplace there is no notice taken of the sharpness or lack thereof of Buffalo nickels. Accordingly, with patience you can form a set with Full Details for no extra cost!

The Full Details reverse of a 1915 Buffalo nickel. Notice the details of the
fur on the bison's head and shoulder. Relatively few nickels are this sharp.

The typical circulation-strike Buffalo nickel such as this 1924-D
has lightness of strike on the bison's head and in some other areas.

Relatively few Buffalo nickels are as flatly struck as this 1925-S.
Third-party grading services take no notice as to whether a
Buffalo nickel is with Full Details or if it is flat, as mentioned earlier.

Buffalo nickels have always been popular. At one time in the 1950s dealer Abe Kosoff took a survey of his clients and found that Buffalo nickels outranked even Lincoln cents in popularity, which was a surprise.[3]

Jefferson Nickels, 1938 to Date

A 1945-D "wartime" Jefferson nickel in silver alloy and with the mintmark over the dome
of Monticello. On the reverse, Monticello has six full steps on sharply struck nickels made
from sharp dies, but in practice some or most of the steps are not visible, as on this coin.

In 1938 sculptor Felix O. Schlag was the winner of a nationwide competition to redesign the nickel. His motif featured President Thomas Jefferson on the obverse and Jefferson's home, Monticello, on the reverse. After some adjustments were made, coins with the new design were struck at the Philadelphia, Denver, and San Francisco mints. The alloy was the standard 75% copper and 25% nickel. Mintmarks were placed on the reverse edge to the right of Monticello. From partway through 1942 through 1945 nickel was eliminated and a new alloy containing part silver was introduced—giving the coins a particularly bright, silvery appearance when new. After these "wartime" nickels were in circulation for a few years many became dark and spotted. In 1946 the regular alloy was resumed.

The reverse of the 2005 Westward Journey nickel says, "Ocean in view! O!
The joy," a quotation from the journal of the Lewis and Clark expedition.
In the original journal entry, the spelling was "Ocian," but the Mint edited it for clarity.

Changes to the design were made in 2004 and 2005 as part of the Westward Journey series. The obverse was redesigned in 2005 to feature a different portrait of Jefferson. Coins of these two years are interesting, attractive, and inexpensive. There is room in every collection for a set of these distinctive pieces. The regular reverse was resumed in 2006. This combination is in use today.

The design of the Jefferson nickel is such that the obverse is usually sharp. Any lightness on the obverse of 1938 to 2004 coins is apt to be toward the back of Jefferson's head and is not particularly noticeable.

On this circulation-strike 1939 nickel five steps (including the top level of the portico) are sharp, and the lowest, or sixth, step is incomplete.

On this 1938-D nickel the steps are not sharp, this being typical of the vast majority of circulation strikes in the series.

The reverse is a different situation entirely. On sharp dies made from sharp hubs Monticello has six discernible steps. These can be seen on some (but hardly all) Proofs and on a very few circulation strikes. Most often, the steps range from indistinct steps to three or four steps, occasionally showing five. There are some varieties, including from the late 20th century, that are not known to exist with Full Steps (FS). At one time there was a passion for collecting Full Step coins by members of the Full Step Nickel Club. That later faded, and the club is currently inactive. Still, seeking nickels with as many steps as possible is an interesting and lengthy pursuit for a number of specialists. When found, nickels with sharp reverses cost no more than those without.

HALF DISMES, 1792

The silver half dismes of 1792 (the predecessors to the half dimes, with an older spelling) represent the first coinage struck for circulation by the federal government. In July 1,500 pieces were struck in the shop of John Harper, on

1792 half disme.

Mint-destined equipment, before the Philadelphia Mint was ready. Although facts are scarce, additional coins were struck in the autumn.

Today most surviving coins show wear, often extensive. Lightness of strike and parallel adjustment marks are common. If you are seeking one, look for the nicest overall quality you can find within your budget range.

Half dimes from 1792 to 1873 (this range including the half disme) form an interesting and challenging specialty. Over the years many numismatists have built notable sets.

HALF DIMES, 1794 TO 1873

Flowing Hair Half Dimes, 1794 and 1795

A high-level Mint State 1795 Flowing Hair half dime. On the illustrated coin the raised dot at the center of the reverse was for one compass point while the other point scratched a light circle near the border, so that the engraver could punch in the letters in alignment. Many 18th century and early 19th century show such center dots.

Half dimes of the Flowing Hair design were all minted in 1795. The 1794 dies were not used in that year and were held over to the next. For a coin club quiz, an entertaining set of questions might be:

Were any half dimes minted in 1794?

No.

Are there any half dimes dated 1794?

Yes, but they were minted in 1795.

The sharpness of half dimes of this type is usually fairly good, but some lightness on the eagle's breast is common. Check the details at the center of both sides. Coins with prominent adjustment marks should be avoided. You are on your own regarding these, as certified holders do not mention them.

Varieties of half dimes of the early years are attributed by LM numbers as described in *Federal Half Dimes 1792 to 1837* by Russell Logan and John McCloskey, 1998.

Draped Bust Half Dimes, 1796 to 1805

Half dimes of the Draped Bust obverse and Small Eagle reverse were made in 1796 and 1797. A die was prepared in 1795 but not used until 1796, when it was overdated 1796, 6 Over 5. The striking quality varies widely on half dimes of this design, as does eye appeal. Some have lightness at the center details on the obverse, and nearly all have lightness at the center of the reverse. Cherrypicking for quality is the order of the day.

In 1800 the Heraldic Eagle reverse was adopted for half dimes, a motif introduced on the $2.50 coins of 1796. This was used through 1803 and again in 1805, after which there was no coinage of half dimes for the next two decades. The 1802 half dime is a classic rarity that is not known to exist in Mint State. Its fame is enduring, beginning in 1883 when Harold P. Newlin published a lengthy essay extolling its virtues and listing all examples known to him.

Draped Bust, Heraldic Eagle, half dimes are usually visually attractive. Some weakness on the obverse star points, occasionally on the hair, and on one or several of the stars above the eagle on the reverse. These can be tolerated if the eye appeal is excellent.

A 1796, 6 Over 5, overdate half dime with Draped Bust obverse and Small Eagle reverse. This particular specimen is exceptionally sharp.

A 1797 half dime with 15 obverse stars. Varieties with 13 and 16 stars were also made. This coin is weakly struck at the centers, particularly on the reverse.

An 1800 half dime with Draped Bust obverse and Heraldic Eagle reverse.

Capped Bust Half Dimes, 1829 to 1837

After a lapse since 1805, half dimes were again struck in 1829. The occasion was the laying of the cornerstone for the second Philadelphia Mint building, and freshly-struck half dimes were given out to those who attended the ceremony. Coinage had begun in the wee hours of the morning. This served to revive the denomination, and half dimes of the Capped Bust type continued to be made into 1837. The motif is a copy of the design by assistant Mint engraver John Reich and first used on half dollars in 1807.

Most Capped Bust half dollars are fairly well struck. Check the star centers on the obverse and the central portrait details. On the reverse check the upper wing at the

A special ceremony held on July 4, 1829, to lay the cornerstone for the second Philadelphia Mint furnished the occasion to strike Capped Bust half dimes for the first time. Shown here is an engraving of it published in 1835.

1829 Capped Bust half dime.

left. As there are no rare dates in this series, forming a date run is easy enough to do. Some LM die combinations are rare, however.

Liberty Seated Half Dimes, 1837 to 1873

The Liberty Seated design by Christian Gobrecht was introduced in the half dime (and dime) series in 1837. Philadelphia Mint coins of 1837 and New Orleans Mint issues of 1838-O lack stars on the obverse—inspired by Gobrecht's silver dollars of 1836. Today the 1837 half dimes are plentiful in all grades, including Mint State. The striking is usually fairly sharp for the 1837 and 1838-O, but check the head of Liberty on this and all later Liberty Seated half dimes through 1873, and check the highest areas of the leaves on the reverse.

An 1838-O half dime, Liberty Seated without stars on the obverse—a design made only at the Philadelphia Mint in 1837 and the New Orleans Mint in 1838. All other Liberty Seated half dimes to 1859 have stars on the obverse.

From 1838 through 1859 the Liberty Seated design has 13 stars on the obverse. For some half dimes of 1853 and all of 1854 and 1855 there are arrowheads at the date. The head of Liberty is sometimes weak, so check this, and also examine the center points of the stars.

1853-O half dime with arrows at the date.

In the early 1960s, before *Coin World* assembled its own numismatic experts on staff, I was their consultant on inquiries for new varieties, numismatic history, and certain other questions. One day I was sent a curious coin—an 1858 half dime with the final date punched over an inverted date. I agreed that this was genuine, and it was publicized. Today it is a standard variety widely listed.

Detail of the 1858 over inverted date half dime.

From 1860 through the end of the half dime series in 1873 the obverse has UNITED STATES OF AMERICA around the border and a restyled wreath on the reverse. These are usually fairly well struck, but check the head of Liberty. On the reverse some are slightly weak at the upper left of the wreath. Proof Liberty Seated half dimes are usually well struck on both sides.

On half dimes of the 1860 to 1873 type there can often be weakness at the wreath at the upper left. Sharp and weak examples are illustrated.

For half dimes as well as other series of this design you may wish to investigate joining the Liberty Seated Collectors Club (http://www.lsccweb.org/), publisher of *The Gobrecht Journal*.

DIMES, 1796 TO DATE

Draped Bust Dimes, 1796 to 1807

Dimes of the Draped Bust obverse and Small Eagle reverse were made in 1796 and 1797, paralleling the styles of half dimes and half dollars for the same years. The striking quality varies widely, as does eye appeal. Some have lightness at the center details on the obverse, and nearly all have lightness on the eagle's breast feathers at the center of the reverse. However, the typical dime is sharper than a half dime of the same design, particularly on the reverse. Eye appeal can vary widely. Cherrypicking for quality is the order of the day.

1796 dime, Draped Bust obverse, Small Eagle reverse.

Die varieties of dimes can be attributed to *Early United States Dimes 1796–1837* published in 1984, the work of a team of five authors.

1798 dime with Draped Bust obverse and Heraldic Eagle reverse.

In 1798 the Heraldic Eagle reverse was adopted. This was used for that year and also for 1801 through 1807, with the exception of 1806. The striking quality can vary all over the place. The first places to look for weakness are the centers of the obverse and reverse. The star centers on the obverse are another place to check. On the reverse the top right of the shield and the nearby part of the wing are often light as are some of the stars above the eagle. Even the best examples usually are a compromise with some weakness.

A flatly struck Mint State 1807 dime with
hardly any border detail in some areas.

At the Mint in 1807 some of the weakest strikes of early silver coins were made. All denominations currently being made that year—the half dime, dime, quarter, and half dollar—were involved. I cannot help but wonder if somewhere among old Mint correspondence there is mention of this. On the other hand, copper and gold coins of 1807 are usually fairly well struck. Perhaps a specific coin press and a single operator were involved. The illustrated coin, a high-grade Mint State piece, is a poster example of weakness. Such a coin would appeal to an investor, as it and like coins are graded without mention of strike. For *you* it should not be considered, even at half of the market price.

Capped Bust Dimes, 1809 to 1837

An 1809 dime, the first year of the Capped Bust type.
This is a typical dime of the early years—with lightness
at the star centers and with the denticles incomplete.

No dimes were struck in 1808. In 1809 the Capped Bust type was introduced—the style by assistant Mint engraver John Reich that made its debut on half dollars in 1807. Dimes of this design in the early style were made in 1809; as an overdate 1811, 11 Over 10; and 1814. Then came a jump to 1820, after which production was continuous through early 1830. Dimes of 1822 are scarce—making it the key date of the decade.

A remarkable Capped Bust dime of 1821 with bold denticles and sharp star centers.
There is, however, slight weakness at the obverse and reverse centers. With beautiful
eye appeal, this coin would attract many buyers if offered for sale.

Many dimes of the 1809 to 1830 years are slightly weak in areas. Check the center of the obverse and the centers of the star points. The latter are often weak, especially on the earlier dates. On the reverse check the neck of the eagle, the higher areas of the claws and leaves. Sometimes the center part of the motto is weak or missing. The denticles on these and other early silver coins are often irregular or partly missing. As these are not major features of the design, such lightness can be overlooked. Eye appeal can vary, but the typical Capped Bust dime is attractive.

Sometime in 1830 the dime was slightly modified. New equipment at the Mint permitted the production of more standardized coins. The denticles are now in the form of small beads instead of teeth, and the coins are more uniform in appearance. These were made continually through 1837. Most are sharply struck. Eye appeal can vary. Finding a coin that is just right should be no problem.

Liberty Seated Dimes, 1837 to 1891

An 1837 dime, Liberty Seated without stars on the obverse—as made only at the Philadelphia Mint in 1837 and the New Orleans Mint in 1838, as can also be said for half dimes of this type. All other Liberty Seated half dimes to 1859 have stars on the obverse, as does the 1860-S.

The Liberty Seated design by Christian Gobrecht was introduced in the half dime and dime series in 1837. Philadelphia Mint coins of 1837 and New Orleans Mint issues of 1838-O lack stars on the obverse—inspired by Gobrecht's silver dollars of 1836. Today the 1837 dimes are plentiful in all grades, including Mint State. The striking is usually fairly sharp for the 1837 and 1838-O, but check the head of Liberty on this and all later Liberty Seated dimes through 1891, and check the highest areas of the leaves on the reverse.

1838 Liberty Seated dime with obverse stars.

From 1838 through 1859 plus 1860 for the San Francisco Mint (1860-S) the Liberty Seated design has 13 stars on the obverse. For some dimes of 1853 and all of 1854 and 1855 there are arrowheads at the date. The head of Liberty is sometimes weak, so check this, and also check the center points of the stars.

A Proof Liberty Seated dime of 1860, the first year with lettering at the obverse border.

From 1860 through the end of the Liberty Seated dime series in 1891 the obverse has UNITED STATES OF AMERICA around the border and a restyled wreath on the reverse. These are usually fairly well struck, but check the head of Liberty. On the reverse some are slightly weak at the upper left of the wreath. Some dimes of 1873 and all of 1874 have arrowheads at the date and are considered to be a different type. Dimes were struck at the Carson City Mint from 1871 to 1878. Those of the first several years are rare today, and the 1873-CC Without Arrows is unique.

Proof Liberty Seated dimes are usually well struck on both sides. There are scattered exceptions in the late 1860s when some lightness and/or lintmarks (from threads or dirt on the dies) can be a problem.

For half dimes as well as other series of this design you may wish to investigate joining the Liberty Seated Collectors Club, publisher of *The Gobrecht Journal*. Information can be found on the Internet.

Barber Dimes, 1892 to 1916

1896-O Barber dime.

Liberty Head dimes, quarters, and half dollars designed by Chief Engraver Charles E. Barber first appeared in 1892. On the dime the reverse wreath type introduced in 1860 was continued.

The New Orleans Mint opened in 1838 and was closed in early 1861.
It reopened in 1879 and produced coins until its final closing in 1909.
Barber coins of the three denominations were struck there starting in 1892.

Production of Barber dimes was continuous from 1892 through most of the year 1916. Most are very well struck. Check the highest areas of the portrait on the obverse and the details of the wreath on the reverse. Most have good eye appeal as well. The Barber Coin Collectors Society (http://www.barbercoins.org/) is devoted to this coinage.

Mercury Dimes, 1916 to 1945

Mercury dimes by nickname, more formally Winged Liberty Head dimes (as Mercury the mythical messenger had wings on his *feet*), were minted from 1916 to 1945 except for 1922, 1932, and 1933. The designer was Adolph A. Weinman, who also created the Walking Liberty half dollar. Key varieties include 1916-D; 1921; 1921-D; 1942, 2 Over 1, overdate; and 1942-D, 2 Over 1, overdate. Mercury dimes have always been one of the most popular 20th century series.

A 1927-S Mercury dime, a common issue
among those struck from 1916 to 1945.

On the obverse check the hair on the portrait and the leading edge of the wing. The last digit of the date is sometimes weak, and the rim can be irregular in that area. On the reverse check the horizontal bands in the fasces. Those with the center pair fully separated are called Full Bands (FB) and sell for a premium. Even if a dime is marked FB, check the other areas for sharpness as well.

Roosevelt Dimes, 1946 to Date

1968-D Roosevelt dime.

Roosevelt dimes designed by Chief Engraver John R. Sinnock have been made continuously from 1946 to date. Those minted 1965 and later are on clad planchets. Earlier dimes are 90% silver. All dates and mintmarks are very affordable in high grades.

Nearly all in the marketplace are well struck. The highest points of Roosevelt's hair on the obverse and the nearly-vertical ribs near the bottom of the torch on the reverse are slightly light on some, but perhaps not worth noticing.

TWENTY-CENT PIECES, 1875 TO 1878

Twenty-cent pieces were introduced in 1875 with the idea that they would facilitate the making of change in the American West. The public soon confused them with quarters of somewhat similar size and appearance. After a generous production in 1875, mainly at the San Francisco Mint, circulation-strike production dropped off sharply in 1875. The last coinage consisted of Proofs for collectors in 1877 and 1878. The Liberty Seated obverse is similar to other silver coinage of the era. The reverse eagle is similar to that found on the trade dollar.

Proof 1878 twenty-cent piece. Proof twenty-cent pieces were struck of all years from 1875 to 1878. Circulation strikes were made only in 1875 and 1876.

On the obverse check the head of Liberty, the word LIBERTY on the shield, and the star centers. On the reverse there is often weakness at the top of the eagle's wings and on the wing to the left.

Believe it or not, twenty-cent pieces can be collected by die varieties. Often the distinctions are microscopic, but under magnification they can be detected. *Double Dime: The United States Twenty-Cent Piece*, by Lane J. Brunner and John J. Frost, 2014, tells all.[4]

QUARTER DOLLARS, 1796 TO DATE

Draped Bust Quarter Dollars, 1796 to 1807

A particularly attractive prooflike Mint State quarter of 1796, the first year of issue of the denomination.

Quarter dollars were not struck until 1796, when the Draped Bust design with Small Eagle reverse was used. The mintage was only 6,146 pieces. Two die varieties are known, Browning-1 and 2. Most coins are sharply struck with strong obverse portrait features and bold denticles. The reverse is usually sharp as well, except for the eagle's breast feathers and head. As the only year of the design type and a coin that is rare in all grades, such pieces are in strong demand. Remarkably, over 100 Mint State coins are known, most of which have partially prooflike surfaces.

Early quarter die varieties are delineated by JR numbers detailed in *Early Quarter Dollars of the U.S. Mint, 1796–1838*, published in 2010.

Draped Bust quarter dollar of 1805, the type of 1804 to 1807.
Weak at the star centers on the obverse and above the center
of the reverse, not at all unusual.

After 1796 no quarters were struck until 1804, at which time the Heraldic Eagle reverse motif was adopted. These were made through 1807.

A detail of the 1806, 6 Over 5, the only overdate in the early quarter series.

All I have ever seen are weak in some areas, and those of 1807 are particularly so. Check the center of the portrait and the star centers on the obverse. On the reverse check the center as well as the stars above the eagle. Search until you find one of above-average striking sharpness, with good eye appeal.

Capped Bust Quarter Dollars, 1815 to 1838

1815 Capped Bust quarter dollar, first year of the design.

After 1807 there was no coinage of quarters until 1815, at which time the Capped Bust type was introduced—the design by John Reich first seen on half dollars of 1815. From 1815 through 1828 the coins were on slightly larger planchets than were used later. The motto E PLURIBUS UNUM was on a band above the eagle on the reverse.

Proof 1827 quarter, the classic rarity of the early quarter-dollar series.

There are several scarce varieties in this range, and the 1827 is a classic rarity. One of the old-time tales is that Philadelphia collector Joseph Mickley called at the Mint this year and obtained four Proofs for face value, but this has never been confirmed. The obverse die started life with the date 1822, then it was overdated to 1823, 3 Over 2, then to 1827, 7 Over 3 Over 2. Later most of the under-digits were removed, the die was polished and Proofs were struck.

Corrected error, 25 over 50 on the reverse die of an 1822 quarter.

Die cutting errors are scattered across early coinage, particularly in the copper and silver denominations. When making a reverse die used on an 1822 quarter the engraver thought he was making a 50-cent piece, entered that denomination, and then corrected it. The striking is usually quite good, but there are many exceptions. Check the details on both sides.

1831 Capped Bust quarter of the modified design with bead-like denticles and slightly smaller diameter. E PLURIBUS UNUM is gone from above the eagle.

In 1831 the design was modified slightly. The diameter was reduced slightly, the details were modified, the motto was eliminated above the eagle, and the denticles were modified to be small beads. These were struck continually through early 1838. Although some varieties are elusive, a collection of one of each date can be formed without difficulty.

With relatively few exceptions the striking details are quite good on quarters of this design type. Eye appeal varies. Finding a nice coin will be no problem.

Liberty Seated Quarters, 1838 to 1891

1838 Liberty Seated quarter dollar.

Quarter dollars of the Liberty Seated design were made continuously from 1838 to 1891. All had 13 stars around the obverse and the date below.

A sharply struck 1853 quarter with arrows at the date and rays on the reverse.

In 1853 there was a slight reduction in authorized weight, and, to signify this, arrowheads were placed at the date and on the reverse a glory of rays was arranged around the eagle. In 1854 and 1855 the arrowheads were retained, but the rays were dropped. This same format was used on Liberty Seated half dollars of these three years. From 1856 to 1865 the style was the same as first used in 1838, although the weight was slightly lighter.

In 1866 the motto IN GOD WE TRUST was added above the eagle on the reverse at the same time as this was done for all of the higher-denomination silver and gold coins.

An 1874-S quarter with arrows at the date, as on some quarters of 1873 and all of 1874. On the reverse is the motto IN GOD WE TRUST, standard since 1866.

On February 21, 1873, there was a slight increase in weight. Arrowheads were added to the date to signify this change, and they were retained in 1874.

From 1875 to the end of the series in 1891 the design was the same as that used in 1866. The weight was slightly heavier. From 1879 onward the mintage quantities for quarter dollars were reduced in some years as the Treasury had enough on hand. Vast quantities of silver coins, which had been hoarded by the public starting in the spring of 1862, came out of hiding.

For the entire Liberty Seated series check the head of Liberty and the star centers for completeness. The reverses are usually quite sharp, but check the higher design parts near the center.

Barber Quarters, 1892 to 1916

The "Liberty Head" quarter designed by Chief Engraver Charles E. Barber, and more commonly known as the Barber quarter made its first appearance in 1892. Mintage was continuous through most of 1916. In the earlier years the Philadelphia, New Orleans, and San Francisco mints struck these pieces. Starting in 1906 the Denver Mint made Barber quarters as well. The low-mintage 1896-S, 1901-S, and 1913-S are the key varieties. The typical member of the Barber Coin Collectors Society (http://www.barbercoins.org/) seeks a high circulated or low Mint State grade for most of the varieties, but opts for lower grades on these three San Francisco rarities.

1895-O Barber quarter dollar.

This detail shows areas of light striking on a 1907-O Barber quarter: the head, shield and part of wing at right, talons at lower left, and talons and arrow feathers at lower right.

The striking quality of most Barber quarters is usually quite good. Check all areas, however. The key spots for weakness are on the reverse in various spots, including at the upper right where the shield joins the wing and also on the eagle's claw at the lower right and the arrow feathers below the claw. With a magnifying glass check all of the details.

Standing Liberty Quarters, 1916 to 1930

A lustrous Mint State 1916 Standing Liberty quarter,
the first year of the design.

Designed by sculptor Hermon A. MacNeil, Standing Liberty quarters made their debut in 1916. Those of that year and of early 1917 are called Type I. Liberty is nude from the waist up and on the reverse there are no stars below the eagle. The 1916 quarter is a rarity. Only 52,000 were struck, and few were saved at the time of issue.

A detail of a 1926-D quarter certified as Full Head.
The hair is flat next to the cheek, and some shield rivets are missing.

The Type II was introduced in 1917 at the request of MacNeil, who desired to show Liberty in a coat of mail, armed for preparedness with the World War raging in Europe. This type was used through 1930, except for the year 1922, when none were coined. As discussed earlier in the text, there is a conundrum regarding the use of Full Head (FH) to describe certain pieces. On the vast majority of so-labeled FH coins some of the head details are flat, and *usually some shield rivets are weak or missing.*

That said, a lot of money can be saved if you cherrypick a coin with complete rivets and with a head that is partially full, perhaps not as full as one called FH. At least that is what I would do. In decades of handling many specialized collections of these beautiful coins, I have never seen a set with all coins having Full Details.

Standing Liberty quarters are one of America's most popular 20th century series. The aforementioned 1916 is rare as is the 1918-S, 8 Over 7, overdate.

Washington Quarters, 1932 to Date

A lustrous Mint State example of the low-mintage 1932-S quarter, the first year of the design.

The Washington quarter was designed by sculptor John Flanagan. The portrait was taken from a marble bust by Jean Antoine Houdon for which Washington posed at Mount Vernon in 1785. The design first appeared in 1932. It was at first conceived as a commemorative to observe the 200th anniversary of Washington's birth. This was changed when the Treasury decided to use it to replace the Standing Liberty design, a motif that had nearly always had problems with striking.

Washington quarters of the new design were made from 1932 through 1998, except for 1933 and 1975. In 1965 the standard alloy of 90% silver and 10% copper was replaced by clad metal planchets without silver. For the bicentennial year quarters dated 1776–1976 were produced. The reverse depicted an early drummer boy. Of the three reverse designs created for three denominations, the drummer boy is the only one that was praised by collectors.

For some reason I could never understand, Jean Antoine Houdon's classic portrait from his famous 1785 bust was "improved" in the late 1990s by adding hair strand squiggles to the head, apparently without knowledge that the original Houdon bust had no such hair details.

A Proof 2000-S New Hampshire quarter in the State series.

In 1999 the series of 50 State quarters commenced with a reverse design relating to Delaware. The new series followed a suggestion made to Congress by Harvey Stack and seconded by others in the hobby. Each year four different states were honored in the order in which they ratified the Constitution. When the states ended, quarters were made with motifs relating to the District of Columbia and American territories. At the launch ceremony for the New Hampshire quarter held at the auditorium of the New Hampshire Historical Society in 2000 I represented the numismatic press and wrote a feature story for *Coin World*. In 2009 several U.S. territories and the District of Columbia were likewise honored.

In 2010 a new series at first called National Park quarters was launched—one for each state, in chronological order of the establishment of the parks. It was soon realized that not all states had national parks, but all had national monuments or other dedicated areas. The coins were renamed the America the Beautiful Series, and they focused on sites of national or historic importance from each state.

Final sketch by artist-sculptor Phebe Hemphill for the 2013 New Hampshire quarter.

Acting Mint Director Richard Peterson and Q. David Bowers at the 2013 America the Beautiful quarter launch. Peterson is holding a model of the coin's reverse.

I was on the spot at the dedication ceremony in 2013 when it was New Hampshire's turn in the America the Beautiful series. There is no national park in the state, so the White Mountain National Forest was honored. Inaugurating the coin, Acting Mint Director Richard Peterson addressed a large room filled with school kids and adults at Plymouth State University. The reverse of the quarter features Mount Chocorua and was designed by Mint sculptor-artist Phebe Hemphill, a fine friend.

Washington quarters of the early years have few problems with striking, as the highest-relief features were not made with delicate details. The later State and America the Beautiful quarters are mostly quite sharp. Not much cherrypicking effort is needed.

The quarters from 1999 onward are a vast panorama of different reverse designs. All are very affordable in Mint State or, for San Francisco, Proof format. You would do well to assemble such a set. Proof coins are mostly gems as issued, whereas Mint State coins vary. MS-65 is an ideal grade. Cherrypick to find coins with only a few marks.

HALF DOLLARS, 1794 TO DATE

Flowing Hair Half Dollars, 1794 and 1795

A lustrous and attractive Mint State 1795 Flowing Hair half dollar.
Some central details are light, as is usually the case with this design type.

The first half dollars were made in 1794 and are of the Flowing Hair type, similar to the motif on the half dime and dollar. This design was also used in 1795. This is a very pleasing depiction of Liberty, and examples in all grades are in great demand.

Striking varies. On the obverse the center of the portrait can be weak. Ditto for the star centers. On the reverse the feathers on the breast of the eagle are usually light or missing in the highest-relief area. Denticles can be irregular.

When cherrypicking for quality, seek the sharpest you can find, bearing in mind that not all details will be full. Perfection does not exist. Avoid any and all coins with distracting adjustment marks. These are very common. Finally, choose a coin with attractive eye appeal.

Early half dollars die varieties are delineated by Overton numbers detailed in *Early Half Dollar Die Varieties 1794–1836* by Al C. Overton, 1967, since updated in several editions. In the early 1960s Overton and California dealer John Cobb were both at work on a listing of varieties. Overton succeeded first, after which Cobb sold his reference collection and other half dollars, including a hoard of the scarce 1815, 5 Over 2, variety, which I bought from him.

Draped Bust Half Dollars, 1796 to 1807

In 1796 and 1797 the Draped Bust design with Small Eagle reverse was used. These were made in small numbers and are rarities today. Even an example worn nearly smooth is worth many thousands of dollars. The striking is usually fairly good except for the feathers on the eagle's breast. One cannot be too picky, as high-grade examples are not offered often. In any event select one with nice eye appeal. The highest across-the-board quality collection of early federal coins ever formed was assembled by D. Brent Pogue (one of his 1796 half dollars is illustrated above), who took nearly 40 years, starting in 1975, to consider thousands of coins to find specimens that were among the very finest of their kind.

Draped Bust obverse, Small Eagle reverse half dollar—the general
type of 1796 and 1797. The illustrated 1796 is the variety with 15
obverse stars. Another 1796 variety has 16 stars.

An 1806 Draped Bust obverse, Heraldic Eagle reverse half dollar,
the type coined from 1801 to 1807. The illustrated example is
above average in sharpness, with excellent portrait and star
details and with the center reverse, including stars above the
eagle, being exceptional.

The next half dollar coinage was in 1801 with the Draped Bust obverse combined
with the new Heraldic Eagle reverse. It was used through 1807, with the exception
of 1804 (though there is an 1805, 5 Over 4, overdate, showing that an 1804 die
was made but not used). Similar to the situation for quarter dollars of the same
type, nearly all show weakness in one area or another. Some of 1806 and 1807 have
indistinct rims. See the sharpest you can find, which for this type may involve examining dozens of images. Eye appeal varies, but there are many attractive pieces in
the marketplace.

Capped Bust, Lettered Edge, Half Dollars, 1807 to 1836

Capped Bust half dollars with lettered edge were made from 1807 through 1836
with the exception of 1816. As silver dollars had last been coined for circulation
in 1804, the half dollar was the largest current silver coin of the realm. They were
struck in large quantities. Many were used as bank reserves. The result is that many
exist today, mostly in higher grades of Extremely Fine to Mint State. Collecting
them by die varieties (Overton numbers) has been a passion for many years. In
terms of popularity, as a specialty only large copper cents have more devotees.

1831 Capped Bust, Lettered Edge half dollar, Overton-109 variety. This is representative of the general type. Notice the lightness toward the left side of the motto. This is because this feature in the reverse die was opposite the high relief of Liberty's drapery on the obverse, and the spacing of the dies was such that metal did not fill both features completely.

The 1817, 7 Over 4, overdate, O-102.

The series is rich with hundreds of varieties, including overdates. The dies were made by hand, by punching in the liberty head and eagle and adding stars, digits, and letters separately. The 1817, 7 Over 4, is famous as a rarity, and only about a dozen are known—all in circulated grades.

The quality of strike is usually fairly good. Those of 1807 and 1808 are often soft in some areas. Half dollars toward the end of the type tend to have better details. Features to check include the portrait and stars on the obverse and on the reverse the upper wing of the eagle at the left, the lettering on the motto ribbon, and the lettering around the edge. Denticles can vary widely. If you pursue these by die varieties, illustrations in the Overton book will guide you as to what to expect.

Capped Bust, Reeded Edge, Half Dollars, 1836 to 1839

Beginning in November 1836 a modified design was introduced for half dollars. The basic obverse depiction of Liberty and reverse motif of an eagle were retained, but now slightly smaller. The overall diameter was reduced, and the edge was reeded. On the reverse the denomination was given as 50 CENTS instead of the earlier 50 C.

A steam-powered press was used for this and later designs (until electric motors became standard in the 1890s). This allowed for more consistent striking pressure and better overall quality. Die-making was improved, and all of the features were provided by the hub and master-hub dies used to make working dies, except for the four-digit date which was added with a special logotype punch. This general process became standard across all denominations.

1837 Capped Bust, Reeded Edge, half dollar. Denomination as 50 CENTS.

Somewhat fewer than 5,000 reeded-edge pieces were made in 1836. Today that date is rare, while examples of 1837 are plentiful. Striking sharpness is usually good, but check the higher points.

1838 Capped Bust, Reeded Edge, half dollar. Denomination as HALF DOL.

In 1838 continuing into 1839 a new type was created by giving the denomination as HALF DOL. Examples of both dates can be found easily. At the New Orleans Mint about a dozen 1838-O half dollars were made, creating a famous rarity. 1839-O half dollars were made in larger numbers and are easily collectible, but scarce in high Mint State grades.

The striking is usually good, but check the parts in highest relief. Eye appeal is usually satisfactory.

Liberty Seated Half Dollars, 1839 to 1891

1846 Liberty Seated half dollar, Tall Date variety.

Types of Liberty Seated half dollars largely echo the types used on contemporary quarters. The first was issued in 1839, with Liberty on the obverse surrounded by 13 stars and with the date below. On the reverse there is a perched eagle with

UNITED STATES OF AMERICA above and HALF DOL. below. This general type was made through early 1866. In the 1840s these were minted at Philadelphia and New Orleans, often in quantity. No numismatic attention was paid to them at the time, and the survival of high-grade examples is a matter of chance.

Apart from the standard dates and mintmarks, many varieties of dates and lettering were made. One variety of 1844-O has a dramatically doubled date, first punched too high and into the base of Liberty, then corrected. One 1846 die has the final digit over an erroneous horizontal 6. Beyond that 1846 half dollars were made in different date sizes, and an 1847 half dollar was struck from a die originally dated 1846, with most of the first date removed.

1844-O half dollar with dramatically doubled date.

1846 half dollar with 6 over horizontal 6.

1853-O half dollar of the early style. Only three are known today, each with significant wear.

1853 With Arrows and Rays half dollar. A brilliant coin with sharply struck details.

In 1853 there was a slight reduction in authorized weight. To signify this, arrowheads were placed alongside the date on the obverse and a glory of rays was added around the eagle on the reverse. Before this took place a small number of half dollars without arrows were made at the New Orleans Mint. Only three such coins are known today, all showing extensive wear.

In 1854 and 1855 the rays were dropped. From 1856 to part way through 1866 the type reverted to that used before 1853, but the weight was slightly more.

1873 With Arrows half dollar. Arrowheads were used on most half dollars of this year and all of 1874.
The motto IN GOD WE TRUST was added to the reverse in 1866.

In 1866 the motto IN GOD WE TRUST was added on a ribbon above the eagle. For most 1873 half dollars, and all of 1874, arrowheads were added alongside the date to signify a slight increase in weight. From 1879 to 1891 the mintages of circulation strikes were low, as the Treasury had a large supply of earlier coins on hand.

Proofs for collectors were made from 1839 onward in small numbers until the late 1850s, when numismatics became very popular and demand, along with Proof production, increased.

Liberty Seated half dollars are a very popular specialty today. More exist than do the quantities of Liberty Seated half dimes, dimes, quarters, and dollars combined. The vast majority of dates and mintmarks are readily collectible, although early coins can be rare in Mint State as are Carson City half dollars from the first several years of mintage, 1870 to 1874.

Sharpness can vary. On the obverse check the head of Liberty and the star centers. On the reverse check the center and slightly above. Eye appeal is generally good.

Barber Half Dollars, 1892 to 1915

1892 Barber half dollar.

Liberty Head half dollars designed by Chief Engraver Charles E. Barber were issued continuously from 1892 to 1915. These are called Barber half dollars in his honor. Of the three Barber denominations, the half dollars are the most economical to collect. In contrast to the dimes with the rare 1894-S and the quarters with the elusive and expensive 1896-S, 1901-S, and 1913-S, there are no especially rare half dollars in circulated grades. In Mint State, especially at higher levels, some are rare.

Many circulation-strike Barber half dollars are weakly struck in several areas. On the obverse the star centers are flat on some. On the reverse it is quite common for the upper right of the shield, the leg on the right, some of the tail feathers, and the arrow feathers to be weak or even flat. Cherrypicking is necessary if you desire to build a set with Full Details on every coin.

An 1893-O half dollar with multiple areas of weakness. On the obverse stars 1, 2, and 3 to the left are slightly flat, and on the right stars 10 through 13 are very flat. On the reverse, areas of flatness are indicated.

There are two items of good news: (1) Every date and mintmark can be found sharply struck, and (2) When found, a coin with Full Details costs no more than a coin without them. Very few collectors and dealers take notice of weakly struck pieces, and weakness is not mentioned on holders. Eye appeal is generally good for all grades.

Walking Liberty Half Dollars, 1916 to 1947

1936 Proof Walking Liberty half dollar.

Walking Liberty half dollars were designed by Adolph A. Weinman, the sculptor who also created the Mercury dime. The Mint described Miss Liberty as *striding* in its news release about the coin. These were struck for circulation from 1916 intermittently to 1929 and continuously from 1933 to 1947. Proofs with mirror surfaces were coined from 1936 to 1942.

Among the earlier varieties several varieties range from scarce to rare in higher Mint State levels. The beauty of the design and the fact that there are no costly rarities have made this a favorite series for a long time.

As a general rule the half dollars of 1916 from all three mints are very attractive, have satiny surfaces, wide rims, and are fairly well struck. From that point quality declined.

The relief of the design is such that the vast majority of circulation strikes are weak in one or more areas. The head of Liberty is often incomplete even on Proofs! On the obverse the weak areas include the head, the center areas of the dress, and her left hand. On the reverse the eagle's feathers are usually weak on the left leg up to the breast.

The 1923-S half dollar is always found with areas of weak striking, as indicated.

Among the different dates and mintmarks, some are weaker than others. The most egregious seems to be the 1923-S, as illustrated, which is usually quite weak in several places.

There are two short sets that have been popular: (1) All coins from 1933 to 1947 and (2) All from 1941 to date. If you are contemplating a full collection from 1916 onward, it is a good idea to start with a short set in order to become familiar with the characteristics of these coins.

Cherrypicking is the order of the day. Examine many illustrations of a given date and mintmark to see what to expect. Some are fairly sharp. Take your time. Building a nice set in, say, MS-63 to 65 or finer, with details as sharp as can be found, may take a year or two.

Franklin Half Dollars, 1948 to 1953

1952 Proof Franklin half dollar.

The Franklin half dollar designed by Chief Engraver John R. Sinnock was minted from 1948 to 1963. At its launch in 1948 collector reaction was an unstifled yawn. Little notice was taken of it. Most felt that the abandonment of the beautiful Walking Liberty design was a mistake. For many years, through the 1950s, most interest in Franklin halves was from investors who bought bankwrapped rolls.

That outlook changed in the 1960s, and many collectors assembled complete sets. There are no rare or even scarce dates and mintmarks, although the 1949-S is considered the key. The coin market was in a slump in that year, and fewer rolls were saved.

Later, the concept of Full Bell Lines (FBL) became popular. On many circulation strikes the horizontal lines at the bottom of the Liberty Bell were incomplete in some sections—sort of like the steps on Monticello on Jefferson nickels. FBL coins were emphasized, and varieties for which these were scarce climbed in value. In my opinion, which may be in the minority, a nice coin with nearly full lines, but at a much cheaper price, is a better buy.

Beginning in a large way in the 1990s some "coin doctors" added rainbow toning to many Franklin halves and also Morgan dollars—these being seldom seen in the marketplace earlier. Today, such pieces are often showcased in auctions and elsewhere.

Most Franklin halves have nice eye appeal. A full set is a nice addition to any collection.

Kennedy Half Dollars, 1964 to Date

1964 Kennedy half dollar.

Following the death of President Kennedy in November 1963, Congress rushed to authorize a commemorative silver coin. The selected denomination was the half dollar. Chief Engraver Gilroy Roberts prepared an obverse design and assistant engraver Frank Gasparro created the reverse. The mints geared up quickly, and the first circulation strikes were released through banks in March 1964.

The public was enthusiastic, and as fast as banks could release them they were snapped up. There was international interest as well. The standard retail price in Europe was equivalent to about $5. Not long afterward, Joseph Segel formed the General Numismatics Corporation (name later changed to the Franklin Mint), and hired Roberts as an officer of the new company. Frank Gasparro became chief engraver, remaining in the post until his retirement in 1981.

The price of silver was rising on international markets. Beginning in 1965, Kennedy half dollars were made of clad planchets with an outer layer of 80% silver and 20% copper, bonded to an inner core of 79.1% copper and 20.9% silver. These figures seem a bit odd until the entire coin is considered—clad exterior as well as the mostly copper interior; taken as a whole, the half dollars of this type are 40% silver and 60% copper.

In 1971 silver was eliminated, and henceforth Kennedy half dollars were made in clad metal consisting of an outer layer of 75% copper and 25% nickel bonded to an inner core of pure copper, the copper being visible when the coin is viewed edge-on. The new composition struck up well, and the pieces made were and are quite pleasing to the eye.

1776–1976-S Bicentennial half dollar with the reverse depicting Independence Hall.

Funny coincidence: the reverse of the 1926 Sesquicentennial quarter
eagle looks a lot like the reverse of the 1776–1976 half dollar.

In observation of the 1976 bicentennial a nationwide competition was held for special designs for the 1776–1976 quarter, half dollar, and dollar. Although the drummer boy on the quarter was widely liked, the half dollar and dollar designs were criticized. As to the half dollar, the Mint might have saved time and effort and not had a completion, for the chosen "winner" was simply a copy of the design used on the 1926 American Sesquicentennial.

1964–2014 Kennedy 50th anniversary half dollar in gold.

In 2014 to observe the 50th anniversary of the Kennedy half dollar special Proof strikings were made in gold with the 1964–2014 double date.

After the initial release of Kennedy half dollars in 1964 the public kept up its enthusiasm, and hardly any coins reached general circulation. Later issues with partial silver content were hoarded as well. By default this caused the quarter dollar to become the highest widely circulating coin in the country, a status quarters still hold today. Half dollars have not been seen in general circulation for a long time. Today, Kennedy half dollars are only made to be sold at a premium to collectors.

There are no rarities among Kennedy half dollars from 1964 to date. A full set of dates and mintmarks of circulation strikes and Proofs is interesting to own. The striking sharpness is good for nearly all, as is the eye appeal.

SILVER DOLLARS, 1794 TO 1935

Flowing Hair Silver Dollars, 1794 and 1795

This 1794 silver dollar from the Cardinal Collection, earlier seen in the Amon Carter Collection, auctioned for $10,016,875 by Stack's Bowers Galleries in January 2013 set a worldwide record for the most valuable rare coin ever to cross the auction block.

The first federal silver dollars were struck at the Philadelphia Mint in November 1794. The hand-operated screw press was designed for no diameter larger than a half dollar. As a result, all were lightly struck at the lower-left obverse and corresponding spot on the reverse. After inspection 1,758 coins were deemed satisfactory and released into circulation. There is no record of even a single piece being saved at the time by someone with numismatic interest.

In time the 1794 silver dollar was recognized as a rarity. By the 1850s they were worth several dollars each and were picked out of deposits by banks and bullion brokers. Today, many generations later, it is thought that about 140 different pieces are known. Even a lightly worn one will sell for well into six figures.

The Flowing Hair design was continued into 1795. In May of that year a large-capacity press was installed, and striking of coins was done with less weakness. Many different die varieties are known today, attributed by Bowers-Borckardt numbers assigned in 1993 or, sometimes, by Bolender numbers published in 1950.

Sharpness varies from coin to coin, but the places to generally check are the center of the portrait and the star centers on the obverse and the eagle's breast on the reverse. Denticles are usually irregular or incomplete, this is expected, and many have adjustment marks from filing the planchet to be the correct weight. Light adjustment marks can be tolerated, but coins with heavy marks should be bypassed. Eye appeal varies widely for these coins, so time and care are needed to select an example that is just right for a type set. Grades of VF and EF are good targets if they are in your budget. If you collect by die varieties you will need to be more flexible in your thinking, though, except for major rarities, a nice coin can usually be found.

There is a special appeal of the Flowing Hair half dimes, half dollars, and dollars, and an attractive coin will be a highlight in a type set.

Draped Bust Silver Dollars, 1795 to 1804

Shown is a 1795 Draped Bust obverse, Small Eagle reverse dollar, BB-51.
This is the very first use of the Draped Bust design that was later adopted
on other silver denominations and copper half cents and cents.

In the autumn of 1795 a new design for silver coins was created and the Draped Bust obverse combined with the Small Eagle reverse made its debut on the silver dollar. In 1796 it was adopted on cents, half dimes, dimes, quarters, and half dollars. For the half dime a 1795 die was prepared, but it was not used until 1796, when it was overdated 1796/5. It was not until 1800 that the design was first used on half cents. The obverse may have been from a portrait by Gilbert Stuart of a Philadelphia society lady, according to some traditional comments, though facts are scarce.

Two obverse dies were made for 1795 Draped Bust dollars, BB-51 (as illustrated) with Liberty positioned slightly left, and BB-52 with the head centered. Both shared a common die known as Small Eagle, Small Letters. This durable reverse die was continued in intermittent use through 1798. Dollars of this type were made in 1796, 1797, and into 1798 (the last being the BB-81 variety). All are fairly scarce today.

A 1798 Draped Bust obverse, Small Eagle reverse with Small Letters—the durable die that was first used in 1795, then in 1796 and 1797, BB-81. The illustrated coin in Very Fine grade is representative of many collectible coins in the early dollar series.

Striking sharpness varies on dollars of this era, so check the center of the portrait and the star centers on the obverse, and on the reverse check the eagle's breast feathers and the feathers high on the eagle's leg to the right. Denticles are often irregular on these issues and heavy adjustment marks should be avoided. The eye appeal of this type is usually fairly good in all grades. Cherrypicking will yield an attractive coin for a type set.

A 1798 Draped Bust obverse, Heraldic Eagle reverse silver dollar, BB-108.

Part way through 1798 the Draped Bust obverse was combined with the new Heraldic Eagle reverse—a style that had been introduced in 1796 on the quarter eagle. Coins of this type were made through early 1804. In the last year of production there were 19,570 silver dollars struck according to Mint records; however, these were from earlier dated dies. No 1804-dated dollars were made at the time.

Silver dollars of this type are the most plentiful among early issues and are found more often than the two earlier types combined. The striking is usually very good, but some weakness here and there is inevitable on certain die varieties. On the obverse check the center of the portrait and the star centers. On the reverse check the top of the shield, the eagle's neck feathers, the top of each wing, the stars above the eagle, and the clouds. Denticles are often irregular, but can be complete on both sides. Eye appeal is usually quite good for various grades. Avoid stained coins and ones with prominent adjustment marks.

In 1834 the State Department desired to present diplomatic gifts to the heads of countries in Eastern Asia. Maps, glass items, engraved weapons, and other items were gathered together as gifts. The Mint was asked to make Proof sets showing the different coin types from the half cent to the $10 gold eagle. This was easy to do from current dies, except for the dollar and the eagle, as these had last been struck in 1804. A search among old dies yielded no 1804, so a new die with that date was made. Adam Eckfeldt, who was in charge of the project at the Mint, did not realize that no 1804 dies were ever made. Eagles were struck in 1804, and new dies were made with that date.

An 1804 Proof silver dollar, part of a set presented as a diplomatic gift to the Sultan of Muscat. This is the finest of eight known Class I coins.

Thus, in 1834 the first 1804-dated dollars were made with little or no notice of the new coins. In 1842 the Mint published *A Manual of Gold and Silver Coins of All Nations*, written by the two curators of the Mint Cabinet, Jacob Reese Eckfeldt and William E. Dubois. Illustrated in their text was an 1804 dollar. This caught the eye of Matthew A. Stickney, a Salem, Massachusetts, numismatist, as he had never heard of a dollar of this date. Desiring to obtain one for his collection, he went to Philadelphia in 1843 and obtained one in trade for other coins. In time, other collectors learned of the coin and wanted one. In the spring of 1859 under Mint Director James Ross Snowden additional dollars were struck, but with a new reverse die. Today there are eight known dollars of 1834 vintage, the Class I coins; a Class II made in 1859 with a plain edge; and six Class III dollars with lettered edges. The last are thought to have been made into the 1870s.

Over the years the rarity of the 1804 dollar was emphasized in articles and auction announcements. No other single coin issue has been so well publicized. Known as "The King of United States Coins," examples of the Class I and III create a lot of attention when offered. The unique Class II is in the National Numismatic Collection in the Smithsonian Institution.

Gobrecht Silver Dollars, 1836 to 1839

This 1836 Gobrecht dollar has a starless obverse and Flying Eagle reverse with 36 stars
(one for each state in the Union). Most were put into circulation. The illustrated coin has light wear.

Christian Gobrecht, a well known and highly accomplished die sinker and engraver, was hired by the Mint in 1835. Not long afterward while Gobrecht's full-time employment was being considered, William Kneass, engraver (today known as "chief engraver," but that term was not used at the time), had a debilitating stroke and Gobrecht was named the "second" engraver, as assistant would imply he was inferior. The Mint desired to redesign the silver coinage and replace the Capped Bust motif then in use. Gobrecht was tasked with creating the Liberty Seated obverse. For the reverse he depicted an eagle in flight, modeled after Peter, a pet bird that lived within the Mint and flew in and out through an opening and was a familiar sight in the city.

A portrait of Christian Gobrecht, engraver at the Mint
from 1835 to 1844, the creator of the Liberty Seated coinage.

The first Liberty Seated coinage was of silver dollars in the amount of 1,000 coins delivered on December 31, 1836. These were of Proof format with mirrored surfaces and plain edges (not reeded or lettered). Most were deposited in a local bank and released into circulation, though two Proofs were given to President Andrew Jackson, and a few others were deliberately saved. In early 1837 an additional 600 were made from the same pair of 1836 dies.

In 1838, pattern dollars were made with stars added to the obverse field and with a plain field surrounding the eagle on the reverse.

This 1839 Gobrecht dollar has 13 stars on the obverse and a plain field on the reverse.

In 1839 300 coins of the 1838 design were made and released into circulation with reeded edges.

Today the above, plus various combinations of restrikes in silver and copper and with plain or reeded edges, are collectively known as Gobrecht dollars. Restrikes were made into the 1860s, possibly even the 1870s. Gobrecht dollars have been the focus of careful study by several scholars in recent years. Their illustration and discussion in the Red Book has added to their popularity.

Liberty Seated Silver Dollars, 1840 to 1873

A Proof 1840 Liberty Seated dollar, the type minted from 1840 to 1865, Without Motto.
Proofs for collectors were struck each year from 1840 onward, except in 1853.
Later, restrikes of the 1853 date were made.

Silver dollars were again made in large quantities for circulation in 1840. The obverse design was a modification of Gobrecht's earlier obverse, now with drapery at the elbow of Liberty and with some other modifications made throughout the years. The reverse depicted a perched eagle.

Liberty Seated silver dollars were distributed through banks, though contemporary records reveal that they never circulated widely, despite generous mintages. It was not uncommon for banks to charge a small premium for them, but silver coins of lower denominations were available for face value. Many of these coins were exported to Europe and to Canton, China.

An 1846-O Liberty Seated dollar: the first branch-mint coinage.

In 1846 59,000 were struck in New Orleans, the first branch-mint silver dollar coinage. These were placed into commerce and were widely used, including in the Mississippi River states and for export. None were saved by numismatists. After 1849 such coins that were in circulation disappeared as the price of silver on international markets increased. All silver coins became worth more as bullion, and large quantities were melted. Mintage quantities in 1851 and 1852 were very low as a result.

The Act of February 21, 1853, reduced the silver content of lower denominations, but not the Liberty Seated dollar. Coinage of these continued in later years, but at the mints they cost more than face value to obtain. Nearly all were exported and were received in foreign lands at values based on their bullion content, the indicated value on the coins being irrelevant.

In 1859 merchants in San Francisco called on the local mint to make silver dollars for the export trade to China. Accordingly, 20,000 were struck for this purpose.

An 1870-CC Liberty Seated silver dollar,
the type minted from 1866 to 1873 with IN GOD WE TRUST on the reverse.

In 1866 the motto IN GOD WE TRUST was added to the reverse. Production continued through early 1873, again nearly all coins going to the export trade. The Carson City Mint struck Liberty Seated dollars each year from 1870 to 1873. Many 1873-CC dollars were melted, with the result that this is the rarest CC issue today.

Proofs of Liberty Seated dollars were made continuously from 1840 onward. The numismatists of the early years and also of the later era who collected silver dollars opted for Proofs and paid no attention to circulation strikes. No numismatic notice was taken when dollars were struck at the New Orleans, San Francisco, and Carson City branch mints either. The Mint Cabinet kept only Proofs. As a result, high-grade circulation strikes are scarce for nearly all Liberty Seated dollars. MS-65 and higher coins are very rare for most. I have never seen a high Mint State dollar of 1855 or 1856.

Branch mint dollars are all scarce in high grades, and most are very rare in MS-63 or higher. The survival of such pieces was strictly a matter of chance, although some 1859-O and 1860-O coins, usually heavily bagmarked, are from small hoards.

Sharpness varies, so on the obverse check the head and the star centers. The reverses are usually sharp, but check all points. Eye appeal is usually quite good.

Morgan Silver Dollars, 1878 to 1921

The Morgan dollars struck early in 1878 at the Philadelphia Mint had eight tail feathers, as shown here. The standard was soon changed to seven tail feathers.

Standard silver dollars had not been minted since 1873, although the silver trade dollar, a different denomination, had been produced for trade in China. On February 28, 1878, the Bland-Allison Act provided that the government purchase millions of ounces of silver metal on the open market in response to political pressure from mining areas of the West. The price of silver had been in a steady decline. The most efficient way to convert the metal into coins was by coining dollars, as less effort was required than to mint two half dollars, four quarters, or 10 dimes.

The Gould & Curry mill in Virginia City, Nevada, was one of the many mining operations that suffered from declining silver prices in the 1870s.

A design that had been created by assistant engraver George T. Morgan for a pattern 1877 half dollar was selected for the new coins. Today these are called Morgan dollars, but in the early years they were generally referred to as Bland dollars, after Richard Bland, co-sponsor of the enabling legislation.

In 1877 assistant engraver George T. Morgan created a number of pattern half dollars. In early 1878 this pattern was selected to be used as the design for the new silver dollar.

The first striking of Morgan silver dollars for circulation took place on March 11, 1878. The first coins had eight tail feathers on the eagle. Someone suggested that the national bird had an odd number of tail feathers, so the design was changed to seven. Coinage took place at the Philadelphia, Carson City, and San Francisco mints. In 1879 the New Orleans Mint struck its first coins. These four mints struck coins continuously through 1893, except for 1886 to 1888 when the presses were quiet in Carson City. The Carson City Mint began coining again in 1889 but production ceased in 1893. In 1900 when it was realized that coinage would never recommence, the dies stored in Carson City were shipped to Philadelphia. Some CC reverses had the mintmark partially removed and then were overpunched with O mintmarks so they could be used rather than wasted. It was not until the 1920s that a numismatist first noticed the 1900-O, O over CC, reverse!

Today, about one in every three 1900-O dollars has this feature. From 1900 through 1904 the Philadelphia, New Orleans, and San Francisco mints struck coins each year consecutively.

Shown is the mintmark on a 1900-O, O Over CC, Morgan dollar.
Traces of the earlier CC mintmark can still be seen underneath.

A view of the Carson City Mint in the 19th century.
Today the building houses the Nevada State Museum.

In 1904 the supply of silver bullion authorized by the 1878 Bland-Allison Act (as well as several later acts) ran out and production ceased. Hundreds of millions of silver dollars remained in storage in Treasury vaults, as the production of these coins far exceeded any call for their use in commerce. In 1918 the government had a call for silver by the British government, then deeply involved in the First World War. Under the Pittman Act of that year 270,232,722 silver dollars of earlier dates were melted into bullion and exported.

In 1921 the Treasury called for more silver dollars, these to provide backing for Silver Certificates. Such bills were issued under the provision that there would be a silver dollar in storage for each dollar of face value of such currency. On a "hurry-up call," more Morgan dollars were issued at the Philadelphia and San Francisco mints, the New Orleans Mint having ceased operations in 1909. The Denver Mint, which opened in 1906, also struck Morgan dollars in 1921. The 1921-D and S dollars were made with tiny mintmarks.

A Mint State 1884-CC Morgan dollar from the Treasury hoard.
Hundreds of thousands of these survive from that source and are widely collected.

In the meantime the Peace silver dollar was designed and would be coined beginning in December 1921. In 1964 some thought was given at the Mint to reviving the Morgan design, and hubs were made. However, no coins are known to have been struck.

Large quantities of silver dollars dating back to 1878 remained stored in various Treasury vaults. Such coins circulated only on a limited basis, such as on gaming tables in Nevada and in commerce in a few Rocky Mountain states. Silver dollars were popular as holiday gifts, and each season there was a call for limited quantities.

At the Philadelphia Mint in November 1962 the supply of silver dollars on hand with the cashier was low. To provide more for distribution for the holidays, a storage vault previously unopened since 1929 was used. In 1929 a shipment of millions of Morgan dollars stored at the New Orleans Mint was shipped to Philadelphia and sealed in a vault (sealed so that it would never have to be opened to take inventory).

The seal was broken in 1962, and quantities of 1,000-coin canvas bags were opened. Included were hundreds of thousands of 1903-O silver dollars, a date and mintmark considered so rare that fewer than a dozen Mint State coins were known! I had never seen one in that grade, nor had any been offered at auction in recent times. In 1941 when B. Max Mehl sold the William Forrester Dunham Collection the 1903-O was singled out as a notable rarity.

The Dunham auction, actually a mail-bid sale, stands perhaps as the strangest sale in American numismatic history. Mehl purchased the collection intact in the late 1930s, whereupon he set about selling the rarities privately, including

Shown is the cover of B. Max Mehl's
1941 Dunham Sale catalog.

the two showpieces—the 1804 dollar and the 1822 half eagle. After the sale he announced that they had been sold at that event and advertised their record prices!

Wait, there's more.

Donald M. Miller, the leading collector of Hard Times tokens and some other series in the 1940s and 1950s, was a bidder in the Dunham sale and bought many pieces later. He learned that for a number of coins Mehl reduced the highest bid to the second or third highest and made up multiple printed envelopes and sent out several of the exact same lot, by adding pieces from his inventory! In one instance, Miller had three tokens each in identical envelopes!

After the unexpected release the price of these former rarities dropped precipitately, and other scarce New Orleans dollars were brought to light, including the 1898-O and 1904-O. The silver rush was on! All across the nation vaults in banks and government facilities were emptied.

Bags of silver dollars, 1,000 coins each, stored in a vault in the Treasury Building in Washington, D.C., in 1904. In the lower foreground on the floor are bags of recently minted (1900) Lafayette commemorative dollars.

The Treasury Building as it appeared in the 1890s.

In the Treasury Building in Washington many bags of long-stored Carson City coins were found among other varieties. The public had a field day! At one time there was a long line of people outside of the Treasury Building with cash waiting to exchange paper money for silver dollars of various dates and mintmarks dating back to 1878.

Finally, by March 1964 silver dollars in bank and Treasury storage nationwide were all gone, except for about three million Carson City dollars that the Treasury held back and later sold to the public at a premium.

The wide availability of Morgan silver dollars caused the prices to fall in 1963 and 1964. That did not last long, as large numbers of collectors began to specialize in the series, endeavoring to get one each of nearly 100 date and mintmark varieties. Within a few years the market prices of all but a handful of varieties rose to well over the values before November 1962. Today, Morgan dollars remain the most widely collected early series.

Striking sharpness varies from date to mintmark. Some such as the 1881-S are usually needle-sharp, while others such as the 1891-O can be weak in areas, such as on the eagle's breast feathers. Cherrypicking for sharpness is easy to do and yields higher quality coins that cost no more. The eye appeal of most coins is quite good.

Peace Silver Dollars, 1921 to 1935

A typical 1921 Peace silver dollar. Note the lightness of strike on the hair at the center of the obverse and on the eagle at the center of the reverse. Nearly all 1921 Peace dollars have these characteristics.

An above average 1921 Peace dollar, and a rarity as such. Center details are still weak, but are better than those usually seen.

To replace the Morgan design the Treasury Department tapped Anthony di Francisci, a talented sculptor, to prepare a new motif for the silver dollar. The design was to emphasize peace, a salute to the Armistice of November 11, 1918, that ended the war, and to the later Treaty of Versailles. For the obverse he created a distinctive Miss Liberty facing to the left, spikes ornamenting her headdress. The sculptor said the face was modeled after his wife, the former Teresa Cafarelli, but a comparison of that with Augustus Saint-Gaudens's Indian Head portrait for the 1907 $10 gold eagle is quite similar.

A portrait of Liberty on the 1921 Peace silver dollar by Anthony di Francisci.

A portrait of Liberty on the 1907 Indian Head $10 gold eagle by Saint-Gaudens.

The reverse, with the top lettering inspired by that used by Saint-Gaudens on his 1907 $20 double eagle, depicts the American eagle perched on a rocky crag from which a pine sapling springs with PEACE lettered below.

Just about everyone admired the beauty of the new dollars when they reached circulation in December 1921. There was an immediate problem with the striking, however—the dies were in high relief. The center of the obverse did not strike up properly, and on *all* examples seen the center hair details are weak. On the reverse the feathers at the top of the right leg and nearby wing are usually but not always weak.

A 1928-S Peace dollar with the low relief used from 1922 to 1935.

To remedy this the relief was lowered considerably, and circulation strikes from 1922 to the end of the series in 1935 are usually fairly sharp. Some that were struck with the dies spaced slightly too far apart, including certain San Francisco dollars of the 1920s (except for 1926-S), show graininess or marks from the original planchet, especially on the upper part of the eagle. Each of the 24 regular-issue Peace dollars has its own "personality." Often, Philadelphia coins are smoother in appearance than are San Francisco issues. The 1928 Philadelphia has beveled rims on both sides—so this particular date can be identified without looking at the obverse.

Peace dollars were struck from 1921 to 1928 and again in 1934 and 1935. The rarest coin in mid-Mint State levels is the 1934-S. In 1964 Peace dollars were struck at the Denver Mint, but were not released due to the rising price of silver. It is said that all were melted, but whether that is the case has never been confirmed. No 1964-D Peace dollar is known to exist.[5]

The pricing structure of certain varieties is such that an MS-65 is valued at multiples of an MS-64. Cherrypicking can pay real dividends here. Some "high-end" MS-64 coins are nicer than those graded as MS-65. Also, cherrypick for sharpness on the 1921 in particular. You will probably never find one with Full Details, but some are sharper than others.

Eye appeal is usually quite good for coins graded MS-63 or higher, but there are exceptions. A full set of Peace dollars is beautiful to behold and is nice to own.

MODERN DOLLARS, 1971 TO DATE

Eisenhower Dollars, 1971 to 1978

A 1971-D Eisenhower dollar.

Following the depletion of silver dollar stocks in banks and in Treasury vaults in 1964, there were no coins of this denomination available. In terms of circulation they were hardly missed, except in Nevada where they had been used on gaming tables. A few years later Congress contemplated issuing a new dollar coin made of clad metal. It was envisioned that these would be popular and would take the place of paper dollars in circulation. The life of a paper bill was less than two years, while it was anticipated that a copper-nickel clad dollar would last nearly 20 years. Chief

Engraver Frank Gasparro was tapped to create designs. For the obverse a portrait of President Dwight D. Eisenhower was chosen and for the reverse a symbolic American eagle landing on the Moon.

The first coins released in the new series were the 1971 issues made at the Philadelphia, Denver, and San Francisco mints. The Philadelphia and Denver coins were copper-nickel clad metal and those of San Francisco were silver clad. The silver coins were made in circulation strike and Proof formats and sold for a premium to collectors. Coinage in the same formats continued in 1972.

In 1971 and 1972 the Mint produced several reverses for Ike dollars, all of the standard Moon, eagle, and Earth design, but with noticeable differences, again observable on the Earth, the eagle, and the Moon craters. The outlines and geography of the Earth in particular permit easy attribution.

- **Reverse A:** Low relief. The State of Maine is huge and with a flat top, and Earth as a whole is flattened at the upper left. The northern part of the Gulf of Mexico has a downward bulge. Mexico appears to be nothing more than a raised blob. This design was used on all copper-nickel coins of 1971 of all three mints, on circulation strike 1971-S silver coins, on a few Proof 1971-S dollars (not identified in this context until 2007), on many 1972 coins, and all 1972-D coins. The details can vary depending on the strike and dies. In the Ike Group (www.ikegroup.info) this is known as the Type 1 reverse.

- **Reverse B:** Earth is flattened at the upper left and the northern part of the Gulf of Mexico is nearly round. California, Oregon, and Washington are a raised lump with Mexico. The eagle has no eyebrow, giving this reverse the nickname "Friendly Eagle," sometimes listed as FEV (Friendly Eagle Variety).[6] In the Caribbean three islands slant down slightly to the right of the tip of Florida. This design is used on the earlier strikings of 1971-D. Coinage using this reverse is small in number.

- **Reverse C:** Higher relief. The Earth is round on this reverse and the continents were redesigned to better match reality, but they are still in the same proportion. A very large low-relief amorphous island extends downward to the right, starting below the tip of Florida. The eagle's eye is different, and the breast feathers have been redone. The Moon craters have been strengthened by giving them higher rims. This design was used on most 1971-S Proofs.[7]

- **Reverse D:** The Earth is round, though the United States are represented as a flat country. The exceptions are Maine and other nearby states which are higher and slightly rounded. Large amorphous low-relief island(s) are seen to the lower right of Florida. South America is also shown to be flat. This design was used on some 1972 dollars. The Ike Group labels this as 1972 Type 2.

- **Reverse E:** Modified high relief. The Earth is round, but the outline of North America has been changed to a very heavy ridge to the left; the southern U.S. coast and Florida are raised and prominent; and a raised ridge is seen along the coast from Florida to Maine. Canada is mostly absent. One large lumpy island is below Florida, a smaller lump is below the left side of the island, and a low-relief island more or less rectangular in shape is to the lower right of the first island. South America is outlined by a ridge, heaviest to the right, and there is a hint of northwest Africa. This design was introduced late in 1972 for most 1972-P copper-nickel coins, and carried over into the next several years of production.[8]

Searching for the above varieties can be fun and all are inexpensive.

Despite aggressive promotion by the Treasury Department the Eisenhower dollars were not popular in general circulation. Even in Nevada their use was limited, as colored chips became increasingly popular. Beginning in 1973, mintages were sharply reduced, though production continued through 1978.

A 1776–1976-S Proof Eisenhower dollar with Bicentennial reverse.

For the Bicentennial a nationwide competition was held for distinctive reverse designs for the quarter, half dollar, and dollar. The winner was Dennis Williams, an art student whose design for the *quarter* was revised and adapted for the dollar. The motif showed the Liberty Bell overlapping an image of the Moon. This design was roundly criticized by many collectors. The Bicentennial coins laid an egg in the marketplace. The coin market was soft across the board, and sales fell short of expectations.

Today the formation of a set of Eisenhower dollars of the basic dates and mintmarks, circulation strikes as well as Proofs, is an interesting pursuit. There are no "impossible" rarities—the more popular and publicized obverse and reverse die varieties range from common to slightly scarce—and all are affordable. Many can be found by cherrypicking at conventions and in coin shops

Uncirculated Eisenhower dollars of the various years 1971 to 1978 vary in sharpness from issue to issue. Most Eisenhower dollars that have circulated, such as in the

Nevada casinos, are rather dull in appearance and, to state it bluntly, are unattractive. There is no particular reason to collect them, in view of Mint State coins being inexpensive. For the most part, the best specimens are represented by Proofs or by hand-selected high-grade Mint State coins.

A degree of connoisseurship is required to build a high-quality set. Eisenhower dollars produced for collectors—including Proofs and those sold in Mint sets—tend to be available in better grades, virtually as issued, which for Proof means Proof-65 or much finer. Circulation-strike coins taken from bags are apt to be a different story and are often heavily marked and fairly unattractive, this being particularly true of those of the first two years.

Elusive varieties include the 1971 (scarcest), 1971-D Variety 1 reverse (second scarcest), 1972 Variety 2 reverse (slightly scarce, once considered a rarity), and 1972-D. The circulation strike 1776–1976 Bicentennial dollars tend to have a lot of bagmarks, but such coins are plentiful in the marketplace and are inexpensive, so tracking down an MS-65 or better will not be difficult.

For extensive background information on all dollars from the 1971 Eisenhower down to the present day, buy or borrow a copy of my Whitman book, *A Guide Book of Modern United States Dollar Coins.* Such coins have fascinating stories, are readily collectible, and, with few exceptions, are very affordable. I found them to be incredibly fascinating when I assembled a set while I was involved in research for the manuscript.

Susan B. Anthony Dollars, 1979 to 1999

Shown is the slightly scarce 1979-P, Wide Rim, variety
(with rim close to the bottom of the date).

When the Treasury Department realized that the Eisenhower dollars were a failure as a substitute for the paper dollar in circulation, the reason given for this was that the coins were too large and cumbersome. A new plan was launched for a dollar smaller than a half dollar but larger than a quarter, surely to be convenient to handle.

Chief Engraver Frank Gasparro created a Liberty Head design with Pole to Cap, a tribute to the copper cents of the 1790s. The idea was applauded by numismatists. Congress, however, had the final say, and suffragette Susan B. Anthony was chosen, a "politically correct" move, it was said. The reverse was a reiteration of the eagle-on-Moon used on the Eisenhower dollar.

Author Q. David Bowers with *Coin World* editor Margo Russell at
the launch ceremony for the Anthony dollar in 1979.

Large quantities of circulation strikes were made at the Philadelphia, Denver,
and San Francisco mints in addition to 1979-S Proofs. Despite extensive publicity,
once again the public ignored the new coins. Production was sharply curtailed in
1980 and dropped much further in 1981, after which the design was discontinued,
seemingly for all time.

In 1999 the Treasury Department was fearful that the nationwide "Y2K"
scare—the shifting of dates on the calendar from starting with 19 to starting with
20—would cause computers to crash with disastrous results in banking and securities. The news media ran baseless articles suggesting that for safety citizens should
get coins to replace paper currency. Although there were still many Anthony dollars in Treasury vaults, additional coins were minted in 1999. Y2K proved to be
an illusion, and there was little to no demand for the additional dollars. By this
time television and the Internet dominated news coverage. Many staffers were
directed to report or create stories that were sensational to increase viewership—
historical accuracy and facts did not matter. Happenings that would have received
little attention a generation earlier in newspaper coverage were now showcased if
they involved violence, racism, religious extremism, money matters, and certain
other controversial or adversarial subjects.

Building a collection of Anthony dollars is easily done and will nicely add to
a collection of modern coinage. There are no rarities and a full set in MS-65 and
Proof-65 or finer grade is easy to assemble and is inexpensive. All Anthony dollars are copper-nickel clad (no silver strikings). There are no significant varieties
except the 1979-P with Wide Rim (the style used on all other Anthony dollars,
but not introduced in Philadelphia until after many Narrow Rim coins had been
struck). Most Anthony dollars are sharp and with good eye appeal, although cherrypicking is needed to find a 1999-P circulation-strike coin with the eagle's talons sharply defined.

Proofs on the market are nearly all high-grade Gems. One as "low" as Proof-65 would be a rarity, not that anyone cares. Mint State coins on the long side of MS-65 are common as well. At the MS-67 or higher levels many are scarce in terms of certified coins, although the vast majority of coins in existence have never been submitted for commercial grading. Auction records for certain early coins in ultra-high grades have run into four figures. *Caveat:* For these and many other series, high prices attract more coins to be certified, and today's rarities may become common tomorrow and valued at a fraction of today's prices. This has happened many times.

Sacagawea Dollars, 2000 to 2008

The Anthony dollars failed to gain significant public interest or support and were rarely seen in circulation. Commerce continued to be conducted with paper dollar bills because there had been many criticisms that the Anthony dollars had been mistaken for quarters when not looked at carefully. The Treasury Department tried one more time. The answer was the "golden dollar" of yellow manganese brass and with a plain (not reeded) edge. Now, at last, here was a coin that could not be confused with a silver-appearing clad quarter.

Shown is a circulation-strike 2000-P Sacagawea dollar.

For the obverse the image of Sacagawea, a Shoshone Indian woman who acted as a translator for the Lewis and Clark Expedition, was chosen. Glenna Goodacre, a New Mexico artist, prepared the design. As there are no contemporary portraits or other illustrations of Sacagawea, Goodacre went to the nearby American Indian Arts Museum in Santa Fe to see if she could find an appropriate model. She settled on Randy'L He-dow Teton, a student at the University of New Mexico. Born in 1976, she is a Shoshone-Bannock-Cree from the Lincoln Creek District within the Fort Hall Reservation in Idaho. This modeling brought her a degree of fame, and she was featured at several numismatic events, the first-ever appearance of a living model for circulating coinage to appear at such gatherings.

The reverse chosen was the work of Mint sculptor-engraver Thomas D. Rogers Sr. depicting a soaring eagle. The obverse and reverse designs pleased the secretary of the Treasury, who made the final choice. Commentary in the numismatic press was very favorable.

The alloy used to make Sacagawea dollars was chemically active, causing many coins to become stained or spotted. Several rinse compounds were tried in an effort to prevent this. One, which was used on about 2,500 coins in 2001, imparted a distinctive pale patina. Faced with many complaints, mainly from collectors and not the general public, the Mint issued this announcement:

> The different hues of the Golden Dollars now circulating are the result of the manganese brass contained in the outer layer of the new coins. Like any brass, its color will eventually become darker, giving your coins an antique finish. As the coins are handled frequently, the darker "patina" may wear off the high points of the coin, leaving golden-colored highlights that accent the darker background around the border, lettering and other less exposed areas. The brighter, brass highlights, in contrast with the darker background, accentuate the profile and add a dimension of depth to the depiction of Sacagawea and her child.

Good try!

No matter. Collectors found them to be ugly.

In 2001 production dropped to 133,407,500, or about one-tenth of the 2000 figure. Beginning in 2002 the Mint limited the mintage to coins and sets sold to collectors. Uncirculated coins dating back to 2000 were available in rolls of 25 and in bags of 2,000. By careful preparation of the planchets, staining and discoloration was no longer a problem.

The prototype circulation-strike with "Boldly Detailed Tail Feathers" reverse has diagonal vanes in the tail feathers. Only 5,500 of these were struck. They were released in Cheerios cereal boxes, and the variety was not noted until 2005. Today only about 100 are known.

Once again the public ignored the new mini-dollars, now with a golden hue. Hardly any were seen in circulation, but the government in distant Ecuador made American dollars legal tender. Hundreds of millions of Sacagawea dollars were shipped there and were a great success. The obverse portrait was thought by many to be a native of that country. This scenario may be unique in the history of American numismatics!

A basic set of dates and mintmarks of Sacagawea dollars can be collected with ease. I assembled one and enjoy it very much. Most circulation strikes can be readily found in MS-65 grade or above. Check the eye appeal, and avoid any of the early issues that are stained or spot-

The regular or "Plain Feathers" reverse later used on all Sacagawea dollars.

ted. Most in the marketplace are very attractive. Proofs as issued are perfection or close to it.

Beyond the basics you may want to add these two key issues, the first being a rarity. I have one of each in my own set:

1. The 2000-P "Cheerios" dollar with the *prototype* reverse. The Mint was eager to promote public interest and acceptance of the new dollar. It arranged with General Mills, Inc., the Minneapolis manufacturer of cereals and other foods, to supply 5,500 coins struck in late summer or early autumn 1999 with a 2000-P obverse and the prototype reverse. The difference in the reverse details was not noticed at the time. General Mills advertised a "treasure hunt"—one in every 2,000 boxes of Cheerios would contain a new Sacagawea dollar, not yet in general release, and a 2000-dated Lincoln cent. "The only place to get either coin is in a box of Cheerios." It was not until 2005 that this variety was noticed![9] Hitherto no one realized that the reverse had been changed before quantities of 2000-P dollars were made for general circulation. Excitement prevailed, and one sold for over $30,000! As word spread, more were discovered. Today about 100 have been certified—making them less expensive, but still the Holy Grail rarity among modern circulation strikes. High-level Mint State coins sell for $5,000 to $10,000—icons among modern coinage. The tail feathers on the prototype have distinctive raised diagonal vanes. Later or regular 2000-P dollars made in large quantities lack this feature.

Shown here is one of nearly 5,000 2000-P dollars struck especially for designer Glenna Goodacre from burnished dies on special planchets.

2. The Glenna Goodacre presentation coins, which are slightly scarce, typically sell into the mid- to high three figures, and are readily found in the marketplace. She requested 5,000 Sacagawea dollars instead of a check as payment for her work. The Mint was having problems with staining and spotting, so gave her coins struck from burnished dies on carefully selected planchets. Not all 5,000 coins had this finish, but most did. Mint Director Philip Diehl accompanied the coins to Santa Fe and presented them to her. She later sold many of these to dealer Jeff Garrett. By now all or nearly all have been widely distributed.

Native American Dollars, 2009 to Date

On September 20, 2007, the Native American $1 Coin Act, Public Law 110-82, was signed by President George W. Bush. The legislation specified that the coins shall have "images celebrating the important contributions made by Indian tribes and individual Native Americans to the development of the United States and the history of the United States." Such images would appear on the reverse and would be different each year. The Sacagawea obverse was to be continued in use.

A 2009 Native American dollar with a new reverse. Each year a new reverse was made. Dates and mintmarks are "hidden" on the edge, making each coin dateless and mintmarkless unless observed outside of a holder or album.

For the first three years circulation-strike Philadelphia and Denver coins were made by the tens of millions and Proofs were struck in smaller quantities in San Francisco. Beginning in 2012 quantities were sharply reduced. These coins are sold at a premium by the U.S. Mint and are not available at face value. Collectors are the main market. In view of that it is sad that the date and mintmark of each coin has been relegated to the edge, where it cannot be seen if in a closed holder or album! Hopefully, the Mint will return to numismatic tradition in the future.

Forming a set of Mint State and Proof coins is easy enough to do. In 2014 and 2015 special limited edition Enhanced Uncirculated coins were struck at the West Point Mint and sold for a sharp premium, as was a 2015-W coin struck at West Point. Still, the overall cost for a complete set from 2009 to date is very modest.

Presidential Dollars, 2007 to 2016

On December 13, 2005, the House of Representatives passed one of the most wide-sweeping pieces of coinage legislation in history. For the bicentennial of Lincoln's birth in 2009 the Mint was to create four special reverse designs for the Lincoln cent; new $10 denomination .9999 fine gold bullion coins for the First Spouse series were authorized; a .9999 fine $50 one-ounce gold bullion coin with James Earle Fraser's buffalo (bison) design used on the 1913 nickel was authorized; and, among other things, the new Presidential series of manganese-brass dollars were set to be minted. The Presidential dollars were to be issued at the rate of four per year and feature the chief executives in chronological order from George Washington onward until the last deceased president had been honored in 2016.

The George Washington presidential dollar of 2007
(date and mintmark are on the edge).

Mint sculptor-engraver Don Everhart created the reverse for the new dollar. Used on all issues, it featured the upper part of the Statue of Liberty. The obverse designs in ensuing years were done by in-house Mint engravers as well as outside engravers who are part of the Artistic Infusion Program.

Each of the varieties from 2007 was stylized with a portrait on the obverse. Dates and mintmarks were placed on the edge where they cannot easily be seen. I and some others suggested at the time that if each obverse featured the president in a different pose or activity and if each reverse depicted an event from his administration the series would have been much more popular.

Reverse Proofs were made for 2016-S Reagan dollars. A full set of Presidential dollars in Gem Mint State and Proof formats is easily obtained. Some issues on discolored planchets can be avoided. On the other hand, some such are called "sintered" on their holders and can be collected if desired.

TRADE DOLLARS, 1873 TO 1885

A Proof 1879 trade dollar.

The Coinage Act of 1873 provided for the discontinuation of the regular or Liberty Seated dollar and the creation of a new denomination—the silver trade dollar of 420 grains of regular silver alloy (90 percent silver and 10 percent copper), or four grains heavier than the standard dollar. These were specifically made for use in the export trade to China, where Spanish-American silver 8-reales coins had been received for many years.

Chief Engraver William Barber prepared a design with Liberty seated on bales of merchandise, looking to the west toward China, with the ocean in the foreground. The reverse, also by Barber, featured a perched eagle holding an olive branch and arrows. He later adopted the eagle for use on the 1875 twenty-cent piece.

Production took place at the San Francisco, Carson City, and Philadelphia mints each year through 1878. Most were struck in San Francisco as it was closest to China and also had large supplies of silver (mostly from Virginia City, Nevada). The Bland-Allison Act of February 28, 1878, abolished the export coinage of the trade dollar and provided for the standard (Morgan) dollar. Proof trade dollars were made for collectors from 1873 onward. These were continued from 1879 to 1883, after which ten 1884 and five 1885 Proofs were secretly struck.

Trade dollars were legal tender in domestic commerce for a dollar until July 22, 1876, when that status was discontinued. During that period from 1873 to 1876 they were used in Western commerce to a limited extent.

Although Proofs were acquired by collectors, there is no record of any numismatists or even the Mint Cabinet having any interest at all in circulation strikes. The survival of Mint State examples is a matter of chance. All dates and mintmarks 1873 to 1878 are available with patience, the exception being the 1878-CC, which is very rare.

Striking quality varies, so check the head of Liberty on the obverse, as well as her left hand and nearby areas, and the star centers. On the reverse the part of the wings and the legs and claws can be weak. Eye appeal varies, but many attractive examples are in the marketplace.

GOLD DOLLARS, 1849 TO 1889

Type I Gold Dollars, 1849 to 1854

Gold dollars made their debut in 1849 and were immediately popular. The engraver was James B. Longacre, who also made the later gold dollar designs. In 1849 the rising price of silver resulted in many coins being hoarded, and for the next several years there were none in circulation (except three-cent pieces of lower silver content). Gold dollars circulated widely in the absence of silver dollars. Production was greatest at the Philadelphia Mint, with additional coinage at Charlotte and Dahlonega. In 1854 gold dollars were struck at the newly opened San Francisco Mint.

An 1849 gold dollar with Open Wreath on the reverse
(later issues had the leaves end closer to the 1)

The Dahlonega Mint opened in 1838 and operated until 1861.
Gold dollars were struck there beginning in 1849.

Type I gold dollars are usually well struck, but check the hair details and star centers on the obverse and the leaves on the reverse. Those struck at the Charlotte and Dahlonega mints often have lightness in areas and need to be examined especially carefully. Most coins on the market are in circulated grades. Eye appeal is usually good.

Type II Gold Dollars, 1854 to 1856

The first gold dollars measured 13 mm and were found by many to be inconvenient. The solution was in the Type II of 15 mm. Coinage took place at Philadelphia in 1854; at Philadelphia, Charlotte, Dahlonega, and New Orleans in 1855; and at San Francisco in 1856.

An 1855-O, Type II, gold dollar.

In the coining press the high parts of the portrait in the obverse die were opposite the date in the reverse die because the metal could not effectively flow in both directions to completely fill the dies unless they were spaced very close together. As a result, Type II gold dollars are often poorly struck. On the obverse check the hair on Liberty and the tips of the feathers in the headdress. On the reverse check for overall weakness. On the vast majority of coins the two central date numerals, 85, are weak. Among coin designs of the mid-1800s, Type II gold dollars are by far the most challenging to find with sharp details.

Type III Gold Dollars, 1856 to 1889

In 1856 the gold dollar design was modified with a new portrait of Liberty in lower relief. The reverse remained the same as on Type II coins.

In 1861 the Dahlonega Mint was taken over by Southern forces after the Confederate States of America was formed. The coinage of an estimated 1,250 1861-D gold dollars, comprising the entire production for the year, was done under Georgia and CSA authorities.

A view·of the Charlotte Mint.

A crudely struck 1857-C, Type III, gold dollar,
representative of most of this date and mint.

An 1861-D gold dollar.

The Civil War started in April 1861. By the end of December of that year the outcome was uncertain, and gold coins were hoarded. Bullion dealers and exchange houses had them available, but only at a sharp premium in terms of paper money. At one point it took over $250 in Legal Tender paper money to buy $100 face value of silver or gold coins. After 1862 the mintage of gold dollars dropped sharply.

> # P. HAYDEN, BANKER,
> ### AND
> ## Dealer in Bullion and Specie,
> ### No. 24 NASSAU STREET,
> (Turner Marble Building.) **NEW YORK.**
>
> **MEXICAN DOLLARS, DOUBLOONS, and all kinds of GOLD and SILVER COIN and BULLION Bought and Sold.**
>
> ### GOVERNMENT SECURITIES
> *Will be Sold or Bought, on Commission, at best current rates.*
>
> The *BULLION AND SPECIE* Department will be under the charge of Mr. J. S. CRONISE, (lately of J. S. Cronise & Co.) and will receive his most careful attention.
>
> *J. S. CRONISE is authorized to sign the firm name by procuration.*

· An 1867 advertisement of P. Hayden, a banker and bullion broker buying and selling silver coins. (*Banker's Almanac*)

The war ended in April 1865 and many people thought that gold coins would return to circulation. The financial position of the Treasury remained uncertain, however, and it was not until December 17, 1878, that gold coins and paper money could be exchanged at par. In contrast, on the West Coast gold coins remained in circulation, and paper money was received only at a deep discount (inverse to the premium in the East). Because of this, gold coins minted in San Francisco often show greater wear than do those made in the East.

Most Type III gold dollars seen today are usually well struck, but inspect both sides. Sometimes the tips of the feather plumes on the obverse are weak. Coins struck at the Charlotte Mint are exceptions to the generally good quality, and many are miserable—poorly struck and on rough planchets. The average grade is usually Mint State.

A Gem 1881 gold dollar.

High-level Mint State coins MS-65 and higher are plentiful for most of the dates in the 1880s. At that time the coin market was very hot, and these low-mintage coins were very popular with collectors and dealers and were saved in quantity.

QUARTER EAGLES, 1796 TO 1929

Capped Bust to Right Quarter Eagles, 1796 to 1807

A 1796 quarter eagle, the first Capped Bust type without obverse stars.

The first 1796 quarter eagles of the Capped Bust to Right design, which I like to call the Conical Cap to Right, had no obverse stars, possibly as there were already stars in the Heraldic Eagle reverse design and more would have been redundant. For whatever reason, the starless obverse, made from a single die, was one-of-a-kind. This die was combined with two reverses, however.

Stars were added to the obverse soon afterward and were retained on various designs for the life of the type and denomination. These were made for most years through 1807.

A 1796 quarter eagle with stars on the obverse (the type made from 1796 to 1807).
All examples in this date range vary from very scarce to rare.

On quarter eagles of this era check the portrait details and star centers on the obverse and on the reverse the central details. Adjustment marks can be a problem on these and early gold coins, but not nearly to the extent of silver coins.

Capped Bust Quarter Eagles, 1808

The 1808 quarter eagle is the rarest of all major U.S. coin designs.

In 1808 John Reich's Capped Bust design, which had made its debut on the 1807 half dollar, was adopted for the quarter eagle. The reverse depicts a perched eagle. Only 2,170 were struck.

No further quarter eagles were made until 1821, at which time a new design was used. The 1808 quarter is thus isolated as the lowest-mintage and rarest issue among major design types of federal coinage. Nearly all show circulation and striking is often weak in areas. Check the high points. The rims can be flat or indistinct in places.

Capped Head to Left Quarter Eagles, 1821 to 1834

An 1821 quarter eagle.

Quarter eagles were next struck in 1821, followed by the 1824, 4 Over 1, overdate; 1825; 1826; and 1827. A Capped Head (mob cap is the correct designation in clothing history, but is a term unknown in popular numismatics) to Left was used, but differently styled than on the 1808. The motto E PLURIBUS UNUM is continued on the reverse. The reverse is a slight modification of 1808. In 1829 the diameter was reduced slightly. Coinage was continuous from that point through early 1834.

By late 1820 the price of gold had risen on international markets to the point that gold coins cost more than face value to produce. Depositors of bullion paid the extra amount and used most of the coins for export, where they were received based on their gold content; the face value was not relevant. None of these coins circulated domestically. The Act of June 28, 1834, lowered the authorized weight, after which time gold coins were struck to the new standard and were again used in commerce.

Most quarter eagles minted from 1821 to early 1834 were well struck. As always, check both sides. The average grade of such coins is high—usually AU or Mint State.

Quarter eagles of the early years, 1796 to 1834, are usually acquired for inclusion in a type set. Due to the combined rarity and cost, very few numismatists have collected them by varieties as a specialty. *Early U.S. Gold Coin Varieties* by John W. Dannreuther and Harry W. Bass Jr. (2006) is the standard reference.

Classic Head Quarter Eagles, 1834 to 1839

Following the Act of June 28, 1834, the authorized weight of gold coins was reduced. The denominations being produced at that time were the quarter eagle and half eagle. The obverse was created by Mint engraver William Kneass. It was not as much a new motif as an adaptation of John Reich's Classic Head used on copper cents beginning in 1808 and half cents starting in 1809. The reverse with a perched eagle was the same as the preceding quarter eagle type, except that the motto E PLURIBUS UNUM was dropped.

Quarter eagles of the Classic Head design were made at the Philadelphia Mint from 1834 to 1839, at the Charlotte Mint in 1838 and 1839, and at the Dahlonega and New Orleans mints in 1839. The mintmark for these coins is above the date. A few years ago John McCloskey published a study of die varieties of Classic Head quarter eagles and half eagles, but the work was not widely distributed.

An 1838-C Classic Head quarter eagle.

The striking sharpness of Classic Head quarter eagles varies. On the obverse check the hair above Liberty's ear and check the star centers. The reverse is usually sharp, but check the center including where the wings join the shield. Most quarter eagles of this design are visually attractive.

Liberty Head Quarter Eagles, 1840 to 1907

An 1848 CAL. quarter eagle, one of 1,389 struck from gold brought from California by a special emissary and counterstamped as such.

Liberty Head quarter eagles designed by Christian Gobrecht were made at the Philadelphia Mint continuously from 1840 to 1907—the longest span without a modification on both sides of any American motif. The Charlotte, Dahlonega, and New Orleans mints struck quarter eagles for most years up to 1860. The San Francisco Mint produced this denomination for most years from 1854 to 1879. The 1854-S is a famous rarity. In 1848 the Philadelphia Mint struck 1,389 quarter eagles from gold received by an emissary from California. On the reverse above the eagle each coin was counterstamped CAL. A number of Philadelphia dates range from scarce to rare. In 1863 the mintage was limited to just 30 Proofs. An interesting subset collection can be made of Philadelphia Mint quarter eagles from 1880 to 1907, a time when it was the only mint striking this denomination. Most survivors are in Mint State, this being particularly true of those made in the 20th century. Some of the low-mintage earlier dates in this subset are challenging to find.

Sharpness varies and is usually best on Philadelphia and San Francisco coins, but no rule fits all. On the obverse check the hair details of Liberty and the star centers. On the reverse the feathers to the left and right and above the shield are often lightly struck. Most coins have nice eye appeal.

Indian Head Quarter Eagles, 1908 to 1929

In 1905 President Theodore Roosevelt commissioned Augustus Saint-Gaudens, America's most famous sculptor, to redesign the entire coinage spectrum from the cent to the double eagle. The artist went to work on the double eagle and eagle, but passed away on August 3, 1907, before they were completed. The other denominations had not received much attention by that time. Through a contact (William Sturgis Bigelow) Roosevelt commissioned Massachusetts sculptor Bela Lyon Pratt to create new designs for the quarter eagle and half eagle so as to have new designs for the four gold denominations then in use.

A 1911-D quarter eagle,
the rarest variety in the Indian Head series.

The result was an Indian Head motif on the obverse and on the reverse a standing eagle, the last adapted from the bird on the reverse of the 1907 $10 gold coin. These features were recessed on both sides, with the result that the highest point was the flat field. Curiously, coins struck at the Denver Mint had their D mintmarks raised on the field surface. This design was also used on the half eagle. Coinage commenced in 1908 and continued intermittently until 1929.

Saint-Gaudens's $10 and $20 coins released in 1907 drew unstinting praise. In contrast, just about all numismatists condemned the 1908 quarter eagle and half eagle, and many letters to this effect were published in the pages of *The Numismatist*. Because of this, not many collectors sought such pieces. The result was that years later when both denominations became popular, high-grade Mint State coins were elusive for some issues.

Proofs were a problem as well. Coins of 1908 and 1909 are Sand Blast Proofs with grainy surfaces made by blasting microscopic sand particles onto the surface of the coins. This technique had been used at the Paris Mint and elsewhere and was thought by Mint officials to be artistic, but collectors disagreed. In 1910 and 1911 the modified Satin Finish was used. That was unpopular at well. The Mint reverted to the Sand Blast style for the last of the Proofs, 1911 to 1915.

Circulation-strike Indian Head quarter eagles are usually fairly sharp, but many have weakness on the band of flowers on the headdress and, on the reverse, on the top of the eagle's left wing. On some examples of the 1911-D the mintmark is quite weak. 1914-D and 1925-D quarter eagles are often lightly struck. The eye appeal of quarter eagles of this type is usually quite good.

$3 GOLD COINS, 1854 TO 1889

A $3 gold coin of 1862.

Three-dollar gold coins were designed by James B. Longacre and are of the same motif as the Type III gold dollar introduced two years later in 1856. The $3 coins were made continuously at the Philadelphia Mint from 1854 to 1889. Most mintages were low after 1862, as gold coins did not circulate in commerce in the East and Midwest. The nadir was touched in 1875 when only 20 Proofs were coined, with 1876 having the second lowest mintage of 45 Proofs. Branch mint coins were made before the Civil War, but after that time the only branch coinage were two 1870-S pieces for the cornerstone of the new San Francisco Mint building. Just one of these has been located.[10]

The striking of these coins is usually good. Check the center hair details on the obverse.

Most $3 coins are fairly sharp. On the obverse check the tips of the feather plumes and the high points of the hair. On the reverse check the higher-relief areas of the wreath. Many coins of the Civil War era have parallel microscopic raised lines from not completely preparing the dies prior to striking. As a general rule, in Mint State the most available Philadelphia Mint dates are 1854, 1874, and 1878. Most of the low-mintage dates from 1880 to 1889 were saved in fair numbers by collectors and dealers of the era and therefore come on the market regularly.

$4 GOLD STELLAS, 1879 AND 1880

An 1879 Flowing Hair pattern $4 gold Stella.   An 1880 Coiled Hair pattern $4 gold Stella.

In 1879 and 1880 pattern $4 coins known as Stellas were made of the Flowing Hair and Coiled Hair types. These are thought to have been designed by Charles E. Barber and George T. Morgan, respectively. Stellas are pattern coins, not regular issues, but because they are listed in the *Red Book* they have been widely collected for many years. All are in the Proof format.

The 1879 Flowing Hair is the only variety seen with frequency. Up to about 500 are known today. The others are rare, with fewer than two dozen gold impressions in existence of the 1879 Coiled Hair and each of the two 1880 varieties.[11]

The hair above Liberty's forehead on the obverse is sometimes lightly struck on both designs. Other features are usually sharp.

HALF EAGLES, 1795 TO 1929

Capped Bust to Right Half Eagles, 1795 to 1807

A 1795 Capped Bust half eagle with Small Eagle reverse.
This type was made from 1795 to 1798.

Half eagles were the first gold denomination to be minted. Their first delivery took place at the end of August 1795. The dies by engraver Robert Scot featured the Capped Bust Right motif of Liberty, possibly more accurately described as Turban Head right or Conical Cap Right. Stars were placed to the left and right, the word LIBERTY above, and the date below. This obverse was used through 1807. The standard star count is 13, but unique 15- and 16-star coins of 1797 were made and are in the National Numismatic Collection in the Smithsonian Institution.

The Small Eagle reverse, as it is called, depicts an eagle perched on a palm branch, holding a wreath aloft in its beak, copied from the motif on an ancient Roman cameo. A large coinage was anticipated in 1795, as evidenced by dies being made with this date. Today half eagles with the perched eagle reverse are easily available for a type set, but certain die combinations are rare. The 1798 Small Eagle $5 coin is a classic rarity with only eight known.

A 1795 Capped Bust half eagle with Heraldic Eagle reverse,
thought to have been coined years later in 1798 by using a leftover 1795 die.

Close inspection is needed for this type. Certain areas of the obverse including hair details and star centers can be weak. On the reverse the feathers on the eagle's breast are often weak or missing. Denticles can be irregular. More than just a few coins have noticeable adjustment marks; avoid those for which such are prominent.

The Heraldic Eagle reverse was introduced on $5 coins in calendar year 1797 but as a die dated 1795 was still usable, a famous variety of that year, it was used in 1798 to create the illogical 1795 Heraldic Eagle $5. Other $5 coins with the Heraldic Eagle reverse were made from 1797 to 1807 with the exception of 1801. These are plentiful as a type, but certain die combinations are rare.

Close inspection is needed for this design type as well. Certain areas of the obverse including hair details and star centers can be weak. On the reverse the neck feathers of the eagle can be weak, as can the areas of the wings adjoining the shield. Stars above the eagle often have light centers. Denticles on both sides can be light or irregular. Avoid coins with distracting adjustment marks. The eye appeal of this type is usually quite good.

Capped Bust to Left Half Eagles, 1807 to 1812

The 1808 quarter eagle is the rarest of all major U.S. coin designs.

Part way through 1807 John Reich's Capped Bust design was adopted as the obverse for the half eagle and half dollar. The reverse depicts a perched eagle. These were made in fairly large quantities through 1812. A representative example for a type set is easy enough to find. Some varieties range from scarce to rare.

Nearly all coins in existence show signs of circulation, including pieces graded MS-60 or slightly higher. True Gems are very rare. Striking is often weak in areas—for sharpness, check the high areas of the hair on the obverse and the star centers. On the reverse check the eagle's feathers near the shield and the horizontal shield stripes. The denticles can be irregular. Avoid coins with significant adjustment marks.

Capped Head to Left Half Eagles, 1813 to 1834

Half eagles of the Capped Bust to Left type were made in slightly higher relief from 1813 to 1815. None were coined in 1816 or 1817, but production resumed in 1819 with a slightly lowered relief.

In 1820 the price of gold rose on international markets, and it cost more than face value to coin a half eagle. Production continued, often in significant quantities. Although depositors of gold paid more than $5 in value for each coin, it made no difference, as nearly all were exported to Europe, where they were received for their bullion worth. The imprinted denomination was of no consequence.

It was the practice in foreign countries to melt incoming coins. In England, gold coins from various countries were melted, the gold refined, and the metal used to coin British sovereigns. Only in that way could the government keep track of the value of gold coins in its vaults. Because of this only a tiny fraction of the half eagles minted during this era survive today. Of the 17,786 half eagles reported to have been coined in calendar year 1822, only three with this date are known today. This comment is modified with the fact that the Mint sometimes used dies with earlier dates (as with silver dollars minted in 1804).

One of three known 1822 half eagles. Shown is the D. Brent Pogue Collection coin.
The other two are in the National Numismatic Collection in the Smithsonian Institution.

A detail of the overdate on the 1825, 5 Over 4, half eagle. Vertical, tiny *raised* lines are seen in the field (very common among early coins) from the die not having been completely smoothed before it was placed into the coining press.

A Bank of England vault for the storage of silver and gold.

In 1829 the style was modified slightly and new half eagles were of a slightly smaller diameter. The denticles were changed to the form of beads. Old and new types were both made in 1829, with coinage continuing into early 1834.

With relatively few exceptions the half eagles of this era are the rarest of the rare. The only numismatist to complete a run of dates was D. Brent Pogue, whose 1822, unique in private hands, was acquired at the auction of the Louis E. Eliasberg Collection of Gold Coins in 1982. The 1815 is a famous rarity, and both types of 1829 are classics as well. Indeed, this can be said for most years in this interval. Most numismatists who have a generous bank balance and are building a type set generally select a single coin of the 1813–1834 type, or one each of the 1813–1829 large diameter and 1829–1834 small diameter.

When found, most half eagles of this era are either at high AU levels or Mint State. Most are fairly well struck, and adjustment marks are not often seen.

Classic Head Half Eagles, 1834 to 1838

An 1834 Classic Head half eagle.

Half eagles of the Classic Head style have the same history as the quarter eagles. Following the Act of June 28, 1834, the authorized weight of gold coins was reduced. The denominations being produced at that time were the quarter eagle and half eagle. A new obverse was created by Mint engraver William Kneass, essentially a copy of John Reich's Classic Head used on copper coins in the first decade of the 19th century.

The mintmark position on an 1838-D half eagle.

Half eagles of the Classic Head design were made at the Philadelphia Mint from 1834 to 1838 and at the Charlotte and Dahlonega mints in 1838. Mintmarks are on the obverse above the date.

The striking sharpness of Classic Head half eagles varies. On the obverse check the hair above Liberty's ear and check the star centers. The reverse is usually sharp, but check the center, including where the wings join the shield. Most half eagles of this design are visually attractive.

Liberty Head Half Eagles, 1839 to 1908

An 1861 Liberty Head half eagle, the type without motto, minted from 1839 to 1866.

Liberty Head half eagles designed by Christian Gobrecht were made at the Philadelphia Mint continuously from 1839 to 1908. In the first year, coins struck at the Charlotte and Dahlonega branch mints had C and D mintmarks above the date. From 1840 onward mintmarks were placed on the reverse below the eagle. In the early years half eagles were struck in Charlotte, Dahlonega, and New Orleans, joined by San Francisco when that mint opened in the spring of 1854. Half eagles of the years 1855, 1856, and 1856 are unique in American numismatics in that a single denomination was struck at five mints: Philadelphia, Charlotte, Dahlonega, New Orleans, and San Francisco. The three Southern mints closed in early 1861 when the Confederate States of America was formed.

As described earlier, from late December 1861 until December 17, 1878, gold coins were not in circulation in the East or Midwest. Bullion dealers and exchange houses had them, but they were available only at a premium in terms of paper money. On the West Coast gold coins circulated and paper money traded at an inverse deep discount.

A Proof 1900 Liberty Head half eagle with IN GOD WE TRUST
on the reverse, the type minted from 1866 to 1908.

Beginning in 1866 the motto IN GOD WE TRUST was added to the reverse. The Carson City Mint opened in 1870 and struck gold coins through 1893, except for 1886 to 1888. New Orleans half eagles were minted for several years in the 1890s. The Denver Mint opened in 1906 and struck gold coins as well.

Today Liberty Head half eagles are popular collectibles. Most are acquired for type sets—two coins, one each without and with motto. Coins of Charlotte and Dahlonega have long been popular on their own as subset specialties. There are no great rarities. Typical coins from these two Southern mints are generally VF to AU. Aspiring to acquire one of each date and mintmark in the Liberty Head half eagle series is a great challenge. The 1854-S is a stumbling block to completion, as only two or three are known, one of which is in the National Numismatic Collection in the Smithsonian Institution. Proofs were minted of the various years and for the most part are rarities today.

The Denver Mint opened in 1906.

Sharpness varies on Liberty Head half eagles and is usually best on Philadelphia and San Francisco coins. On the obverse check the hair details of Liberty and the star centers. On the reverse the feathers to the left and right and above the shield are often lightly struck. Most coins have nice eye appeal.

Indian Head Half Eagles, 1908 to 1929

A 1909-D Indian Head half eagle with recessed designs on both sides.
This is one of the more rare varieties of the type.

From 1908 to 1929 Indian Head half eagles were made. The designer of these unusual coins with recessed surfaces was Bela Lyon Pratt, as described under the quarter eagles section of the same design and era on page 123.

Indian Head half eagles were struck from 1908 to 1916 and again in 1929. In 1909 the New Orleans Mint coined half eagles.

Proofs were made at the Philadelphia Mint from 1908 to 1915. Those of 1908 and 1911 to 1915 are of the Sand Blast format, while those of 1909 and 1910 are Satin Finish.

The key issues of this type are the 1909-O in high grades and the 1929, the last always seen in Mint State. Circulation-strike Indian Head half eagles are usually fairly sharp, but many have weakness on the band of flowers on the headdress and the top of the eagle's left wing on the reverse. Bagmarks can be a nuisance, but eye appeal of half eagles of this type is usually quite good.

EAGLES, 1795 TO 1933

Capped Bust to Right Eagles, 1795 to 1804

A 1795 Capped Bust eagle with Small Eagle reverse.
This type was made from 1795 to 1797.

Eagles were first delivered in autumn 1795. The dies by engraver Robert Scot featured the Capped Bust Right motif of Liberty, possibly more accurately described as Turban Head Right or Conical Head Right, and were of the same style as used on half eagles. Stars were placed to the left and right, the word LIBERTY above, and the date below. This obverse was used through 1804.

The Small Eagle reverse, as it is called, depicts an eagle perched on a palm branch, holding a wreath aloft in its beak, and was used on half eagles as well. Today eagles with the perched eagle reverse are easily available for a type set, but are expensive. The *Red Book* describes these varieties as challenging: 1795 with 13 leaves in the palm branch, 1795 with 9 leaves (scarcer), 1796, and 1797.

Mint-caused adjustments at the center of the
eagle on reverse of an early $10 gold coin.

Close inspection is needed when considering coins of this type for purchase. Certain areas of the obverse including hair details and star centers can be weak. On the reverse the feathers on the eagle's breast are often weak or missing. Denticles can be irregular. More than just a few coins have noticeable adjustment marks. Avoid those for which such are particularly prominent.

The Heraldic Eagle reverse was introduced on $10 coins in 1797 and was used continuously until 1804. Eagles of 1798 are overdates (8 Over 7), and are known with two star arrangements: 9 left and 4 right and 7 left and 6 right (scarcer). Eagles minted in 1804 have a crosslet 4 in the date. Years later restrikes of the 1804 were made in 1834 for inclusion in Proof sets for diplomatic presentation (see 1804 silver dollar on page 95). These later $10 coins have a plain 4 in the date.

A 1798, 8 Over 7, Capped Bust eagle with Heraldic Eagle reverse, the type of 1797 to 1804.
This is Bass-Dannreuther variety BD-1 with 9 stars left and 4 right.

When the Philadelphia Mint was established its purpose was to provide coins to facilitate domestic commerce. Frustrating to the Treasury Department, many of the large-denomination silver and gold coins were exported. Merchants and banks in foreign countries wanted coins and would not accept paper money. By 1804 the vast majority of gold eagles had been shipped abroad. To end this, the denomination was discontinued, but it didn't matter by that point. The $5 gold half eagle became the largest gold coin of the realm, and these were exported in quantity. Eagles were not coined again until 1838.

Careful inspection is needed when considering purchasing an eagle of this type. For some unexplained reason, nearly all survivors of the 1804 date have rough or problematic surfaces. The other dates are usually satisfactory in eye appeal.

Certain areas of the obverse including hair details and star centers can be weak. On the reverse the neck feathers of the eagle can be weak, as can the areas of the wings adjoining the shield. Stars above the eagle often have light centers. Denticles on both sides can be light or irregular. Avoid coins with distracting adjustment marks. Avoid those for which such are prominent.

Liberty Head Eagles, 1838 to 1907

Liberty Head eagles designed by Christian Gobrecht were made at the Philadelphia Mint continuously from 1838 to 1907. Those of 1838 and 1839, 9 Over 8, have the head differently aligned.

An 1839, 9 Over 8, overdate Liberty Head eagle, the type without motto minted from 1838 to 1866. Coins minted in 1840 and later show the date position aligned differently with relation to the portrait.

A rare Proof 1862 $10 gold coin, one of 35 struck, of which only about a dozen are known today. Runs of Proof Liberty Head gold coins of the several denominations are in the National Numismatic Collection in the Smithsonian Institution and in the collection of the American Numismatic Society, most of the last from a donation by J.P. Morgan.

This represents the first appearance of the design that was later used on half cents (starting in 1840), cents (1839), quarter eagles (1840), and half eagles (1839). In the early years eagles were struck every year at the Philadelphia Mint and most years at the New Orleans Mint, the 1860-O being the last early issue from the Southern mint. The San Francisco Mint opened in 1854 and struck eagles for most years after that time. As noted earlier, gold coins did not circulate in the East and Midwest from late December 1861 until December 17, 1878.

A Proof 1890 Liberty Head eagle with IN GOD WE TRUST on the reverse, the type minted from 1866 to 1907.

Beginning in 1866 the motto IN GOD WE TRUST was added to the reverse. The Carson City Mint opened in 1870 and struck gold coins through 1893, except for 1886 to 1888. New Orleans eagles were minted intermittently from 1879 to 1906. The Denver Mint opened in 1906 and struck gold coins as well.

Today Liberty Head eagles are popular collectibles. Most are acquired for type sets—two coins, one each with and without motto. Over the years only a few numismatists have aspired to collect these by date and mint. For some early issues no Mint State coins are known. Proofs were minted of the various years and for the most part are rarities today.

Sharpness varies on Liberty Head eagles and is usually best on Philadelphia and San Francisco coins. On the obverse check the hair details of Liberty and the star centers. On the reverse the feathers to the left and right and above the shield are often lightly struck. Most coins have nice eye appeal.

Indian Head Eagles, 1907 to 1933

In 1905 President Theodore Roosevelt commissioned Augustus Saint-Gaudens to redesign the American coinage from the cent to the double eagle. In a visit to the Smithsonian Institution in 1904 he had admired the beauty of ancient Greek coins and thought that current U.S. designs were insipid in comparison. Working from his studio in Cornish, New Hampshire, Saint-Gaudens began work on the double eagle. While that was in process he created the eagle design as well.[12]

A 1907 Indian Head $10 with periods before and after the inscriptions on the reverse. These were made with rolled (as seen here) and wire rims and are rare today.

For the $10 gold coin he created an imaginative portrait of a young lady wearing the feathered bonnet of an Indian chief. The model for the portrait is unknown, but a popular speculation is that Davida Clark, one of the artist's lovers, was the one.

The reverse depicted a bold perched standing eagle, a motif he had used earlier on the 1905 inaugural medal for Roosevelt. The earliest strikings had dots or periods before and after the inscriptions on the reverse. Many of these With Periods coins were struck, and some were even made available to numismatists and others, though most were melted.

A 1907 Indian Head eagle without periods, the type used for 1907, 1908, and 1908-D coins.

The design was soon slightly revised to eliminate the periods on the reverse. Coins were struck in quantity at the Philadelphia Mint in 1907 and at Philadelphia and Denver in 1908.

In the summer of 1908 the motto IN GOD WE TRUST was added to the reverse. Mintage was continuous through 1916, then resumed with the

A 1920-S eagle, a rare issue. This is of the With Motto type minted from the summer of 1908 intermittently to 1933.

issues of 1920-S, 1926, 1930-S, 1932, and 1933. Today the 1907 coins with periods and the 1920-S, 1930-S, and 1933 are the key rarities. Sandblast Proofs were made in 1908 and 1911 to 1915, and Satin Finish Proofs were the format in 1909 and 1910.

Circulation-strike Indian Head eagles are usually fairly sharp, but many have weakness on the hair at the center and, on the reverse, the top of the eagle's left wing. Eye appeal of eagles of this type is usually excellent. This design has been a numismatic favorite for a long time.

Roosevelt's 1905 inaugural medal made for him by Augustus
Saint-Gaudens. The *official* inaugural medal was made at the Mint by
Chief Engraver Charles E. Barber, but was rejected by the president.

DOUBLE EAGLES, 1850 TO 1933

Liberty Head Double Eagles, 1850 to 1907

Following the discovery of gold in quantity in California in 1848 and 1849, there was a call for a new high-denomination coin to economically convert the metal to coins. In 1849 the $20 gold double eagle was authorized. At the same time the gold dollar became a reality, a necessity as silver dollars were being withdrawn from circulation due to the high price of silver.

1850 double eagle, type of 1850 to 1866 Without Motto.

Chief Engraver James B. Longacre prepared the designs. For the obverse of the gold dollar and double eagle the motif of Liberty facing left, wearing a coronet inscribed LIBERTY was chosen. On the double eagle 13 stars were placed around the border, and the date was below. The reverse displayed a wingspread eagle with a shield and ornaments, with a glory of rays above. The denomination below was given as TWENTY D.

Coinage commenced in 1850 at the Philadelphia and New Orleans mints, joined by San Francisco in 1854. The New Orleans Mint closed in early 1861 after quantities of 1861-O double eagles were struck by the Union and, later, under Louisiana and Confederate jurisdiction.

An 1866 double eagle, With Motto type of 1866 to 1876,
with denomination as TWENTY D.

In 1861 modified reverse dies with tall letters, by assistant engraver Anthony C. Paquet, were briefly used at the Philadelphia and San Francisco mints. After December 1861 gold coins were no longer seen in general circulation in the

East and Midwest, but remained in commerce on the West Coast as noted earlier. All the while depositors of gold could receive double eagles on demand, accounting for continuing coinage during the Civil War and afterward. Such coins were used in the export trade. Gold coins and paper money did not achieve par with each other until December 17, 1878.

The added motto.

In 1866 the motto IN GOD WE TRUST was added to the larger silver and gold denominations. Thus was created a new design type. The Carson City Mint opened for business in 1870 and struck silver and gold coins, a production that continued through 1893, with the exception of 1886 to 1888.

In 1877 the reverse of the double eagle was modified to change the denomination to TWENTY DOLLARS. This style was used for the remainder of the type. In the early 1870s several European countries abandoned the silver standard; old coins were melted, placing quantities of the metal on the market. In the same era increased silver production in the United States resulted in the price dropping.

An 1877-CC double eagle, With Motto type of 1877 to 1907,
with denomination as TWENTY DOLLARS.

What to do about the sagging price of silver? Mining interests and others in the Prairie States, in the Rocky Mountain States, and in the West started the Free Silver Movement, often in print as the Silver Question. By the late 1870s Free Silverites, as they were called, were a powerful force in politics. Their call was for Uncle Sam to prop up the market by purchasing tons of silver and converting the metal into coins. On February 28, 1878, the Bland-Allison Act accomplished this goal, at least in part, by providing for millions of ounces to be purchased and coined into the series we know today as Morgan silver dollars.

Still, the price of silver declined. There was too much metal and too little demand, even with the new coinage of dollars. Free Silver advocates stated that silver coins should take the place of gold in large transactions, never mind that a $20 double eagle had full bullion value in gold, while a Morgan dollar of 1878 had only 89 cents worth of silver.

The coining of millions of silver dollars that nobody wanted severely disrupted both politics and international finance and caused double eagles to be hoarded. (*Harper's Weekly*, December 15, 1880)

Foreign merchants, banks, and other commercial entities in the import-export trade with America became fearful that international debts would be settled in silver dollars. A great rush to acquire double eagles began in the 1870s, resulting in millions of coins being exported. In early 1895, when a Morgan dollar had just 51 cents value in silver, the Treasury Department reserve of double eagles reached dangerously low levels, and financier J.P. Morgan and others were called in to help.

In the meantime, Silverites remained powerful in politics. In 1896 William Jennings Bryan secured the Democratic nomination for president on the Free Silver platform. His "Cross of Gold Speech" predicted that mankind would be "crucified" unless silver coins became more important than gold. Bryan was nominated again in 1900 and a further time in 1908, but lost in each contest. In the early 20th century the Free Silver movement expired.

A Free Silver cartoon in *Harper's Weekly*, April 27, 1895. Foreign banks, merchants, issuers of gold bonds, and others were fearful that silver dollars would be used instead of gold to pay off debts.

More of the same: a cartoon in *Harper's Weekly*, May 25, 1895. "How to make two dollars out of one"—a reference to a silver dollar containing only about 50 cents worth of silver.

The result of all of this is that millions of double eagles exported to Europe, South America, and elsewhere from the 1870s onward remained there. Had there been no Silver Question double eagles that are common today would range from scarce to rare. In 1933 when President Franklin D. Roosevelt commanded that the public surrender its gold coins (numismatists excepted), foreign governments held onto their double eagles more tightly than ever!

Beginning in a significant way with Paul Wittlin traveling to Europe in 1949, huge hoards of double eagles were found in foreign banks and treasuries. Over a long period of time many of these were repatriated, forming by far the largest part of the double eagle supply available to collectors today.

In a buying trip to Zurich, Switzerland, in 1961 I visited the leading banks there on Paradeplatz, each of which had a department that traded in gold coins in bulk. I was always ushered to a private room, where I met with a specialist. The banks had copies of the *Red Book* and were familiar with rarities, which were therefore priced at a premium.

Among common dates of Liberty Head and Saint-Gaudens twenties, there was no differential in price between an EF coin and one that was Gem Mint State. One price, such as the Swiss equivalent of, say, $40.25 applied to one and all. Buy and sell prices were posted daily, but did not seem to change much. I asked how many I could buy at the "ask" price, and the officer said that right now he could confirm an order for 100,000 coins, but for a larger quantity he would have to leave the room to check! Of course, I could not afford more than a small percentage of such a number.

Liberty Head double eagles have always been popular with my customers. Going back to the 1950s when my dealership was beginning, there were always a few clients who enjoyed owning gold, and obtaining one each of every affordable date and mint-mark of double eagle was an interesting way to do this.

In later times beautiful Mint State double eagles recovered from the undersea wrecks of the SS *Brother Jonathan* (lost in 1865), SS *Central America* (1857), and SS *Republic* (1865) came on the market beginning in 1999 and yielded quantities of Mint State coins, most spectacularly 5,305 mint-fresh 1857-S twenties from the *Central America*. Excitement prevailed, and in a relatively short time all were gone. The availability of Choice and Gem double eagles catalyzed more interest, with the result that Liberty Head coins became more popular than ever before.

Today, Mint State coins from the treasure ships reappear on the market and find easy sale. Mint State double eagles after 1865, continuing into the mid-1870s, are fairly rare at this level, especially if accurately graded MS-63 or higher. Many AU and low-level Mint State coins exist, mostly with extensive bagmarks. Many Mint State coins that were exported in quantity starting in the mid-1870s have been repatriated and most dates and mintmarks with high mintages are readily available in MS-63 or higher. Certain issues of the late 1890s and early 1900s are very common as such.

The New Orleans Mint struck double eagles in 1879 in limited numbers. The Denver Mint began coining twenties in 1906.

The striking quality of Liberty Head double eagles varies. Check the hair of Liberty, although on some dies it was not strongly defined, this being particularly true of those minted from 1866 into the late 1870s. Sometimes areas of the hair have few if any details. Check the star points as well. The reverse is usually well struck, but check the center.

Saint-Gaudens Double Eagles, 1907 to 1933

An MCMVII (1907) High Relief double eagle by Augustus Saint-Gaudens.

Theodore Roosevelt, in office from 1901 onward, remains the only American president to have taken a deep interest in coinage designs. As related above, in 1905 he commissioned Augustus Saint-Gaudens to redesign all of the denominations. The double eagle received the sculptor's earliest and most extensive attention. Selected for the obverse design was Liberty in the form of *Fame*, also called *Victory*, as created by Saint-Gaudens for the *Sherman Victory Monument* (an icon in New York City at the south edge of Central Park opposite the Plaza Hotel). For the reverse an eagle in flight was created, inspired by but different from that on the 1857 Flying Eagle cent, which the sculptor said was his favorite design from the past. Adding a classical touch, the release year of 1907 was given in Roman numerals as MCMVII.

Work on the design continued in 1906 and went into 1907. Early patterns were in what we know as Ultra High Relief and had wire rims. By early summer 1907 the design was nearly ready. Saint-Gaudens had been ill with cancer for some time, and on August 3 he passed away. The MCMVII design was finessed and completed by his assistant, Henry Hering. The relief was lowered slightly but was still very high.

Hering interfaced with Chief Engraver Charles E. Barber at the Mint, who protested that the relief was too high for use on regular high-speed presses and requested that the dies be modified. Otherwise multiple impressions would be needed on a special press intended for medals. President Roosevelt dismissed this and other complaints from Barber, calling the double eagle his "pet crime" and stated that if the Mint could only strike one coin *per day* that is how it would be!

In December, continuing slightly into January 1908, the MCMVII High Relief dies were used to strike 12,367 coins. These were done on a medal press with three blows per coin in order to bring up all of the details. The coins went into circulation and caused a nationwide sensation as they were paid out by banks. They were gone almost overnight, and the market price rose to about $30 each. Years later after the passion and novelty passed, many were returned to circulation. Today an estimated 6,000 or so exist, most of which are in grades from AU-58 to MS-63.

These coins are in great demand as many numismatists consider them to have the most attractive American coin design ever made for circulation. The striking is generally very good, but a few have some lightness on Liberty's bosom. The eye appeal is nearly always excellent.

A 1907 "Arabic date" double eagle,
type of 1907 and early 1908, Without Motto.

In December while the MCMVII coins were being struck, modified dies in shallow relief and with the date as 1907 were coined in quantity. Production continued with dies for 1908 and 1908-D.

A 1913-D double eagle, type of 1908 to 1933, With Motto.

Detail of the lower right obverse of a double eagle of the 1907–1908 type.

Detail of the lower-right obverse of a double eagle of the 1908–1913 type
with two added stars for Arizona and New Mexico.

In the summer of 1908 the motto IN GOD WE TRUST was added to the reverse. This remained the type throughout the rest of the series. In 1912 Arizona and New Mexico became states, raising the count from 46 to 48. To reflect this, in 1912 two stars were added at the lower right of the obverse. Technically, this can be considered a separate type, but few people do.

Double eagles of the 1907 to 1933 design in low relief are usually found in grades from AU through lower Mint State, although MS-64 and MS-65 coins are very common for some of the higher-mintage dates. Many have areas of light striking on Liberty's bosom and on her knee to the right—areas that should be checked. The eye appeal is usually excellent.

NUMISMATIC
EXCURSIONS

An undated NE Massachusetts silver XII pence or shilling struck in 1652,
representative of the very first coinage made in what is now the United States.

Beyond the federal series I have discussed in the preceding chapter, there have been many little journeys and excursions I have taken through American numismatics in regards to other coin specialties It is often the case that after enjoying coins of the various U.S. mints, collectors turn to tokens, medals, and other subjects, most of which offer many opportunities to combine collecting with history.

EXCURSION NO. 1

Colonial and Early American Coins

When I first discovered the world of numismatics I learned that coins had been struck in America beginning in 1652. I had heard of Massachusetts Pine Tree shillings, but did not know much about them and had never seen one. I soon learned that there was a comprehensive book about the field known as colonial and early American coins. Written by Sylvester S. Crosby and published in

Boston in 1875, *The Early Coins of America* was still the standard reference even then. While a comment like this might seem surprising today, back in the 1950s most standard references were long out of print. As other examples, the pivotal work on early half dollars by M.L. Beistle had been published in 1929—that on pattern coins by Edgar H. Adams and William Woodin in 1913, and that on copper coins of New England by Henry Miller and Hillyer C. Ryder in 1918.

Fortunately, with a little bit of asking around and scouting, it was easy enough to find such books. Members of the Wilkes-Barre Coin Club gave me a lot of old magazines and auction catalogs they no longer needed and gave or sold me quite a few reference books. Others I ordered by mail, such as from Charles and Ruth Green in Illinois. Stack's in New York City had several shelves of reference books for sale on just about every imaginable subject.

The Early Coins of America, which today is a standard reference, if no longer *the* standard reference, was a delight to read. It is a combination of technical and sometimes tedious listings of early legislation, plus interesting descriptions of how and where certain coins were minted (in Vermont, in several places in New Jersey, at a secret mint in Upstate New York, and so on), plus illustrations and descriptions of the coins themselves. It was and is a numismatic smorgasbord—not to be consumed all at once, but to be picked at, enjoyed, and then returned to. I still consult my copy regularly.

A 1652 Pine Tree shilling, probably the most famous early American coin.

As mentioned, the first coins struck in what is now the United States were silver coins made in Massachusetts beginning in 1652. Types include the NE (for New England), Willow Tree, Oak Tree, and Pine Tree designs. Although certain coins were minted until 1682, the original date of authorization, 1652, is on most varieties. Nathaniel Hawthorne penned a fanciful tale about Pine Tree shillings that was published in 1840. It told of mintmaster John Hull whose daughter Betsey was about to be married. For her dowry he had her sit on one platform of a large balance scale, and on the other side he piled freshly-minted Pine Tree shillings equal to her weight, and Betsey was a plump lass. The coins served them well after their marriage.

Most coins from the 1652-dated Massachusetts coinage were made under rustic circumstances and can vary widely in sharpness, planchet quality, and other features. This gives them a special cachet of desirability, much like folk art. NE, Oak Tree, and Pine Tree coins are often found fairly well struck. In contrast, Willow Tree coins are nearly all miserably struck with many details indistinct. If you become interested in these and seek to buy some, Massachusetts coins should be examined carefully in connection with reading about what is to be expected for certain varieties.

I myself don't have a collection of such pieces, but I do have a very nice Pine Tree shilling, say in VF to EF grade, of the die variety known as Noe-1, attributed to the study of these pieces published by the American Numismatic Society in 1943.

A 1737 Higley copper made from native metal in Simsbury, Connecticut. Surviving pieces, all very rare, are nearly all in low grades. No Mint State coins are known to exist, nor are any even close to that grade.

In Simsbury, Connecticut, in 1737, Dr. Samuel Higley struck copper threepence pieces made from metal taken from local mines, a coinage that was continued after his death the same year. Higley, a medical doctor with a degree from Yale College, also practiced blacksmithing and made many experiments in metallurgy—an early Renaissance Man of sorts. In 1727 he devised a practical method of producing steel. In 1728 he purchased property on a hill in Simsbury (the area later known as Granby) which furnished the site for many copper mines, the most famous being the extensive mine corridors and shafts which were later used as the Newgate Prison. Mines on the hill were worked extensively during the early and middle 18th century.

Following his purchase, Higley operated a small but thriving mining business which

Shown are ruins of the copper mine and Newgate Prison as photographed in 1910.

extracted exceptionally rich copper. Much if not most of the metal was exported to England. Sometime around the year 1737 Higley is thought to have produced copper tokens, perhaps using his own copper, but this is not verified. The obverse depicted a standing deer with the legend THE VALUE OF THREE-PENCE. The reverse showed three crowned hammers (derived from the arms of the English blacksmiths' guild) with the surrounding legend, CONNECTICUT, and the date 1737.

Legend tells us that drinks in the local tavern sold at the time for three pence each, and Higley was in the habit of paying his bar bill with his own coinage. There was a cry against this for the Higley copper threepence was of a diameter no larger than the contemporary English halfpence which circulated in the area; coins which had a value of just 1/6th of that stated on the Higley coin. Accordingly, Higley redesigned his coinage so that the obverse legend was changed to read VALUE ME AS YOU PLEASE. The pieces still bore an indication of value, the Roman numeral III below the standing deer. Sylvester S. Crosby tells us that one reason these coins are so rare is that jewelers sought them to melt as a source of especially pure copper.

I have never owned a Higley threepence personally, but over the years I have handled quite a few at auction and otherwise. Nearly all Higley coppers in existence are well worn, and VG-10 would be an outstanding grade for such a coin. The Connecticut State Library in Hartford has a marvelous collection of these.

A silver shilling struck in London for the colony of Maryland.

In addition to coins made in America, many were imported, especially from England. The silver fourpence (groats), sixpence, and shillings struck at the Tower Mint in London in 1658 for circulation in Maryland circulated widely in that colony.

1773 copper halfpennies intended for circulation in Virginia were struck in quantity in England. Today, Mint State examples are very common. In contrast, well-worn coins are rarely seen.

At the Tower Mint in 1773 copper halfpence were made for circulation in Virginia. By the time they arrived on this side of the Atlantic the fires of the Revolution were about to spark. As nearly all known pieces today are Mint State from an old-time hoard of thousands of pieces once owned by Colonel Mendes I. Cohen of Baltimore, numismatic tradition had it that with the current unrest of Virginia and the patriots dislike of tyrant King George III (who was depicted on the obverse of each coin), very few ever reached circulation. That view changed in the late 20th century when detectorists, as they are called, used Fisher, Garrett, and other electronic metal finders to unearth quite a few Virginia halfpennies that showed extensive circulation in their time.

Coppers were struck under contract for the State of New Jersey from 1786 to 1788. They are attributed by numbers arranged by Dr. Edward Maris in the late 19th century. This is Maris 10-G.

Especially popular today and to a large extent affordable are the various copper coins dated in the 1780s, including coppers authorized by Vermont, Connecticut, New Jersey, and Massachusetts. These are fairly well delineated as to when and under what circumstances they were struck. In contrast, many coppers associated with New York have little documentation, and some well-worn coins have been called "patterns," which they probably are not. In the same era 1787 Fugio cents were struck private under federal contract. Imported from England, 1783–1785 Nova Constellatio coins circulated in America in quantity. Today, excellent reference books exist for most of the above and are key to knowledge and enjoyment.

The coppers of Connecticut of the 1780s are often crude and rustic. This has made them especially appealing to many specialists. Over 300 different die combinations are known, and every now and again a new one is discovered. Attributions are to Miller numbers assigned by Hillyer Ryder and Henry C. Miller in *The State Coinages of New England* (1920).

The Miller die variety letters and numbers were inked on the obverse of this 1785 Connecticut copper many years ago, a popular way at the time to keep track of coins stored face-up in a cabinet drawer. Such ink can be easily dissolved today, but most collectors prefer to keep the numbers intact. Planchet fissures such as are seen here are common on Connecticut coins, particularly for those of 1785 and 1786.

A 1787 Connecticut copper, the so-called Muttonhead variety (Miller 1.2-C). This is a contemporary counterfeit crudely made from dies with purposely unclear lettering, so as to give it the appearance of having been accepted in circulation for many years. Among copper coins of the 1780s contemporary counterfeits are avidly collected and have values equal to or greater than genuine coins of comparable rarity and grade.

Striking took place under state contract and also unofficially by counterfeiters, the identities of whom are largely unknown. Numerical grades, while important, take second seat to quality and eye appeal. A Connecticut copper with smooth, evenly worn surfaces graded Fine-12 is preferred by most everyone to a VF-30 with dark and porous surfaces. Besides, no grading standards, not even approximate, exist that are widely agreed upon.

In the 1950s I collected Vermont and Connecticut coins by die varieties. Well-worn pieces drew little interest from most dealers at the time as they had little value and were a nuisance to attribute and describe. Even if attributed, not many people had a copy of the long-out-of-print *State Coinages of New England* book. One day while visiting Stack's in New York City I asked Morton Stack what he had for sale in such pieces. He showed me a box filled with them, each coin in a paper envelope with various markings—pieces culled from collections that had been purchased. I said I would be interested in buying some, but would have to study them first. We came to an agreement that I could take the box of coins, buy any common to slightly scarce ones for $6 each, and assign and pay a higher price for any rarities. This worked out quite well for both of us. Later, I had a similar arrangement with Art Kagin, partner in the Hollinbeck Coin Company in Des Moines.

A Massachusetts copper half cent of 1788 with all features sharply struck.

In contrast to the usually well worn and often crudely struck coins of Connecticut, most half cents and cents struck by the State of Massachusetts at its own mint in 1787 and 1788 are sharply struck and in higher grades. Most have Full Details, but exceptions to this general rule are usually sharp except in the very highest-relief areas.

Shown is a 1787 Massachusetts cent. The highest-relief features near the center show slight weakness. The copper coinage of 1787 and 1788 was the first in America to use the word CENT.

The history of the Massachusetts mint is detailed by Crosby and others, but in brief, all went well at this particular facility until an audit revealed that each coin cost twice face value to produce. The mint closed its doors.

A Washington Success to the United States token. These can vary widely in sharpness and eye appeal.

Several dozen varieties of coins depicting George Washington were struck in America and, mostly, in England during the late 18th and early 19th centuries and are listed in the Red Book under early American issues. These are a numismatic specialty unto themselves. Over the years a number of numismatists have studied these carefully and have written books on Washingtonia (or is Washingtoniana a better term?). Authors include James Ross Snowden, William S. Baker, George J. Fuld, Jack Collins, Russell Rulau, and Neil Musante.

Some of the Washington coins are dated 1783 but were struck later. These have been a popular specialty for many years, with grades varying widely. Those minted especially for collectors, such as the 1783 Draped Bust and 1792 Roman Head issues in Proof, are usually preserved in high grades. Those made for circulation, including many used in commerce as halfpennies in Great Britain and later acquired by numismatists, can be rustic and show considerable wear.

Washington Roman Head cents of 1792 were made in Proof format and sold to collectors. All are sharply detailed.

The 1794 Washington Ugly Head token, a major rarity, is a candidate for the crudest issue in the Washington series. No one knows who issued it.

The 1795 Washington North Wales halfpennies were crudely struck from rustic dies. These circulated in the British Isles.

Some, such as the 1784 Ugly Head and the undated Success tokens, are from unknown makers, are usually seen with wear, and their original purpose is unknown.

EXCURSION NO. 2

Eureka! Treasure Coins from the Deep Blue Sea

Lost treasure found! How exciting! This is the story of three Eureka! moments, the word said to have been uttered by John Marshall when he spotted the history-making flake of gold in the tail race of Sutter's Mill on the American River on January 24, 1848. Eureka means "I found it!" in Greek.

Shipwrecks have long been a source for gold treasure—what with pirates, doubloons, and other such tales. All or nearly all wrecks that yielded coins were of Spanish galleons, usually wrecked off the coast of Florida or elsewhere in that area, while traveling in fleets laden with silver and gold coins struck in the Spanish dominions in South America. As is still true now, in the 18th century hurricane season began in late July or August and continued into early October. There was no way to forecast them, so they could not be avoided. In some years the tropical storms were mild, while in other years they spelled disaster. On July 31, 1715, 11 out of 12 ships in the treasure fleet were lost off the coast of Florida, a disaster that also claimed more than a thousand lives.

The finding of Spanish wrecks has gone on for many years. In August 1954 at the American Numismatic Association convention in Cleveland, Lieutenant Commander Mendel Peterson of the Navy, and the curator of the Smithsonian Institution in Washington for 25 years, told of his search for wrecks in the Caribbean and in the vicinity of the Florida Keys.

Once in the 1960s when I was visiting well-known numismatist Amon G. Carter Jr. at his office in Fort Worth, Texas, the phone rang on his desk while I was prowling through his safe looking at his collection. I overheard snatches of Amon's conversation—about gold, treasure, and shipwrecks. When he hung up he said to me, "That was Art McKee, who has a treasure museum in Florida. He wanted to know if I would invest in his recoveries from a wreck site he had just found. I said, 'Sure. I have invested in just about everything else. Why not treasure hunting?'"

I don't know how the Carter-McKee connection turned out. I visited Art later and he showed me many artifacts and coins he had found over the years. Ed Link, of Binghamton, New York, was a fine friend of mine for many years. He did much treasure hunting in and around the Florida Keys using submersible craft. Some years later another treasure hunter, Mel Fisher, located the wreck of the *Atocha*, lost in a hurricane in 1715. Excitement prevailed as silver and gold coins were brought to the surface and sold to investors and others.

Other accounts of Spanish wrecks were numerous, but there were no stories of significant discoveries of *American* gold coins. That changed in 1989 when news was published of the finding of the wreck of the SS *Central America*, a sidewheel steamer lost in 1857 with tons of American gold coins and ingots aboard. (I will return to that ship later.)

Double Eagles of the SS *Brother Jonathan*

The first ship was the SS *Brother Jonathan*, one of dozens of vessels engaging in the Pacific Coast trade in the Gold Rush era and the decade afterward.[1] Launched at the shipyard of Perrine, Patterson & Stack, in Williamsburg, New York, on November 2, 1850, the 1,181-ton ship was made of locust, white oak, live oak, and cedar and cost about $190,000. Her measurements were 220-feet 11-inches long by 36-feet wide with a draft of 13 feet 10 inches. Power was provided by a vertical steam engine made by the Morgan Iron Works. Accommodations, including 24 staterooms, were provided for about 365 passengers. The staterooms offered extra amenities for those who wished to pay a higher fare, but most voyagers were content with simple berths in a dormitory-like arrangement.[2] In 1861 the ship became the property of the California Steam Navigation Company.

Her most eventful and last voyage commenced on July 28, 1865.[3] Overloaded with freight far beyond her 900-ton capacity and riding low in the water, the *Brother Jonathan* left San Francisco headed north toward its intended destination of Vancouver Island. Captain Samuel J. DeWolf had strongly protested the overloading, but was told

The cover of my book, *The Treasure Ship SS* Brother Jonathan: *Her Life and Loss 1850–1865.*

153

that if he complained further, there were many other ship captains who would like to have his job at the helm.

The SS *Brother Jonathan*.

No sooner had she gone through the Golden Gate marking the entrance to San Francisco Bay than the *Brother Jonathan* ran into a fierce gale. High winds continued through July 30 as she passed Crescent City on the coast of Northern California. Shortly after 1:45 on the afternoon of the 30th, under clear skies in a sea whipped by the still-heavy winds, the ship ran onto rocks hidden beneath the surface off St. George's Point.[4] The concussion ripped a great hole in front of the engine room, causing the auxiliary foremast to topple across the deck. Three cannon shots were fired, alerting citizens on the nearby shore, which soon became crowded with spectators.

It is believed that her cargo was valued at $300,000 to $500,000, including machinery for a woolen mill, mining apparatus for the Owyhee district in eastern Oregon and Idaho, 346 barrels of whiskey, and $200,000 in payroll for U.S. troops at Fort Vancouver, Washington. One account stated that the payroll was in federal "greenback" notes, part of a shipment totaling $250,000 in such currency.[5]

In ensuing years several salvage attempts were made on the SS *Brother Jonathan*, but none with success. In 1991 Donald G. Knight and Harvey Harrington, both formerly of another exploration company, Sea-Epics Research, and an experienced diver, James Wadsley, founded Deep Sea Research to recover coins and whatever else of value that could be found. Others joined the firm in 1991 and 1992, including Sherman Harris and David L. Flohr. Later, Messrs. Wadsley, Harrington, Harris, and Flohr would become the four officers of the company, and Knight would leave in 1994.

Using side-scan sonar and other technology, searches for the wreck were made for the next two years. Finally, on October 1, 1993, the remains of the ship were located and confirmed. In the summer of 1996 some artifacts were recovered. Efforts were conducted with the M/V *Cavalier* as the mother ship, *Xanadu* as the dive ship, and the assistance of the one-man mini-sub *Snooper* and the two-man *Delta*. Gold coins were nowhere to be found, however.

A beautiful Mint State 1865-S double eagle recovered from the wreck of the SS *Brother Jonathan*.

Eureka! That moment happened on August 20 when Harvey Harrington spotted a large quantity of double eagles on the surface of the wreck. Subsequent dives brought hundreds of coins to the surface, mostly $20 pieces. Specimens were handled with care and transported by Brink's to a San Francisco area bank vault, where they were conserved by Robert Johnson, a well-known numismatist. By the last day of the 1996 search, 875 coins were found, mostly $20 double eagles.

In 1997 my son Andrew and I went to Crescent City and climbed aboard a recovery ship, the *American Salvor*, which was still being used to seek additional items. Most of the coins were consigned by DSR in 1999 to Bowers and Merena Galleries.

Here in New Hampshire my staff and I studied and described the recovered coins. The sale was widely publicized, including a special display at the Treasures

The *American Salvor* in the Pacific Ocean off the coast of Crescent City, California, as photographed by the author in 1997.

of Mandalay Bay Museum in the Mandalay Bay Resort & Casino in Las Vegas. For that exhibit I wrote a script that was recorded by James Earl Jones and was played to visitors.

At the auction there were 842 lots, of which 793 were double eagles dominated by mint-fresh 1865-S coins. How exciting! The event, held in Los Angeles on May 29, 1999, created a lot of attention and resulted in strong prices. In connection with the event I wrote a book, *The Treasure Ship SS* Brother Jonathan, which garnered favorable reviews.

This event was a catalyst for the creation of a numismatic subculture of enthusiasts who desired to obtain one or more coins documented as coming from shipwrecks. This movement went into high gear soon afterward when large quantities of double eagles from the SS *Central America* became available.

Gold on the SS *Central America*

Now to the *Central America*. The treasure of treasures!

In late August of 1857 several hundred passengers and over $1.2 million in registered gold coins and ingots left San Francisco aboard the SS *Sonora*, the first leg of a trip to New York City. The voyage in the Pacific Ocean, south along the coast of California, Mexico, and Central America, was uneventful. The ship reached Panama City, where passengers disembarked and went to the station of the Panama Railroad for a 48-mile trip over land. The rail connection had been completed and opened in 1855. Earlier, the trip across Panama involved several days by wagon and small boats.

Arriving at the railroad station in the city of Aspinwall (today's Colon) the passengers and cargo were soon loaded aboard the SS *Central America*, name just changed from the SS *George Law*, for the trip north to New York City. The departure was under clear sunny skies and a stop was made in Havana, but most passengers remained on board due to a cholera epidemic there. Several people boarded, except for one man who was at a hotel and missed the connection.

The trip resumed northward, a pleasant voyage made all the more so by a 12-miles-per-hour breeze from the ship's forward motion. In time, clouds were seen, a tropical storm that the crew thought for sure would pass quickly. It did not. The wind increased to gale force, and by Thursday, September 10, the waves were mountainous and the ship had sprung leaks.

Matters went from bad to worse, and on Friday the fires in the boilers had been extinguished and the ship was helpless. On Saturday the conditions were such that some lifeboats were set off with women passengers who reached two small sailing ships and were saved. Finally, at eight in the evening the ship slipped beneath the waves, with Commander William Lewis Herndon standing on a wheel box. In time a number of survivors on rafts and makeshift floats were rescued, but over 400 souls perished.

In time the *Central America* was forgotten.

In the early 1980s Thomas ("Tommy") G. Thompson, a student of shipwrecks, who worked as a scientist at the Battelle Memorial Institute in Columbus, Ohio, learned of the *Central America* and began directing his efforts toward trying to find the ship. In 1985 with two associates, Robert Evans and Barry Schatz, he formed the Recovery Limited Partnership to finance the search. Most of the investors were business leaders in Ohio. In time $12.7 million was raised.

Evans and Thompson compiled the passenger and crew information from historical accounts including newspaper stories, reports by survivors, and other contemporary sources. The resulting matrix would provide clues leading to the location of the *Central America*. They entered the data on a 12-by-

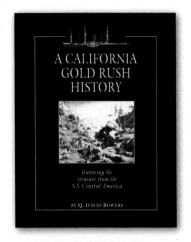

A California Gold Rush History featuring the treasure from the SS Central America.

The Panama Railroad.

A depiction of the loss of the SS *Central America* at eight in the evening on Saturday, September 12, 1857.

12-foot sheet of paper, arranging the historical accounts into three-hour time slots covering the period of the storm and the sinking. The matrix also included information about the weather, the progress of the hurricane, and the physical deterioration of the steamship. The treasure hunters called themselves the Columbus-America Discovery Group (C-ADG).

An area of about 1,200 square miles was targeted for exploration by equipment and sophisticated scanning technology, including side-scan imaging. In the summer of 1988 a new ship, the R/V *Arctic Discoverer*, was prepared and the first iteration of *Nemo*, a remotely controlled mini-submarine that could carefully photograph the surroundings and grasp objects and gently bring them to the surface, was built. In late August they set out, finally diving on the new target on September 11, 1988. Eureka! Remains of a rusting steamer sidewheel were seen—a distinctive feature on ships of the U.S. Mail Steamship Company. In time her identity was confirmed by the recovery of the ship's bell which was marked "MORGAN IRON WORKS NEW YORK 1853" by the ship's manufacturer. The treasure finders registered their discovery with a federal court.

A gem 1857-S double eagle recovered from
the treasure aboard the SS *Central America*.

In 1989 the recovery recommenced on a grand scale by the C-ADG. The *Arctic Discoverer* was outfitted with additional gear, including a vastly upgraded *Nemo*, now standing over 7-feet tall, 15-feet long and weighing more than six tons. The find was announced in general terms in September. Additional funds were needed, and in 1990 Columbus Exploration, LLC, was established and raised an additional $10 million. Given the golden prospect, investors were eager to participate. Recovery operations extended into 1991, and details of the find were kept secret.

That changed, and by 1992 the finders were eager to share information. *Coin World* ran front page stories and editorials about the effect of the news on collectors and dealers. "The numismatic community teemed with excitement," said editor Beth Deisher.[6] "The thought of being able to identify, recover, and preserve the SS *Central America's* coins and bars produced a wave of enthusiasm among numismatic researchers and collectors." *Numismatic News* was equally enthusiastic in its news coverage, and other periodicals followed suit.

It was finders keepers, and those who financed the recovery were set to make a fortune!

No appraisal had been done yet, but that did not slow down the excitement. When pressed as to the potential worth, Tommy Thompson stated that $1 billion "isn't out of the realm of possibility."

Oops! This and other glowing stories attracted dozens of people who claimed they had a vested interest in one or another of the companies that insured the wreck, or helped Tommy Thompson and others with information, or otherwise were entitled to a share of the treasure. This unexpected consequence resulted in a wave of lawsuits that tied up the treasure for years and cost millions of dollars in legal fees.

Finally, in 1999 the parties reached an agreement. Claimants were awarded 7.6% and the treasure finders 92.4%. Debts were heavy, and the finders in combination with Christie's art auction house, which had also put up money, decided to sell their share outright in order to recover their costs. After all of the legal hassle, prospects for a profit were slim. On January 19, 2000, it was revealed that the California Gold Marketing Group (CGMG), headed by Dwight Manley, had purchased the entire 92.4% interest held by the finders, and that all claims had been settled.

A selection of *Central America* gold ingots.

As part of that arrangement, CGMG consigned a selection of gold coins and ingots to Christie's. They did not have an in-house expert, and I was tapped to write the entire catalog from start to finish.

Along the way Christine Karstedt, Ray Merena, and I at Bowers and Merena Galleries acquired a small share of the CGMG, which was in the process of constructing a large "show front" display, "The Ship of Gold," measuring 50 feet from left to right. This was a representation of the side of the ship, with portholes through which gold coins and ingots could be observed. The "Kellogg

Dwight Manley, Bob Evans, and author Q. David Bowers at "The Ship of Gold" exhibit at the August 2000 ANA Convention.

Andrew Bowers and the largest gold ingot found, nicknamed the Eureka bar.

& Humbert Assay Office" was set up nearby, and other exhibits were put in place. A small theater consisting of a large screen and several rows of seats was assembled for continuous presentation of the History Channel's *Ship of Gold* film. This was the sensation of the 2000 American Numismatic Association convention in Philadelphia. Over 20,000 people attended—an all-time record that stands today.

The author (seated) being interviewed by the History Channel.

Bob Evans presented a program as part of the Numismatic Theatre, and I helped. The large room was filled with 400 people, more than ever attended such a program before or since. The History Channel film crew was back to do a second feature on the treasure.

"The Ship of Gold" exhibit on tour, shown here at the Tucson Gem and Mineral Show.

"The Ship of Gold" went on tour, including to the Tucson Gem and Mineral Show where, for the first time in the history of that famous event, crowd control needed to be put in place in the form of stanchions and ropes. Previous attractions including the greatest collection of Fabergé eggs and the Hope Diamond required no such precautions.

Christine Karstedt and I helped with the marketing and other publicity, a memorable and unique experience. In time everything was sold, and by a decade later almost all of the coins and ingots had increased in market value. Or perhaps all, without exception, did.

I wrote the definitive book on the find, *A California Gold Rush history: Featuring the treasure from the SS* Central America: *a source book for the Gold Rush historian and numismatist*, a title suggested by Eric P. Newman. With 1,055 pages the book weighed more than 12 pounds, and the print run of 4,400 copies sold out. Today on the Internet and through booksellers copies typically bring much more than the issue price.

Working with Bob Evans, Dwight Manley, Larry and Ira Goldberg, and others in marketing the treasure, doing research for the book, traveling, and giving programs combined to make this one of the most exciting adventures of my life. Every once in a while I go to the bank safe deposit department and take out my Gem 1857-S double eagle in its special PCGS gold seal holder and again reflect on the agreatest treasure of all time and my part in it. Then I put it back. Today it is easy to enjoy, in a way, coins and other items by bringing their images up larger than life on a computer screen.

As an epilogue, in 2014 the original investors from Columbus, Ohio, and others tapped Odyssey Marine Exploration to make another trip to the treasure site. This was accomplished with success, and 45 more ingots, 1,153 additional 1857-S double eagles, and many other coins were recovered, including a large cluster of silver dimes. As of press time for this book, marketing plans have not been announced.[7]

The SS *New York* Coin Discovery

The third treasure ship with American coins that I was directly involved in was the SS *New York*. Constructed in 1837 at the yard of William H. Brown on the East River, New York City, she was a side-wheel steamship with auxiliary sails, a smaller class of vessel generally known as a steam packet. She was 160.5-feet long, had a 22.5-foot beam, and a 10.5-foot draft or displacement. There was one main deck with a cabin section in the center, with decks fore and aft. The fore deck had a canvas cover. Above the aft or promenade deck was an open-air deck, essentially a platform, where passengers could relax if the passage was smooth, enjoying themselves under the sun and in the open air, cooled by the breeze of forward motion.

The Treasure Ship SS New York: *Her Story 1837–1846.*

On Saturday, September 5, 1846, the SS *New York* departed Galveston, Texas, at 4:30 in the afternoon, heading to New Orleans carrying 30 passengers and a crew of 23. The weather had been foggy and rainy for nearly three weeks, and at departure time a light haze covered the harbor. At the helm was the owner of the ship, Captain John D. Phillips, a seasoned commander. The load was far short of capacity, foretelling a pleasant voyage with more than usual attention to the passengers by the crew. Fare was $15 for cabin passage, less for steerage. Money in the estimated amount of $30,000 to $40,000 was aboard, although no authoritative figures were ever published. This consisted of gold and silver coins and, it is likely, many bank notes. We know that among the cargo was a woodworking machine. Probably there were barrels and crates of other goods as well, normal for the route, although one later account stated the hold was empty.

The voyage was expected to take two days, including overnight, with arrival in New Orleans on Sunday evening. The ship headed to the open sea, with no indication of anything unusual. Once the bar—a ridge of sand about 12-feet below the surface—was crossed, a stiff breezed kicked up waves. Soon it began to rain heavily. The going was choppy, as sometimes happened. No doubt the roughness would soon pass. It did not. On Sunday the storm worsened, and the ship was tossed about even more violently. The passengers huddled together and tried to cheer each other. Surely the winds would subside and the sea would become quiet and then on to New Orleans, as planned.

This did not happen. The worst was yet to come.

At about midnight or within an hour afterward, a cable snapped, and part of the structure gave way on the starboard side. Water rushed into the hold, the boiler fires were extinguished, and for the first time, passengers seriously feared for their lives. Into the night men manned pumps, but to no avail. Early the next morning the ship sank, while some deck parts and the wheelhouse floated away. Survivors included 19 passengers and 18 crewmembers including the captain. Lost were 11 passengers and 8 of the crew. One of the survivors, John Todd, published a detailed account of the tragedy. In time the ship was forgotten.

Fast forward to the 20th century.

Avery Munson, of New Iberia, Louisiana, a man who loved scuba diving and exploring the sea, wondered whether there might be any historical accounts of lost ships with treasure aboard in the Gulf of Mexico within reach of his port. For several years he combed through old newspapers and other accounts. Lightning struck! He found the telltale story of the loss of the *New York* in a news article in the *Daily Picayune* of September 10, 1846. With this as a beginning, he enlisted several friends, forming a group of four styling themselves as the Gentlemen of Fortune, including Craig DeRouen and the husband and wife team of Gary and Renée Hebert.

The team studied newspaper articles, survivor accounts, charts, and underwater data. The Gulf of Mexico is a center for offshore oil rigs, and much mapping had been done. They consulted shrimp fishermen and others familiar with the Gulf to seek clues and ideas. The group took measurements and made estimates. In time, success was theirs. Finally, in early 2005 they had their "Eureka!" moment: the ship's bell was found. In due course their ownership was successfully registered in a federal court, and recovery commenced. Several hundred gold coins and nearly 2,000 silver coins were found.

An 1826 Capped Bust half dollar from the SS *New York.* Half dollars dating back to a 1795 Flowing Hair coin gave insight as to what coins were in general circulation in Galveston, Texas, in 1846.

This rare 1842-O, Small Date, half dollar was among the coins recovered.

This 1839-O Classic Head quarter eagle
was among the many gold coins found.

This 1840-D half eagle retains nearly all of its original mint luster.

The *Night Moves* and its tender in the
distance as we leave the recovery site.

Aboard the *Night Moves* recovery ship
Andrew Bowers gets ready for a dive to
the wreck of the SS *New York* while
scuba diving expert Tom Wachsmuth will
be next to jump overboard.

On August 13, 2007, I had the pleasure of spending some time at sea with the finders, while my son Andrew, a certified scuba diver and his friends, Tom Wachsmuth and Cris Dow, joined them aboard the *Night Moves* yacht in dives to the wreck. All of this was a memorable, indeed unique experience. Later I wrote a book, *The Treasure Ship SS* New York, and our company sold the coins at auction, each in a special holder made by the Numismatic Guaranty Corporation.[8]

Hunting for Treasure

I was involved in a slight way with the treasure from the SS *Republic* discovered in the early 21st century by Odyssey Marine Exploration. I contributed information on coins and other artifacts to Ellen Gerth, the firm's curator.

How can you become involved with shipwreck treasures? One way is to search auction and other listings and seek one coin from each of the different wrecks that have been discovered. Opportunities for U.S. coins are limited to just a few ships, but worldwide there are many others, including in particular Spanish ships that departed from South America in the 18th century and were lost in hurricanes. There is a lot to read about treasures and explorations even if you don't have any of the coins.

Just for fun, but not numismatically related, is Edgar Allan Poe's 1843 short story, "The Gold Bug," which gave its name to a later generation of gold aficionados.

EXCURSION NO. 3

Let's Go to the Fair!

O dear, what can the matter be?
Dear, dear, what can the matter be?
O dear, what can the matter be?
Johnny's so long at the fair.

World's fairs, or national exhibitions drawing sponsors, displays, and features from different countries, are said to have begun with the French Industrial Exposition of 1844. The best-known early such event is the Great Exhibition of 1851, opened by Queen Victoria in London in 1851. It was centered in the Crystal Palace, a huge glass and steel structure 1,851-feet long (a significant number), and with an interior height of 128 feet. Merchants, manufacturers, artists, associations, governments, museums, and others set up displays, some 40,000 in all.

In America the first world's fair was the Centennial Exhibition held in Philadelphia in 1876. Before then there were many other fairs of varying sizes in the United States.

The Crystal Palace, not officially a world's fair but often called such in various accounts, was built in New York City for the 1853 Exhibition of the Industry of All Nations, inspired by the structure in London. The building made of steel and glass was two-stories high. The first story was octagonal in outline and the second was in the shape of a Greek cross. In the center was a dome 148 feet high. Each of the four corners was octagon shaped, and each front had two towers 70-feet high topped with flagstaffs. This building comprised 170,000 square feet. A two-story annex 450-feet long and 21-feet wide was devoted to art and other exhibits and refreshment stands. All told there was an estimated 206,000 square feet of glass panels. George J.B. Carstensen and Charles Gildemeister designed the buildings. Subscriptions for stock were sold by the banking house of Duncan, Sherman & Co., there being no official government or city sponsorship, although the land was leased from the city for a period of five years, and various help was provided by the state and the federal governments.

The Crystal Palace was erected on the south side of 42nd Street in New York City, between 5th and 6th avenues on what later became known as Bryant Park. Exhibit space amounted to 173,000 square feet comprised of 111,000 on the main floor and 62,000 in galleries. The arrangement of the main categories was essentially the same used in London in 1851: machinery, raw materials, manufactures, and fine arts. There were 4,100 exhibitors, with more than half from foreign countries. Costs for the building and related expenses amounted to $640,000.

Opening day was July 14, 1853. The featured guest was President Franklin Pierce, who arrived at two in the afternoon in a rainstorm, while a band played *Hail Columbia* and *Yankee Doodle*. Later, the Crystal Palace officials fêted the chief executive at a banquet at the Metropolitan Hotel.

The Crystal Palace in New York City.

An interior view of a section of the Crystal Palace.

Nearby, Warren Latting constructed the wood and steel Latting Observatory, on 6th Avenue between 42nd and 43rd streets, which jutted 350 feet into the air and permitted visitors to look down upon the Crystal Palace and have a bird's-eye view of the surrounding city. It burned in 1856.

The Crystal Palace remained open to various exhibits, retail displays, and small businesses. Phineas T. Barnum, the indefatigable showman, was deeply involved and helped with promotions, showcasing it in his *Illustrated News.* On view in 1853, and possibly at later times, was a display of coins and medals known as the Crystal Palace Collection. On Friday, October 14, 1856, these were described on a "large sheet" and offered at auction by Bangs & Bro., New York City.[9] There was not enough business, however, to cover expenses, and the building was unprofitable, and the stockholders lost about $300,000.

In October 1858 *Harper's Monthly Record of Current Events* included this:

> The Crystal Palace in New York, built in 1853 for the "Exhibition of the Industry of all Nations," was burned on the afternoon of October 5. The Exhibition, it will be remembered, proved a pecuniary failure, the stockholders losing their entire investment. The Fair of the American Institute had just been opened in the Palace, which was filled with objects for exhibition, some of which were of considerable value.

Many works of art, sent to the Exhibition of 1853, still remained in the Palace. The principal of these were Thorwaldsen's colossal group of "Christ and the Apostles," and Kiss's "Amazon and Tiger." These were consumed with the building. The fire is supposed to have been the work of an incendiary, and a reward of $3,000 has been offered for his apprehension. The entire loss is estimated a fully half a million of dollars, besides the value of the building, which cost $635,000, and might probably have been sold for a quarter of that sum.

In July and August of that year a passion for collecting medalets of about 31-mm diameter started when those relating to the Atlantic Cable, completed in August, sold like the proverbial hotcakes. This inspired Augustus B. Sage, a teenaged dealer in rare coins who in March 1858 had been the founder of the American Numismatic Society, to commission local diesinker and coiner George H. Lovett to make medalets showing the Crystal Place in flames.

Augustus B. Sage's 31 mm copper token showing the Crystal Palace ablaze.

These were the first in his planned Odds and Ends Series, which, as it turned out, expired after two other subjects were created.

The Crystal Palace featured on the reverse of a 28 mm
brass token of 1853 advertising a team of trained dogs.

All told, over a dozen varieties of tokens and medals relating to the Crystal Palace were issued by various entities, but they have never been studied as a group.

During the war various sanitary fairs, as they were called, took place in such locations as New York City, Philadelphia, Springfield (Massachusetts), Cincinnati, and even on the island of Nantucket. These were set up to raise funds for the relief of wounded Union soldiers. Donated merchandise was sold, contests and events were held, and for some of them, tokens were issued.

Shown is a silver token (17.9 mm) from the Great Central Fair, the variety known as Fuld PA-750-Lf. The portrait of Washington was by Mint engraver Anthony C. Paquet.

A stereograph card showing the token-coining setup at the fair.

The best-known numismatic items connected with these fairs are the cent-size tokens sold at the Great Central Fair held in Philadelphia in June 1864, an event that drew visitors from all over the North, including President Lincoln and his family. Struck on a steam-driven coining press provided by the Mint, these tokens featured George Washington on the obverse and on the reverse was an inscription in several lines. Copper tokens were sold for 10 cents each, silver for 50 cents. Large numbers were made, as is evidenced by more than two dozen die combinations known today.

Fairgrounds at the Great Central Fair.

In 1876 the Centennial International Exhibition was held in Fairmount Park in Philadelphia—the first American event to be recognized as a world's fair. Different states and other entities put up buildings to showcase their assets, and nearly 10 million visitors went through the gates. The nearby Philadelphia Mint was invited to set up an exhibit with items from the Mint Cabinet, but declined, stating that visitors to the city could stop by if they wanted to. An official medal was made (38 mm) and sold in bronzed copper (13,000 struck), gilded bronze (10,500), and silver (10,133), with appropriate legends. Many smaller medals and tokens were issued privately, but no comprehensive study of them has ever been made. Today the official medals appear on the market often.

The official 1876 Centennial Exhibition medal struck at
the Philadelphia Mint made of gilded copper (73 mm).

An admission ticket to the fair.

Aerial view of the World's Columbian Exposition in Chicago in 1893,
comprising 600 acres on the shore of Lake Michigan.

The gigantic Ferris Wheel and a view of the cars.

Although various fairs, industrial expositions, and other events were held during this era, the next world's fair was the World's Columbian Exposition held in Chicago. The event honored the 400th anniversary of Christopher Columbus's discovery (not that it was lost) of America. About 200 buildings were made faced with "staff," as it was called—a white composition in imitation of stone—intended for short-term use after which structures would be torn down. Katherine Lee Bates, a visitor to the event who later went to the top of Pikes Peak in Colorado, memorialized these white buildings in "America the Beautiful," "Thine alabaster cities gleam, undimmed by human tears."

Set to open in 1892, delays ensued, and it was not until May 1, 1893, that the gates were thrown open to the general public. The prime attraction was the gigantic rotating Ferris Wheel that towered over the fairgrounds. Buildings were devoted to art, science, industry, and other subjects. On the slightly naughty side by standards of the time was the "Streets of Cairo" section with Egyptian dancers and games of chance. There had never been a fair like it anywhere in the world.

An 1893 Isabella quarter.

An 1893 Columbian souvenir half dollar.

From an early time I have had a connection with the exposition. The first "rare" coin I had as a kid was a worn 1893 Columbian *souvenir* (as stated on the inscription) half dollar. Later, it and the two other commemoratives, the 1892 half dollar and the 1893 Isabella quarter, became stock in trade in my coin business inventory. Today they are among the most popular of American coins. My great grandmother Frances Mumaugh, a professional artist, exhibited five of her paintings at the fair in various places, including one listed in the exposition catalog.

The Mermod Frères exhibit at the exposition. A very special music box is circled in red at the lower right.

The music box today.

Description of the Eroica by Sotheby's, London, 2000.

The award-winning Symphonion three-disc Eroica music box with clock that was displayed at the Columbian Exposition.

Mermod Frères, the world-famous maker of music boxes based in Sainte-Croix, Switzerland, had a large exhibit there. A few years ago I made the delightful acquisition of one of the music boxes that was on view. It had survived in nearly mint condition and still had its golden "Highest Award at the Columbian Exposition" plaque on the underside of the lid.[10] It plays as beautifully and brightly as it did for convention visitors!

Another Columbian Exposition item that I treasure is a tall hall clock that includes a special musical mechanism that plays three discs simultaneously, a virtual trio! Made by Paul Lochmann's factory in Leipzig, Germany, it was sold as the Symphonion Eroica Model 38B. This particular one had been set up at the exposition and played for visitors. Later, it went back to Germany where Paul Lochmann placed it in his home.

Years later his family consigned it for auction to Sotheby's in London, where it was purchased by Mark Yaffe, from whom I acquired it. Along with it came the official award medal.

The 77 mm medal struck at the Philadelphia Mint awarded to the Lochmann factory, maker of the Eroica, and detail of the award. The obverse design was by Augustus Saint-Gaudens, the reverse by Charles E. Barber.

There were dozens of different medals and tokens made for the Exposition. Among my favorites are rolled-out coins made by at least four machines, or at least four dies were made with inscriptions. Coins could be inserted into such device, a crank turned, and a rolled-out coin emerged. Many coins of different denominations and dates are known today, with Indian Head cents and Liberty Head nickels being the most common. Two representative rolled-out coins are shown below.

An 1891 Indian Head cent rolled out at the Columbian Exposition.

A rolled-out 1886 Liberty Seated dime.

Tokens and medals known to Nathan N. Eglit as of 1965 are described in his book published that year, *Columbiana, the medallic history of Christopher Columbus and the Columbian Exposition of 1893*. Collecting items from this event can be a specialty on its own.

The Trans-Mississippi Exposition held in Omaha in 1898 (in which my great grandmother was an exhibitor), the Pan-American Exposition held in Buffalo in 1901 (at which President William A. McKinley was fatally shot), and other fairs of the late 1800s and early 1900s were popular attractions, with tokens and medals issued in connection with each.

In 1904 the Louisiana Purchase Exposition, popularly known as the St. Louis World's Fair, was the occasion for issuing two commemorative gold dollars dated 1903—one with the portrait of Thomas Jefferson and the other depicting William A. McKinley.

The Art Palace at the 1905 Louisiana Purchase Exposition in St. Louis.

Farran Zerbe, a numismatic salesman of the era, gained the concession for these coins, and the Philadelphia Mint struck 125,000 of each. They were over-promoted at $3 each and laid an egg in the marketplace. All but 17,500 of each design went into the melting pot. Time usually makes all things right in the rare coin market, and today Gem Mint State commemorative gold dollars sell for over a thousand dollars each!

In terms of commemorative coins the 1915 Panama-Pacific International Exposition held in San Francisco outdid all others. The purpose of the event was to celebrate the recent opening of the Panama Canal and also the rebirth of San Francisco after the great earthquake and fire. Farran Zerbe held the coin franchise and offered a half dollar, gold dollar, quarter eagle, and two shapes of $50 coin at his exhibit.

Shown are obverses of the 1903-dated Louisiana Purchase commemorative gold dollars and their shared reverse.

Dozens of different postcards were issued to promote the exposition.

The Palace of Fine Arts as depicted in 1915.

The same building as photographed by the author in August 2001.
This is the only remaining structure from the fair.

A 1915-S Panama Pacific commemorative half dollar.

The commemorative gold dollar featuring a worker on the Panama Canal, popularly thought to be a baseball player by those who bought the coins.

The obverse of the 1915-S quarter eagle features Liberty riding a mythological hippocampus and was designed by Chief Engraver Charles E. Barber. The reverse with an eagle atop a Roman-style standard is the work of George T. Morgan.

An 1877 pattern half dollar designed by Morgan had the same reverse motif that he used on the exposition quarter eagle.

An octagonal $50 with Athena (Minerva) on the obverse and an Athenian owl on the reverse.

The round commemorative $50 gold coin.

Farran Zerbe's display at the exposition.

Once again, his expectations proved to be optimistic, and many were melted. In time, their values increased, and today each is expensive and highly prized with Gem examples of each of the $50 style crossing the $100,000 mark at auction.

The two female figures on the reverse of the official exposition medal by
Robert A. Aitken were modeled by Audrey Munson in the sculptor's New York studio.

Audrey Munson, a young lady whose profession was posing nude for sculptors, modeled for Robert A. Aitken who created two images of her for the official Panama-Pacific International Exposition medal. Munson acted in several silent films, often taking the part of a model. There were dozens of statues exhibited at the fair, and most were created on the other side of the country in and near New York City by sculptors with Munson as the model going from studio to studio.[11]

Audrey Munson posing for a film.

Other expositions, fairs, and celebrations furnished many occasions for later issues of silver half dollars through 1954 and gold coins in 1916, 1917, 1922, and 1926.

The commemorative half dollar issued for the 1926 Sesquicentennial International Exposition held in Philadelphia to observe the 150th anniversary of American independence.

A bird's eye view of the 1926 exposition grounds.

The year 1936 is the 100th anniversary of the State of Texas. Commemorative half dollars were issued starting in 1934 (as shown here) and were kept into production though 1938, a situation that was displeasing to many collectors. Mintages were low in the later years.

Publicity for the 1936 Texas Centennial Exposition.

A 1936 commemorative half dollar observing the 100th anniversary of the city of Cleveland (founded by Moses Cleaveland, shown on the obverse) and the Great Lakes Exposition.

An artist's conception of the Great Lakes Exposition in Cleveland on the shore of Lake Erie.

There are two main categories of commemorative coins. The first group consists of classic silver coins and (to a lesser extent) gold coins from 1892 to 1954. These include the 1893 Isabella quarter, the 1900 Lafayette silver dollar, and 142 dates and mintmarks of half dollars. Although collecting a full set of these has been popular for a long time, many collectors have opted to acquire the 48 different design types of half dollars instead of all of the varieties. Not as many people collect gold due to the higher prices of such coins, but if you can afford such, a set of the nine different gold dollars, the two quarter eagles, and the two $50 coins is well worth owning.

A 1936 Cincinnati half dollar commemorating the city's 50th anniversary as a musical center of America, one of 5,005 struck. Today a Gem Mint State coin is valued at about $500. In late 1989 the price was $1,750.

When I was a teenager I visited Edmund Karmilowicz, a local collector, who showed me his type set of silver commemorative coins. I was quite impressed and set about building my own collection, coin by coin. By that time, I had all of the issues of *The Numismatist* going back to 1893 (the magazine started in 1888). I had read about how each commemorative was created, advertised, and distributed—a very enjoyable experience—and now it was exciting to see the actual coins.

A 1939-S Oregon Trail half dollar of which 3,005 were coined. Today a Gem sells for about $700. In 1989 the price was about $1,600.

Today the market for commemoratives is, well, weird. It has been such for a long time. Until the late 1980s they were a hot ticket, very popular, and in the mainstream. At that time a great interest in rare coin investment took place on the part of people, including Wall Street brokerages setting up funds to buy Mint State and Proof silver and gold coins. Classic commemoratives were a natural choice, as nearly all are Mint State, most have enticingly low mintages, and most of them are attractive and interesting to behold. A great rush to buy them took place, and prices increased sharply. Collectors were squeezed out. Then reality struck. The investment market collapsed in 1989 and never recovered. Today, nearly all silver commemoratives are much cheaper than they were back then. They have never returned to the mainstream of collecting.

The second category consists of modern commemoratives that have been issued, starting with the 1982 Washington half dollar commemorating the 250th anniversary of his birth, continuing down to the present day. A flood of coins has inundated the market—some honoring meaningful people and events, others obscure—all as ordered by Congress under the influence of various constituents. These have been good, bad, ugly, and beautiful—take your choice. Issue prices are nearly often made higher by surcharges mandated by Congress—extra money that is given to those who sponsored the coins. The result has, in many instances, been pricing at the outset that has not been supported by a meaningful aftermarket. The overwhelming quantities of these seems to have dulled the market for classic commemoratives of the 1892 to 1954 years.

A 1991-P commemorative dollar issued to observe the 38th anniversary of the "end" of the Korean War. Though an armistice was signed to return prisoners to their homes, a peace treaty has never been signed, so the two Koreas are still technically at war.

If you select modern issues of interest (few people want them all), check prices on eBay and elsewhere before buying. Also remember that nearly all have been issued in very high quality—MS and Proof 67 to 70—and that high grades are normal, not special. Beware of pieces in holders marked with high grades that are priced at high prices. Check the aftermarket for these on eBay and other Internet sites.

EXCURSION NO. 4

Civil War Tokens

There are *so many* other specialties in American numismatics that I could devote hundreds of pages—as, indeed, I have done in a number of Whitman books on tokens, medals, and paper money (check the Whitman Publishing site on the Internet, or visit your favorite shop or coin dealer and start with *Coins and Collectors: Golden Anniversary Edition*).

My excursions into Civil War tokens are shorter than the previous three—side trips they might be called. Summaries of some of my favorites, in no particular order, might invite you to explore further.

Tokens with a dog and GOOD FOR A SCENT made by Joseph H. Merriam of Boston exist in several different die combinations. They are scarce but not rare. For many years these have been among the most popular in the Civil War series, with the result that nice examples can sell into the hundreds of dollars.

When the very first issue of the *American Journal of Numismatics* was published in May 1866, the showcased subject was Civil War tokens. From that point down to the present day they have been among the most popular series. Today the Civil War Token Society (found online at www.cwtsociety.com) and its lively *Civil War Token Journal* (published quarterly) keep up the pace. As is the case with all specialized groups I mention in this book the Internet gives more information.

The Civil War began in April 1861 and ended in April 1865, so from a technical viewpoint such tokens are those issued during that interval. In practice, some outside of those parameters have been adopted as standard, such as the Wealth of the South tokens dated 1860.

One of the most illogical Civil War tokens is Fuld 506/514a, featuring Abraham Lincoln on the obverse and a pro-South motif on the reverse. Only a few of these exist.

By late 1861 the outcome of the Civil War became increasingly uncertain, and citizens hoarded coins, first gold, and then silver. By the second week of July 1862 even one-cent pieces had disappeared from circulation. It was impossible to find a coin to buy a newspaper, get a haircut, or take a ride on a horse-drawn car.

One of many varieties of The Flag of Our Union tokens (1863),
choice examples of which can be purchased for less than $50 each.

Filling the gap, many merchants, towns, and others issued tickets and scrip bills. In time, many merchants issued bronze tokens, the size of a cent, which served for that value. Today these tokens are avidly collected. They are divided into two categories:

(1) Patriotic tokens with inscriptions relating to that subject—depicting flags, cannon, ships, Washington and other historical figures, Lincoln and McClellan from current news, and more.

Civil War tokens made by Merriam for C.F. Tuttle's Restaurant are unique in that the dies are modular. A common obverse with the head of a steer was combined with a reverse die into which four different round slugs could be inserted to change the denomination.

(2) Store cards, which are mostly cent-sized copper or brass tokens issued by merchants and giving their name and location—depicting hotels, taverns, ferries, breweries, patent medicine vendors, horses and coaches, railroads, groceries, clothiers, book stores, and more. A few years ago at a Civil War Token Society meeting John Evans gave an interesting program on tokens issued by establishments mentioning oysters as a specialty.

Attributions are by Fuld numbers, derived by George Fuld and his father Melvin in the mid-1900s, which have since been updated and finessed. More than 10,000 different die combinations and metal varieties are known today. A common token is one for which, say, 500 or more are known to exist. Many if not most can be bought in grades from Extremely Fine to Mint State for less than $100 each, including many VF and EF pieces under $25. Great rarities of which just a handful are known can be bought in Mint State for less than $1,000. Unique pieces can cost less than a couple thousand dollars or so.

Store cards are often collected by merchant and subject—such as one of each different issuer from New York City, Zanesville (Ohio), or Boston. Beyond that is similar to real estate—a key to the value of store cards is location, location, location. A popular pursuit is to acquire one token from each of the hundreds of towns in which tokens were issued.

One of my favorite tokens is that issued by C. McCarty of Urbana, Ohio. A few years ago I tried to find as much as I could about its background. Published December 1866 in Urbana was this:

> Capt. McCarty has named his new hotel the "Washington House." If the hotel is as good as the man was its named after it will deserve much custom. The Captain is competent to keep a No. 1 house.

The store card of C. McCarty of Urbana, Ohio, is a notable rarity in the Civil War
token series. The Prairie Flower die is known combined with several dozen
different reverses. Over a period of many years I have tried to collect one of each.

The name should have been spelled as McCarthy. This brings up a question: If the hotel was opened for the first time in 1866 and was new, this was after the Civil War. And yet the several token dies combined with the Washington House die are dated 1863 and 1864.

Possibilities include McCarthy ordering tokens in, say, 1865, in advance of opening his hotel; or the tokens being made later as numismatic strikes. Such puzzles add much to the appeal of Civil War tokens.

Waldo C. Moore in "The Washington House Token," 1931, included this:

> A pioneer tavern was the Washington House. It was the great resort of the surrounding community and the news emporium where all the male gossips met to smoke their pipes and exchange their daily experiences. How few now know the importance of the frontier tavern. It was, of course, the place of rest for the pioneer weary traveler or the transient guest, whether on foot or on horse. It was the market place for all; the hunter with his venison and turkeys, the trapper with his furs and skins, and the knapsack peddler here gladdened the hearts of all with his boughten wares.
>
> At the inn, too, were all the public gatherings called to arrange for a general hunt, to deal out justice to some transgressor, or to put up the stakes for the horse race. But this pioneer institution is among the things of the past, and as we all sit at the well-laden boards of the more modern hostelry it is hard to realize the frugal fare of the earlier dining place.
>
> Among the rarest Ohio Civil War tokens are those bearing this inscription: WASHINGTON / HOUSE / C. McCARTY / URBANA / O.

I have enjoyed and collected Civil War tokens since I first discovered the series in the 1950s. Many cost me just a few dollars each back then. Since that time prices have advanced slowly and steadily, and across the board all cost multiples of yesteryear. One of the most expensive in my collection is that issued in the Elmwood District of Cranston, Rhode Island, a "rare location." Described as Fuld RI-220-A-1a, I graded as MS-63 BN and bought it from the Steve Tanenbaum Collection for $17,466. Expensive, yes—but pocket change, so to speak, in comparison with many federal coins of which hundreds are known.

The curious and very rare store card issued by Theodore Pohle when he operated a vineyard in Cranston, Rhode Island, a suburb of Providence.

As I like to do, I set about trying to learn of its history (which is undocumented in numismatic literature for most issuers).

The following is from Mr. J.T. Myers of the Division of Archives and History, Providence, Rhode Island:[12]

> In 1863, the Elmwood Vineyard in the Elmwood section was located in Cranston. This area was annexed to Providence on June 10, 1868.
>
> The name of Theodore Pohle does not appear in the 1864 *Providence Directory,* but does appear in the 1867 *Providence City Directory* as the owner of a saloon at 91 Westminster Street. In 1878, Theodore Pohle is living at 116 Clifford Street. In checking the Index of Deaths in Providence, I noticed the death of a Theodore Pohle on July 17, 1886. The details of his death are on the enclosed sheet.
>
> Death Certificate Information: Name: Theodore Pohle. Date of Death: July 17, 1886. Age: 66 years, 11 months. Place of Death: 116 Clifford Street. Married. Occupation: Boarding House keeper. Place of Birth: Germany. Parents: Christian and Mary. Cause of Death: Apoplexy.

I have yet to learn about Pohle and his activities as a vintner that prompted him to issue a store card. As to my cost, it was not exactly pocket change, but it was a tiny fraction of what a 1793 cents of which hundreds are known would have cost. Most of the tokens in my collection cost less than $100 each, some much less.

A City Fruit Store, Providence, Rhode Island, store card (Fuld RI-700-G-4) from hand-engraved dies. On the detail view compare the circled Rs and note that there was not quite enough to spell out the name of the street!

The State of Rhode Island was a veritable playground for a Civil War token coiner, the identity of whom is not known today. For the city of Providence dozens of die combinations and metal varieties were made. The lettering on these is wonderfully crude and in many instances seems to have been engraved by hand, rather than made by using letter punches.

A store card issued by Skidmore's Hotel of Seneca Falls, New York. The dies were created by William Bridgens. The reverse shows the American eagle smoking a cigar, one of many interesting motifs in the series.

Much more affordable than the Lincoln, McCarty, and City Fruit Store tokens that can run into the high hundreds or low thousands of dollars and the expensive Pohle classic rarity are the hundreds of different patriotic tokens with various motifs. The cards issued by William Bridgens, Emil Sigel, and others in New York City are at once diverse and mostly inexpensive. Ditto for the prolific store cards of Shubael Childs of Chicago and William Lanphear and John Stanton, both of Cincinnati. A large and impressive collection of Civil War tokens can be built for less than $100 each, and a memorable collection can be formed without spending more than a few hundred dollars per token.

EXCURSION NO. 5

Private and Territorial Gold Coins

Fasten your seat belt! This is a very expensive specialty, and a well-fortified checkbook is needed!

The *Guide Book of United States Coins* gives a nice overview of these coins, mostly privately minted, but some were produced under state or

In Rutherfordton, North Carolina, the family of Christopher Bechtler struck gold coins of $1 (as shown), $2.50, and $5 denominations.

federal authority. These include the Templeton Reid coins of Georgia (1830) and, starting in the same era, the Bechtler family gold coins and the many varieties of $1 to $5 made in Rutherfordton, North Carolina, from 1831 to 1852.

The most diverse and extensive coins were issued in California during the Gold Rush, starting with Norris, Gregg & Norris $5 gold coins in Benicia City (but imprinted San Francisco) in 1849 and continued by various coiners.

$5 gold coins by Norris, Gregg & Norris, formed by entrepreneurs who came from New York, were in circulation by June 1849.

A Baldwin & Co. $10 "Horseman" or "Vaquero" of 1850. The coins of Baldwin were unfairly discredited as to gold content in early 1851, after which the coinage ceased. At the Mint in Philadelphia large numbers of privately minted coins were received in deposits. Choice examples such as this one were reserved for the Mint Cabinet display.

Private mints included those of Baldwin & Company; Wass, Molitor & Company; Moffat & Company; Miners Bank; J.S. Ormsby; and others.

Under arrangements set up by the Treasury Department, Augustus Humbert was designated as the U.S. assayer of gold in California. Under license with the facilities of Moffat & Co., octagonal $50 gold coins were minted in 1851 and 1852.

Moffat was the largest, and in addition to coinage for its own account it arranged with the Treasury Department to produce coins for Augustus Humbert and the United States Assay Office of Gold.

In 1853 the Moffat coinage equipment and building were sold to the Treasury, which enlarged the structure and opened it as the San Francisco Mint in March 1854.

The branch mint in San Francisco, opened in 1854, was in the modified premises of Moffat & Company. This facility was used until 1874.

An 1860 gold $10 struck in Denver by Clark, Gruber & Co., bankers, assayers, and the operator of a private mint.

Gold coins were made in Oregon by a partnership, in Salt Lake City under the authority of the Mormon Church, and by several private minters in Colorado. All range from scarce to very rare today.

The Clark, Gruber & Co. mint was purchased by the Treasury Department in 1862, but no federal coins were ever struck there.

EXCURSION NO. 6

"Good for One Tune" Tokens

In contrast to the previously mentioned coin types, the contents of a piggy bank could have paid for one of my favorite specialties. Well, almost but not quite. In the 1960s through the early 1970s I set about collecting tokens, mostly brass, that were used to play coin-operated pianos and other music machines when dropped into a slot. These had inscriptions such as GOOD FOR ONE TUNE, sometimes the name of a particular instrument given, such as the Pianolin or Mandolin Quartette. Often a token would lead me to a trail of history—the story of where it was used and related information. This multiplied my fascination for a given token, as with the Cliff House example shown here. The results were published in a softcover book, *A Tune for a Token*, published by the Token and Medal Society (online at www.tokenandmedal. org). It was well received and won the TAMS book of the year award. My total cost for all of the tokens involved was less than $1,000!

A dime-sized token used to play the large Welte orchestrion at the Cliff House at Seal Rocks overlooking the Pacific Ocean in San Francisco. "Orchestrian" is a misspelling.

The French-chateau style Cliff House
opened in 1897 and burned in 1907.

A nickel-sized brass token issued by the Peter Apostle Piano Co.

ORCHESTRION IN THE DINING ROOM OF THE CLIFF HOUSE.
SAN FRANCISCO, CAL

The Welte orchestrion in the dining room
of the Cliff House. At the drop of a coin it
played music for the patrons.

I don't (yet) know much about the Peter Apostle Piano Co. of Chicago and Taylorville, Illinois (research on various issuers is ongoing), but I am quite familiar with the Coinola coin-operated pianos and orchestrions he sold and serviced as advertised on his brass tokens.

Drop such a nickel-size token in an instrument and the reward was two minutes of lively music. From the 1890s through the 1920s coin-operated pianos and orchestrions were set up in hotels, restaurants, railroad stations, bordellos, amusement parks, and other locations all across America.

The Coinola Style X orchestrion contained a piano, mandolin, orchestra bells, drums, and traps and had a beckoning slot to entice nickels.

After electronically amplified music became a widespread reality in 1926, record-playing jukeboxes took over most of the market. By the mid-1930s most coin-operated pianos were gone. The first person to build a significant collection of these was Alden Scott Boyer of Chicago, who in the early 1930s served as president of the American Numismatic Association after having been secretary for many years.

EXCURSION NO. 7

A Numismatic Library

There is a little secret that really is not a secret at all: build your own basic working library of interesting and informative books and read them. One enlightened dealer suggested that for every $100 spent on coins, $15 should be spent on books. Today there are more good titles in print than ever before.

Pledges of History by William E. Dubois (1846) was one of the first texts on coins published in America.

Coin collecting and related books on display at the Books-A-Million (BAM) store in Florence, Alabama.

A part of Kenneth Bressett's fine library covering all aspects of numismatics from ancient times to the modern era.

From day one I bought every numismatic book, old catalog, and magazine that I thought would be interesting or useful to own. These included runs of *The Numismatist*, *The Numismatic Scrapbook Magazine*, the *American Journal of Numismatics*, *The Coin Collector's Journal*, *Numisma*, auction catalogs of B. Max Mehl, Stack's, Numismatic Gallery, and more, to a run of *The Annual Report of the Director of the Mint*.

The *Coin Collector's Journal,* first published in 1877, kept readers up to date on new coins, such as in 1878 the silver dollar and also auction prices, articles on history, and more. The publisher was J.W. Scott & Co., the New York stamp and coin dealer.

The *Coin Collector's Journal* also included its share of errors and misinformation—not unusual in an era with few standard reference works or guides. Here it is stated that the 1842 dollar is known in two date sizes; today all dollars of this date seen have the same size of date numerals. The notice also says that dollars were last coined in 1866. The correct year is 1873.

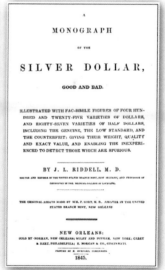

One of the rarest books about U.S. coins, but not a numismatic text, is *A Monograph of the Silver Dollar: Good and Bad,* by J.L. Riddell, M.D., 1845. It describes the weight and silver content of U.S. and other coins and has a large section on counterfeits. The illustrations closely follow die varieties of the coins themselves, quite unlike artists' sketches, and may have been made by some sort of a transfer process.

I also collected a room full of publications on American history—ranging from *American State Papers* and bound copies of *The Congressional Globe,* to *Banker's Magazine,* a full set of *Scientific American* through the early 1900s, bound copies of *Harper's Weekly,* all of the Civil War issues of the *New York Tribune,* and city directories from Gold Rush San Francisco to New York City and Boston.

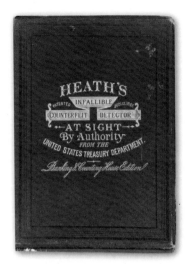

Heath's Infallible Counterfeit Detector was issued in a popular pocket edition and in a larger banking and counting house edition (pictured). The Treasury Department allowed Laban Heath to use sample proof notes from official plates, which caused problems when some sharpers adjusted them and paid them out. Issued in the 1860s these are popular as a collectible today, not as much for their informational content.

I spent a small fortune on my reference library, the cost of which was not only provided for but repaid many times over in connection with my rare coin dealership and writing many books on numismatics and other subjects—over 50 titles in all. Today with Google Books and other Internet sites and the Newman Numismatic Portal, much equivalent information can be had for free! Beyond that, historical newspapers, books, news accounts, and other sources are searchable.

As previously mentioned, if I wanted to learn more about the Peter Apostle Piano Co. of Chicago and Taylorville, Illinois, I would start on the Internet. Decades ago I would have begun by writing to historical societies and buying or borrowing old directories.

Still, there is something nice about a hardbound book. Not far away at any given time when I am writing about numismatics is the latest edition of *A Guide Book of United States Coins*, commonly referred to as the Red Book. Although I can find the information on the Internet, I am not about to sell my collectible original copies of Montroville W. Dickeson's *American Numismatic Manual* of 1859 or Crosby's *Early Coins of America* (1875).

The omnipresent *Guide Book of United States Coins* is a treasure house of good information, particularly in the front section and in other narratives. When I was a teenager I read it carefully from cover to cover, then reread it every now and again. Jim Ruddy, who was a business partner for nearly 20 years starting in 1958, and I used to quiz each other on *Guide Book* trivia. We each got to the point where we knew just about every fact in that book, except for mintage figures and current prices.

Using the current Red Book I have created a modern version of a similar quiz. See how many you can get right:

A launch ceremony for the 2005 Red Book. Mary Burleson, president of Whitman, is to the left, editor Kenneth Bressett is to the right. For many years this has been the one-volume standard source for pricing and other information.

RED BOOK QUIZ

1. What did Glenna Goodacre do?
2. Why is February 28, 1878, numismatically important?
3. When was a bison depicted on a *Jefferson* nickel?
4. What early American coin is called the "Baby Head" variety?
5. Why were there no Liberty Seated coins in circulation in New York City in 1851?
6. Where did John Chalmers privately mint coins?
7. Why is David Parsons, a University of Wisconsin student, mentioned in the *Guide Book?*
8. What does S.M.V. on the reverse of certain private gold coins mean?
9. What commemorative half dollar was struck at the San Francisco Mint, but had the S mintmark inadvertently omitted?
10. From what date was an obverse die altered to read 1804 for a "restrike" cent?

ANSWERS: 1 She designed the obverse of the 2000 Sacagawea dollar. 2. For the Bland-Allison Act that authorized the Morgan dollar. 3. 2005. 4. A certain 1786 Vermont copper. 5. At the time their melt-down value was more than their face value, and speculators withdrew them from commerce. 6. Annapolis, Maryland. 7. He designed the obverse of the 1936 Wisconsin half dollar. 8. Standard Mint Value. 9. 1925 Fort Vancouver. 10. 1803.

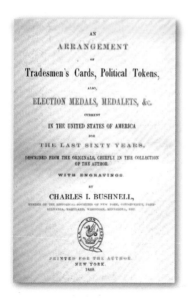

The cover of Charles I. Bushnell's study of election medals and related items was published by the author in 1858. This is one of the first specialized numismatic references issued in America.

A medalet honoring Bushnell issued by Augustus B. Sage in 1859.

A shelf with interesting books is the ideal passport to enjoying the coins you already have as well as learning about items you might like to acquire. Hard copies are a better start than is the Internet, in my opinion. I would not trade my *Guide Book* in hand for an Internet view. On the other hand, if I were to start over I would not spend several thousand dollars for a San Francisco city directory of the early 1850s. In fact, I might sell the one I have.

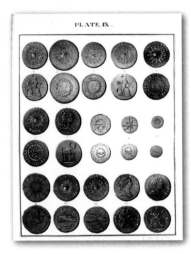 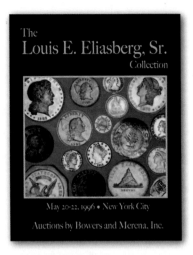

A color plate from the *American Numismatical Manual* by Montroville W. Dickeson (1859). It was the first comprehensive numismatic book issued in the United States; original copies are relatively inexpensive today.	The 1996 catalog of the Louis E. Eliasberg Collection, one of several sales offering estate of the only collector ever to complete the federal coin series by date and mintmark, is a popular addition to a reference library.

For starters today the Whitman Publishing Web site offers many possibilities, including quite a few books that I have written. I could cite many instances in which buyers of a book on an American numismatic specialty have used it to form a collection of such coins, tokens, or medals.

As collecting specialties, runs of auction catalogs and periodicals can be interesting to search for. Try as I might I was never able to find some of the catalogs issued by Thomas L. Elder. His cataloging style was hodge-podge, arranged, it seems, in the order that consignments arrived.

Of the books I have written, the one that has brought the most enthusiastic comments from readers who have felt they learned a lot is a favorite of mine, *The History of United States Coinage as Illustrated by the Garrett Collection* (1979). Over 12,000 copies were issued, but it has been out of print for many years. You can easily find one from a seller of antiquarian books or on the Internet. Another is *The Expert's Guide to Collecting and Investing in Rare Coins*, published by Whitman and still in print. The ANA Library has copies to loan by mail for no charge except postage.

Your assignment: Spend several hundred dollars on a small library of titles with *historical and numismatic information*, not so much on pricing, population reports, and the like (although those are essential). Devote several evenings a week to reading them.

EXCURSION NO. 8

Hard Times Tokens

Hard Times tokens have been popular since the 19th century. To me these are incredibly interesting, and I have enjoyed them for many years.

An 1837 Hard Times token, one of many different varieties satirizing
the fiscal policies of President Andrew Jackson and his successor
Martin Van Buren (who followed in the steps of his illustrious predecessor).
The jackass was the punning substitution for Jackson on many varieties.

This anti-Jackson token satirizes him as custodian of the nation's money and
on the other side derides the honorary doctorate awarded to him by Harvard.

This 18 mm Feuchtwanger cent is smaller than a typical Hard Times token.
Cents of Feuchtwanger's Composition, a variety of German silver, were made in quantity.
At one time samples were given to congressmen in an effort to have them adopt the alloy
for regular coinage. The plea was ignored.

Some Hard Times tokens recorded history, as did this one that observes
the stopping of specie payments (the exchange at par of paper notes for
silver and gold coins) on May 10, 1837. This copper token of November 1837
was a "substitute for shin plaster" (private currency printed on paper).

Although the Hard Times era in American economics began in a significant way in late 1836 and lasted until the spring of 1843, it was numismatically defined in the 1880s by Lyman H. Low, author of the first book on such tokens, as beginning in 1832 with the reelection campaign of Andrew Jackson. It extended to 1844, so as to include a cent-size token of J. Cochran, a bell founder in Batavia, New York. Somewhat more than 400 varieties are known.

This anti-slavery token was issued in quantity in Baltimore in 1838. Later, many stories were made up about them, including their being used as secret passes on the Underground Railroad.

A Hard Times token issued by Francis L. Brigham, who in 1833 had a dry goods store in the Cheapside row of buildings in New Bedford, Massachusetts.

This token issued by William H. Milton of the Faneuil Hall Clothing Warehouse in Boston is inexpensive and readily available. His store was in the front left of Faneuil Hall, illustrated, a building that still stands today.

Gustin & Blake, who operated a copper and tin works shop in Chelsea, Vermont, made dies for their own Hard Times token—a candidate for one of the most rustic in the series.

A Hard Times token issued by Beck's Public Baths in Richmond, Virginia.

Each Hard Times token stands on its own, and examining both sides carefully is recommended as some were never well struck to begin with. An examination of images online and in texts will reveal what is generally available.

Most are fairly inexpensive, with VF and EF examples selling for in the very low three figures. Some but not many rarities sell into the several thousand dollars. Each one has its own story.

EXCURSION NO. 9

Encased Postage Stamps

  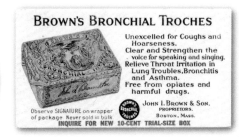

An encased postage stamp for Brown's Bronchial Troches and an advertisement for the same. This remedy was sold for many years.

As the Civil War progressed, uncertainty as to the outcome increased. Concerned citizens began to hoard gold coins in late December 1861, and in the spring of 1862 all silver coins had disappeared from circulation as well. This engendered many monetary substitutes including Civil War tokens discussed in the previous excursion. On July 17 the government decreed that ordinary postage stamps could be used as money. Some were housed in paper envelopes, others pasted to cards.

Among the entrepreneurs with an eye open to profit was John Gault, a Boston inventor and entrepreneur who had moved to New York City earlier in the year. Recognizing that stamps would soon become discolored or damaged, and that those in envelopes would be clumsy to inspect, he felt that "encased postage stamps" would serve a need.

Basically the unit consisted of a multiple-part arrangement displayed in a circular encasement or frame made of brass. On the face under clear mica a postage stamp was displayed. The back was embossed with advertising. Made by the Scovill Manufacturing Co., production com-

The Treasury issued Postage Currency notes with postage stamp designs, after which the interest in encased postage stamps faded.

menced after patent No. 1627 was granted on August 2, 1862, and lasted through spring 1863, at which time Postage Currency notes issued by the Treasury Department flooded circulation. These had postage stamp designs and rendered the encasements redundant.

An encased postage stamp advertising Ayer's Sarsaparilla. J.C. Ayer & Co.
also advertised Ayer's Pills and Ayer's Cathartic Pills.

During this time 31 different merchants signed up to advertise. Featured were patent medicines, hotels, food, wine, dry goods, and other products and services, including messages for Ayer's Sarsaparilla and Pills, Brown's Bronchial Troches, Aerated Bread, Drake's Plantation Bitters, Lord & Taylor, the Tremont House, and Mendum's Family Wine Emporium. Most stamps were of lower denominations such as 1¢, 3¢, and 5¢, but higher values included 10¢, 12¢, 24¢, 30¢, and 90¢.

A trade card advertising the same product.

In time these became very popular with collectors. Believe it or not, at the turn of the 20th century more people collected encased postage than did Morgan silver dollars by mintmarks!

An encased postage stamp offering Burnett's products.

In January 1902 *The Numismatist* printed this:

> The fad just now seems to be the collecting of encased postage stamps that were in circulation for a brief period during the Rebellion. At this time small change was scarce and the current unused postage stamps of the various denominations were enclosed in a round metallic case to protect them from wear and injury and passed current as small change. They were issued in July and August of 1862 under the patent of J. Gault, and in this day are quite scarce and bring high prices. We have been asked to furnish a list of these encased stamps and shall do so at an early day.

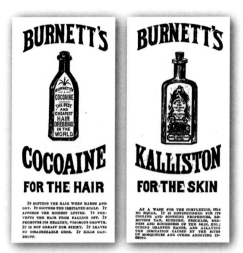

Advertisements for two of the products mentioned on the advertised postage stamp.

In the May and June issues of the same magazine, Albert R. Frey studied encased postage stamps, listing different known varieties and their auction records. In the June issue appeared the following lines: "According to reports there is an effort being made to corner the market on encased postage stamps. Many will remember, no doubt, a similar effort made about a year ago on the 1856 Flying Eagle cent, and we think this should be a warning."

Today, encased postage stamps are enthusiastically collected, although as a niche specialty. While hundreds of thousands of numismatists seek mintmarked Morgan dollars, the number of serious collectors of encased postage is probably no more than a few hundred.

A popular objective is to acquire one from each merchant, the three rarest being B.F. Miles (a Peoria, Illinois, druggist), Arthur M. Claflin (a Hopkinton, Rhode Island, clothier), and Sands Ale. There are not many of these three rarities to go around, and if two dozen millionaires decided to form sets, a dozen of them would come up empty handed.

Fortunately, the encased postage stamps of most issuers exist by the hundreds, and for J.C. Ayer and Drake's Plantation Bitters there are at least several thousand. Nice examples range from a few hundred dollars up.

An encased postage stamp issued by George G. Evans, a Philadelphia entrepreneur who sold many products, including wine and books. In the 1880s and 1890s he published many editions of a book on the history of the Mint.

The Evans building at 439 Chestnut Street in Philadelphia.

Some time ago I put together a set by merchants while at the same time tracking down original advertisements. To be economical I chose lower denominations from 1 cent to 10 cents, with just a few higher. I do not own a 90-cent example. With Michael Hodder in 1989 I wrote *The Standard Catalogue of Encased Postage Stamps* and assigned HB numbers to the varieties. Today with the Internet offering so many possibilities for research, one of these years I might go back and get much more information about the history of the various issuers.[13]

EXCURSION NO. 10

Society of Medalists Issues

Conceived by America's leading sculptors under the aegis of the American Federation of Arts, the Society of Medalists was intended as a forum for experimentation with medallic sculpture. The Medallic Art Company, with its Janvier pantographic equipment for the engraving of hubs to make dies, was the ideal choice for a mint, because it allowed artists to model their designs in a 9- to 12-inch format, to be mechanically reduced onto medal dies. Almost every important sculptor in the country submitted potential designs to the Society's review committee, which extended the invitation to create a medal to just two artists per year. Each medal struck in silver and bronze was edge-marked with the issue number and year, and the number of medals issued was governed by, but not limited to, the number of current subscribers.

The first five participants, Laura Gardin Fraser, Paul Manship, Hermon A. Mac-Neil, Frederic MacMonnies, and Lee Lawrie, were thrilled to have total control over subject matter, design, shape, metallic content, and finish—something not available to them as commissioned makers of commemorative and award medals. They were joined by a stellar lineup of successors: John Flanagan, Herbert Adams, Carl Jennewein, Chester Beach, Walker Hancock, Adam Belskie, Marcel Jovine, Karen Worth, Alex Shagin, Don Everhart, and many more.

"The Hunter" by Laura Gardin Fraser, No. 1 in the Society of Medalists series.

"Africa" by Anna Hyatt Huntington, wife of numismatist Archer Huntington
(who donated funds to pay for the beautiful headquarters building of the American Numismatic
Society opened on Audubon Terrace at 155th Street and Broadway, New York City, in 1908).

"Pony Express" by James Earle Fraser, husband of Laura Gardin Fraser. The reverse design is similar in some ways to the reverse of the 1926 to 1939 Oregon Trail commemorative half dollars designed by Mr. and Mrs. Fraser. James Earle Fraser also designed the 1913 Buffalo nickel.

The result of all that unleashed talent and imagination was a 65-year-long emission span representing 129 different artistic approaches and as many creative visions. From time to time, as artists often do, the medalists provoked controversy with their subject matter. At the height of Prohibition in 1930, Paul Manship saluted Dionysus, WHO FIRST DISCOVERED THE MAGIC OF THE GRAPE. In his 1971 medal the cautionary statement PANDORA ONE, PANDORA TWO, was used by Elbert Weinberg to associate the atomic bomb with Pandora's box, the ancient epitome of evil. Aside from thematic content, the impact of modern design, photography, Art Deco, and other stylistic innovations through the decades is apparent throughout the series.

Anna Hyatt Huntington.

Although there were exceptions, most medals were struck in copper or brass to the extent of hundreds of examples, and fewer than 100 were made in silver. I much prefer the copper and brass examples and have one of each in my collection, to which a few silver medals have been added. This series is not widely known and its unique "museum" of free-rein sculpting talent has been appreciated by very few. The result is that many examples are available on eBay and other sources for less than $100 each! Most others cost less than $200 in copper and brass.

With the retirement of Joseph Veach Noble, the Society's administrative guiding light in the final 30 years, the series came to an end in 1995. The dies survived in the possession of the Medallic Art Co., a company which changed hands several times after the last medals in the series were issued.[14]

EXCURSION NO. 11

Medals and More Medals

While the Society of Medalists series has a beginning and an ending, and while completion is possible, that is not so for most American medal series. Those that were made for presentation rather than for numismatic sale can be great rarities. Silver Indian Peace medals given by government agencies to tribal leaders are an example, although it later years restrikes in copper were made available.

American medals begin with the hundreds listed by C. Wyllys Betts, published posthumously in 1894 under the title of *American Colonial History Illustrated by Contemporary Medals*. Frederic H. Betts, brother of the deceased author, gave this rationale for the desirability of medals:

A rare medal of General James Wolfe, hero of the 1759 Battle of Quebec, in which he vanquished the French. It is unlisted in Betts as it is a relatively new discovery.

The value of coins and medals, as enduring records of events, has often been emphasized. All original documents and contemporary accounts of occurrences are of peculiar importance to the conscientious historian. Medals are original documents in metal. In studying them we study history at its source. As contribution to the knowledge of the history of portraiture, dress, and habits, as indices of then existing information in architecture, geography, and the natural sciences, and as means of restoring the knowledge of structures long destroyed, medals are not to be underestimated.

Medals are a body of history, or, perhaps, a collection of pictures in miniature, or so many maps for explaining ancient geography. One is to look upon a cabinet of medals as a treasure, not of money, but of knowledge.... "It is safer," it has been said, "to quote a medal than a historian."[15]

Remarkably, the 1894 Betts book is still the standard text on the series today! It has never been updated or superseded. Many new varieties have been discovered and have been listed here and there in auction catalogs and elsewhere, but not in one single place.

A silver medal commemorating the Peace Treaty of Versailles (1783), officially ending the Revolutionary War (Betts-608, 45.1 mm).

The book describes medals that have subjects relating to discovery and exploration in the Americas, not just the land that eventually became the United States, most of which were struck in Europe. Voyages, wars, treaties, and more are discussed. Most Betts medals, as they are called, are at least scarce, and many are rare. The number of serious specialists in the field is rather small, with the result that prices can be modest. Most sell for the hundreds of dollars, and relatively few cross the $5,000 mark.

The Token and Medal Society organized in 1980 and established in 1981, and of which I was a founder, treats all areas of its title subject—from medals of colonial America down to modern arcade and turnpike tokens.[16]

An issue of the MCA Advisory.

Medal Collectors of America (online at www.medalcollectors.org), a group formed in 1998, is the leading edge today for study and appreciation of Betts and other early medals, although later issues are often treated as well. The *MCA Advisory* is one of my favorite publications. I have said on several occasions that if a numismatist were given three or four copies and commanded to read them from cover to cover, he or she would become a medal collector.

A New Haven medal (1838) by Charles Cushing Wright, considered to be one of the most beautiful and important American medals of the early 19th century (55.5 mm).

William Elliot Woodward, generally conceded as the most authoritative numismatic cataloger from the 1860s through the 1880s, presented the J.N.T. Levick Collection of tokens and medals at auction May 26–29, 1884, and included this comment:

> Many of these cards and tokens are amongst the very rarest of all American issues, and if the word *rare* with its superlatives is thought to occur too frequently, let it be attributed to the fact mentioned, which every collector knows is perfectly correct. The 1804 dollar and the 1802 half dime are actually common in comparison with many of these pieces, and I confess, that apart from their money value, I regard them as much less interesting. These pieces and the political series, now so much neglected, are an epitome of the political and business history of the country, while the Mint series is money —that's all.

Collecting medals is like collecting art. You do not aspire to completion, and for nearly all series that is not possible. Instead you review books, catalogs, magazines, and other sources, view exhibits, and look around to find what subjects interest you the most. There are many delightful discoveries to be made, including if your budget tops out at $100 per medal.

As is true with so many things, medals have stories.

Many years ago in a visit with John J. Ford Jr., at his home in Rockville Centre, New York, John showed me a specimen of the variety he described later in the foreword to my 1979 book, *Adventures With Rare Coins:*

> Ted Craige was once offered a specimen of the extraordinarily rare Lady Washington and Columbia medal. It fascinated him, and after establishing what it was, he located a book titled *Voyages of the "Columbia" to the Northwest Coast, 1787–1790 and 1790–1793* by F.W. Howay.
>
> Early on, he and I discovered that the particular piece he had been offered was spurious, a cast copy, but Ted read the book from cover to cover (all 518 pages) anyway. Once he got started, he couldn't stop. Once he completed the book he couldn't bear to part with it; it just had to be in his library. He even wanted to keep the fake medal, but the price prohibited it.
>
> His enthusiasm grew as he researched the origin of the medal, the controversy concerning the diesinker, the purpose of issue, and other details. To my knowledge, he never owned a genuine specimen of this rare medal, but he certainly knew as much about it as any numismatist of my acquaintance.

A 1787 Lady Washington and Columbia medal in the Massachusetts Historical Society.
The "Lady" part of the ship name is usually dropped from descriptions of the medal.

The 40.2 mm Washington and Columbia medal (also called the Columbia and Washington medal, for the *Columbia* was the larger ship) was so exciting to me that I just had to have one! Desire was the easy part. Finding one was the challenge. In time I acquired a well-worn example, then upgraded it to one in, say, Extremely Fine condition.

A sketch by George Davidson of the
Lady Washington and *Columbia*
in the Pacific Northwest in 1890.

A Libertas Americana medal in silver (Betts-615).

In 2007 Whitman Publishing issued *The 100 Greatest American Medals and Tokens* compiled by Katherine Jaeger and myself. We sent out questionnaires to leading collectors, scholars, museums, and dealers and asked them to rank their favorites. Number 1 was the Libertas Americana medal made in Paris under the direction of Benjamin Franklin to commemorate American independence.

One of many medals commemorating Admiral Vernon of Great Britain capturing
the Spanish town of Portobello in South America "with six ships only" (Betts-230, 37.2 mm).

Washington C.C.A.U.S. (Commander in Chief, Army of the United States) medal.

To see the 100 greatest list and learn more about any of the illustrated coins,
borrow or buy the book or search on the Internet.

The American Numismatic Society award to the author,
silver medal by Alex Shagin, in connection with the yearly Gala in 2006.

A medal for the second inauguration of President Barack Obama
and Vice President Joseph Biden, by Marc Mellon.

Medals continue to be made for special occasions. Presidential inauguration medals can be easily collected from the past several decades. The American Numismatic Society awards medals such as the one I received at a special dinner held at the Waldorf-Astoria Hotel in 2006.

Most modern medals are inexpensive. Subjects range from well known, such as the 2001 World Trade center disaster, to the obscure. Lots of possibilities!

Sculptor Marc Mellon in his studio in Greenwich, Connecticut.

EXCURSION NO. 12

Counterstamped Coins

As you know by reading this far, forming a fine collection of coins, tokens, or medals need not be an expensive venture. Among those that have brought the great pleasure are many that cost very little. In the case of counterstamped coins, when I first started acquiring them in the 1950s most had little or no market value. Some dealers used to save them for me, charging just a few dollars or giving them to me for free. Maurice Gould of Boston was the only other person I knew who was interested in these. As

A 1793 Wreath cent, a numismatic classic in its own right, counterstamped "BRADBURY" in a hallmark punch by Theophilus Bradbury, a Newburyport, Massachusetts, silversmith and jeweler. The coin is also stamped with a punch depicting an eagle in a vertical oval.

he was in the twilight of his interest I obtained many from him.[17] The standard reference was "A Trial List of the Countermarked Modern Coins of the World," by Frank G. Duffield, the first installment of which was printed in *The Numismatist* in July 1919.

An 1825 cent, worn nearly smooth, but counterstamped with this legend: MESCHUTT'S / METROPOLITAN / COFFEE ROOM / 433. BdWAY. It is a souvenir of a long-forgotten restaurant in New York City. The stamp MESCHUTT'S / METROPOLITAN / COFFEE ROOM / 433. BdWAY is large and contains many letters. As a corollary to conventional thinking, the more worn a coin was when counterstamped, the sharper the message was impressed on it!

Dr. Shattuck's Waterford Water Cure advertisement on a Canadian token that circulated in the United States in the mid-1800s. Intrigued by these I visited Waterford, Maine, where the buildings still stand, and wrote a book on this establishment. At the time John J. Ford Jr. said it was his favorite of all the books I had written. (It was hardly a best-seller, however!)

By the 1960s I had many pieces, my favorites being large copper cents with advertising, political slogans, or other inscriptions that could be tracked down. I added some other denominations as well. Counterstamps included Meschutt's Metropolitan Coffee House, Gold Pile Salve, Oil of Ice, Washington and Lafayette 1824, G.G.G. & G.G.G.G., VOTE THE LAND FREE, Shattuck's Water Cure, Kidder's Family Pills, Dr. G.G. Wilkins, and Houck's Panacea in a list of hundreds. For many I was able to track down their histories in city directories, advertisements in old newspapers, and elsewhere.

Today with the Internet such a search would take much less time, but would it be as much fun? Instant gratification often learns to the lessening of interest in any numismatic specialty I learned from my customers long ago!

As the years passed, more and more people became interested in counterstamps. In the mid-1980s Dr. Gregory Brunk, who was researching the series, camped his motor home in the Bowers and Merena Galleries parking lot and spent a week studying my collection. This and his other investigations led to the publishing in 1987 of *American and Canadian Countermarked Coins,* followed in 2003 by an updated version under the title of *Merchant and Privately Countermarked Coins: Advertising on the World's Smallest Billboards.* In the meantime Russell Rulau listed and priced many counterstamps in his *Standard Catalog of U.S. Tokens 1700–1900.* When we sold the John J. Ford Jr. Collection at auction in the early 2000s a number of scarce or particularly interesting counterstamps sold for several thousand dollars each.

A Washington/Lafayette counterstamp on an 1824 Capped Bust half dollar from the Belden E. Roach Collection (B. Max Mehl, 1944).

Many years ago I paid a strong four-figure price to Stew Witham for the 1824 Washington-Lafayette half dollar, in beautiful Mint State, that in 1944 had brought $132.50 in the Belden E. Roach Collection sold by B. Max Mehl. By way of comparison in the same sale a Proof 1856 Flying Eagle cent brought $15.75. The half dollar was described as lot 2030:

WASHINGTON-LAFAYETTE HALF DOLLAR
Really the First Commemorative Half Dollar Issued

1824 over 21. U.S. half dollar with counterstamps of portraits of Washington and Lafayette. Portrait of Washington to left, with semi-circle, GEORGE WASHINGTON. Reverse, counterstamp portrait of Lafayette facing right, date 1824 below. Around. GENERAL LA FAYETTE.

The counterstamps are about the size of a U.S. half dime and struck in the center of coin. Perfect Uncirculated with the counterstamps in Proof. Struck to commemorate the visit of Lafayette in 1824. This specimen is the only one I have ever seen or heard of. As far as I know it is unique. I have handled this identical specimen when I purchased some dorms from the great collector, Mr. Granberg of Wisconsin. It then went into the Newcomer Collection of Baltimore, a million-dollar collection, then to the Colonel Green Collection.

I believe this is the first time coin is being offered at auction. It is difficult to place a value on a coin of this kind, but if late commemorative coins have brought over $50 each, this coin is certainly worth very near if not above the $100 mark, especially in its beautiful gem condition.

If anything, such comparisons indicate that many tokens, medals, and other things outside of the main federal series may be very inexpensive today. Don't tell anyone!

An 1854 half dollar with punning double-entendre counterstamp by
Yankee Robinson, FREE TICKET TO YANKEE ROBINSON'S QUADRUPLE SHOW.
To gain "free admission" the half dollar had to be surrendered!

EXCURSION NO. 13

Other Tokens from Here and There

Of the tens of thousands of tokens issued in America from the 18th century to the present time, only a fraction have ever been cataloged. For those that have been studied and published, books are often out of print.

Such can be collected by topics, locations, use, and other ways. Over a long period I have acquired many that are interesting to me. Most are inexpensive, with relatively few being otherwise. I have often gathered postcards, brochures, and other material about them, enhancing their appeal. You can do the same.

A 24.4 mm aluminum token issued by W.P. Young, a Portsmouth, New Hampshire, collector. In the early 1900s many collectors and dealers issued tokens—a fad at the time—and quite a few were described in *The Numismatist* in the early 1900s.

A notice about tokens in *The Numismatist,* April 1902.

Why, when, and where was this 16 mm brass token issued? Depicted on one side is Liberty Seated, as on a contemporary half dime. On the reverse an airship and a hot air balloon are high over a city.

In 1860 William Leggett Bramhall issued this 19.1 mm token on occasion of Lincoln's being nominated for president. The reverse inscription caused controversy. Accordingly, the reverse die was expertly altered to read WIDEAWAKES.

Many modern tokens cost a dollar each or less, exist in infinite variety, and have not been researched. New Hampshire highway toll tokens such as this (22.8 mm) were discontinued years ago. The design is the same on both sides. This one dates from about 1990. Such tokens exist from many states.

The Old Man in the Mountains motif was also used on a token (24..4 mm, nickel) issued by Clark's Trading Post.

Gallery of American Traitors No. 1 (there never was a No. 2) issued in 1861 by George H. Lovett. Listed are prominent Americans who stood with the South during the Civil War.

A brass one-cent token (19.1 mm) that could be spent in one of many Mills Edisonia penny arcades set up in America in the early 1900s.

The entrance to the Mills Edisonia at 278 State Street, Chicago.

Joseph Merriam, die sinker in Boston, made many tokens in the 1860s. This one was struck of metal taken from the ruins of a turpentine works in New Bern, North Carolina, and is made of copper (27.2 mm).

This aluminum Moxie Bottle Wagon token could be exchanged for the soft drink (31.9 mm).

An advertising token made of white metal issued by Augustus B. Sage (31 mm). Sage was very prominent in numismatics in the late 1850s, founded the American Numismatic Society, issued tokens, and conducted auctions.

The Moxie Bottle Wagon in Flag Staff Park, Mauch Chunk, Pennsylvania circa 1908.

Augustus B. Sage in his Civil War uniform.

The 1778-dated Non Dependens Status copper (29.1 mm) is one of the more enduring mysteries in American numismatics. Was it hand-engraved by Paul Revere? Does it actually date from 1778? Early notice of it appeared 1858 in *Norton's Literary Letter* No. 2, a 46-page offering of coins, autographs, etc. The coin attracted the notice of Montroville W. Dickeson in his *American Numismatical Manual* (1859) who described it in detail and illustrated it on a plate. In 1875 Crosby illustrated the coin and gave it a half-page description, concluding with, "Nothing is known of the origin or history of this piece." A copy version was made circa 1859 by, it is thought, George H. Lovett.

In my *Coins and Collectors* book, Golden Anniversary edition (2014) I devoted a chapter to the mysterious "Let the Egle Fly" token made of copper (26 mm). The attribution of this token has been a matter of considerable discussion. The Mormons did not establish Great Salt Lake City until 1847, the year after the date of the token. And yet, the letters J.S.G.S.L.C. are sufficiently distinctive that it would be difficult to assign any other attribution. As to the initials J.S., these letters could relate to the founder of the religion, Joseph Smith, who was killed in 1844. At least a dozen or so examples are known today, and nearly all show signs of circulation. These are not numismatic issues made for collectors but in their time were used in circulation. What is their true story?

Other excursions can be self-guided. On your own explore as many different highways and byways of numismatics as possible.

One of the themes of this book, a mission statement, is that great coins, tokens, and medals do not need to be expensive, and a great collection within many specialties can often be assembled for modest cost. While 1804 silver dollars that we and others sell at auctions make front-page headlines, inexpensive items are the true backbone of numismatics and the pleasures thereof.

Variety is the spice of life, they say. Coins, tokens, and medals offer infinite possibilities.

COIN COLLECTING AND MARKET TRENDS

This chapter tells of numismatics in America from the earliest years of interest down to 1952, when I first became involved in the hobby. Reading of the different events will add to the basic information given earlier. As mentioned in my preface, this will acquaint you with the lessons of history.

NUMISMATICS IN THE EARLY TIMES

Interest in numismatics—the art and science of collecting coins—dates back to times of antiquity when emperors and others acquired Roman and Greek coins. By the 1600s and 1700s interest in coins and medals was widespread in Europe, and many books were published, mostly on the ancient coins of Rome and Greece.

In England, starting in a large way in the 1780s, a great passion arose for collecting halfpenny-size copper tokens. In that decade and in the 1790s countless varieties were made with motifs ranging from political satire to advertising for services and products to depictions of buildings. Today these are known as Conder tokens, after James Conder, who wrote a book illustrating many varieties. Some of these, such as the Theatre at New York token, 1794 and 1795 Talbot, Allum & Lee cents, and several tokens with images of George Washington are included in *A Guide Book of United States Coins.*

The Coventry halfpenny with Lady Godiva, one of the most famous and popular Conder tokens.

A Token Collectors Halfpenny of 1796 with a numismatist being watched by Father Time.
On the reverse is the inscription ASSES RUNNING FOR HALFPENCE, a parody on the collecting craze.

At the time there was relatively little interest in numismatics in America. When the Philadelphia Mint first produced coins in 1792, continuing to the turn of the century, there was no known person or museum that systematically saved the nation's new copper, silver, and gold coins. There was, however, some interest in these on the part of collectors in England, as much of America had earlier consisted of British colonies.

NUMISMATICS IN THE EARLY 19TH CENTURY

In the United States in the early 1800s at least two dozen historical societies, museums, and libraries included coins and medals in their holdings. Some were called athenaeums, from the wisdom of ancient Athens, and were repositories for historical items. Popular museums such as those conducted by Charles Willson Peale and his sons, John Scudder, Phineas T. Barnum, and others charged admission and emphasized attention-getting curiosities including coins. Today, little is known about their specific contents.

Scudder's American Museum, circa 1829. This exhibit was the successor to several earlier museums dating back to one formed in New York City by the Tammany Society in the 1790s. Later, Scudder sold out to P.T. Barnum.

John Allan, a Scottish immigrant who in New York City became an accountant and bookkeeper, is thought to have been the first professional numismatist in America and was active by 1820. Among his clients was Philip Hone, a wealthy gentleman who at one time was mayor of the city.

A token honoring early American numismatist John Allan, struck in 1859 from dies engraved by George H. Lovett. The Latin inscription translates to "John Allan, Scottish antiquarian. Born Feb. 26, 1777."

Although many important collections of coins had been auctioned in Europe since earlier decades, today numismatic historians believe that the first significant public sale in America was that of the private collection of Benjamin H. Watkins, auctioned in Salem, Massachusetts, on June 12 and 13, 1828. By later standards the descriptions were rudimentary at best, consisting of grouped lots with sparse descriptions. John H. Nichols, 17-year-old son of auctioneer John Nichols, created the listing, which comprised 530 lots of coins, books, engravings, and other items, among which were several Massachusetts coins, including two New England shillings, a silver three-pence, and a two-pence, these being the only pieces outside of bulk lots, 21 lots taking care of 350 coins altogether.[1]

Among earlier collectors was Robert Gilmor Jr., son of a prosperous Baltimore merchant, who collected American coins systematically by date. In the 1830s he enlisted Adam Eckfeldt, coiner and long-time employee of the Philadelphia Mint, to restrike for him certain needed coins, using old dies in storage. In 1839 Reverend Joshua B. Felt of Salem, Massachusetts, was the author of the first book in America that was of numismatic importance—*An Historical Account of Massachusetts Currency*, an impressive 248 pages in length (first edition). The book was generally historical rather than numismatic, but included valuable information on coins and paper money that is still useful today. Dr. James Mease of Philadelphia, a polymath whose knowledge spanned many categories

John Allan.

Published in *The Casket* in 1830, this is one of the earliest large illustrated articles on American coins.

and whose articles were numerous (not to overlook his guide to the city of Philadelphia), was an early numismatist. An article he wrote for the New York Historical Society included descriptions of 17 medals relating to America, supplemented by a study of 33 medals presented to the officer of the War of 1812 and four other medals.

Charles Willson Peale of Philadelphia opened a museum of curiosities, including coins, in Philadelphia in the 1820s. His sons later conducted museums in Baltimore (its building still standing) and New York City. Coins and medals were among the items exhibited. In Pennsylvania near Pittsburgh the Harmony Society settlement had coins in its museum. Of these various early institutions no detailed numismatic inventories have been found. Joseph Mickley of Philadelphia compiled a major collection, said to have been begun in 1816 when he was perplexed that he could not find a copper cent of his 1799 birth year. All told there were probably 50 to 100 numismatists in the United States by the late 1830s.

In 1838 the Mint Cabinet was authorized by Congress with a $1,000 contribution plus a promise of $300 per year for maintenance. The co-curators were Mint employees Jacob Rees Eckfeldt and William Ewing Dubois. Adam Eckfeldt contributed some coins he had saved. Most pieces were saved from deposits made at the Mint of gold and silver coins. In 1842 the Mint published *A Manual of Gold and Silver Coins of All Nations*, written by the two curators. In 1846 Dubois's 138-page *Pledges of History* described coins and other items in the Mint Cabinet.

The Long Room in Peale's Philadelphia Museum in the 1820s.

The Mint Cabinet as it appeared in 1885.

The first truly important rare-coin auction was that conducted on February 20, 1851, in the sale room of Moses Thomas & Son, Philadelphia. The catalog was titled *Executors' Sale. Valuable Collection of Gold and Silver Coins and Medals, Etc., Catalogue of the Entire Collection of Rare and Valuable Coins, Medals, Autographs, Mahogany Coins Case, Etc., Late of Doctor Lewis Roper, deceased.* Roper, a medical doctor, had gone to California to participate in the Gold Rush, became ill on the way home, and died aboard a steamship in Panama. The catalog provided that the coins had to be examined prior to the event as they would not be shown at the sale itself.

A medal depicting P.T. Barnum's American Museum in New York City, by Allen & Moore, medalists, Birmingham, England. On the reverse, below the image of Barnum, some of the attractions are listed, including COINS, MEDALS. (38.6 mm)

In 1853, Barnum's Museum, also called the American Museum, which had its roots as the Tammany Museum decades earlier, published a novel-length catalog which included coins.[2] Years later in 1867, Augustus B. Sage recalled:[3]

"About seven years ago the old Museum (Barnum's) contained a very fair cabinet; a miscellaneous collection it is true, but scattered here and there in the cases were some very rare specimens of our earlier coinage. At the time of the 'clock excitement,'[4] I believe, the rarer specimens were purchased at 'one dollar each all round' by a prominent collector of New Jersey. There can be no question, I take it, that the exhibition of the cases of coins in Barnum's at the time I have referred to, was an incentive for a great number of present collectors to turn their attention to the subject; and the public exhibition of such frames in all museums tends greatly to stimulate the study."

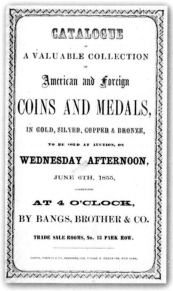

Cover of the June 6, 1855, sale catalog of the collection of Peter Flandin, although his name is not mentioned. The sale was held at Bangs, Brother & Co.

A playbill for the Boston Museum, June 23, 1857. Among its attractions were coins and medals, as noted on ribbons at the lower-right border.

Interior of the Bangs, Brother & Co., sales room in Park Place, New York City. This was a popular venue for selling books (especially in trade wholesale quantities), antiques, art, and other items. (*Frank Leslie's Illustrated Newspaper,* April 5, 1856)

In 1855 the Peter Flandin auction, a key event in its time, offered many important rare coins for sale.

THE PASSING OF THE LARGE COPPER CENT

The Act of February 21, 1857, abolished the copper half cent and cent and mandated other changes, including the planned expiration of the legal-tender privilege for certain foreign silver and gold coins. New cents of the Flying Eagle design, of smaller diameter and made of

The last large copper cents were minted for circulation in January 1857.

copper-nickel, soon began rolling off the presses. On May 25, the first small cents were available to the public in exchange for old coppers and Spanish silver.

This engendered a wave of nostalgia. All across America thousands of citizens contemplated that the copper pennies of childhood would soon disappear, and endeavored to find one of each date in change when they were still available. In his *American Numismatical Manual*, published in 1859, Dr. Montroville W. Dickeson noted that cents dating back to 1793 were still in circulation, although most of those early cents were worn nearly smooth.

In 1857 *Historical Magazine* made its debut. Issued monthly, it contained many items of numismatic interest. Jeremiah Colburn penned coin articles for the Boston *Evening Transcript*, and teenaged Augustus B. Sage did the same in his "Gleanings of Coins" column in the *New-York Dispatch*, which began on June 28 of that year. Knowledge spread.

The passion for coin collecting expanded rapidly, with numismatologists, as they were called, seeking rare early cents such as those dated 1793 and 1799, while noticing other interesting old coins as well. Thus was born an active market for rare coins, tokens, and medals. There were at least five or six scattered dealers in rare coins

A medalet honoring Jeremiah Colburn, issued by Augustus B. Sage in 1859.

in America by 1857, most of them handling autographs, prints, and other items as well. In addition, many bullion dealers and exchange offices kept an eye out for scarce coins and set aside many. Gobrecht silver dollars dated 1836 were a favorite item to find and were worth two or three dollars each.

On January 1, 1858, the Philadelphia Numismatic Society was formed, becoming the first such group in the United States. In March, Augustus B. Sage and friends founded in New York City the American Numismatic Society, which rose into great prominence. By late summer 1858 there were nearly a dozen dealers active in the United States, including, in New York City alone, the venerable John Allan and at least three young men: Sage, Henry Bogert, and John Curtis. Ezra Hill was soon on the scene as well.

Late in 1858 Edward D. Cogan, an art dealer in Philadelphia, was asked to sell a friend's collection of copper cents, and he sent out listings, inviting bids by mail, closing on November 1. Bids were received from 19 people. A 1793 Chain cent sold for $12.67, a 1793 Wreath cent brought $5.13, a 1793 Liberty Cap cent realized $7.25, a 1799 cent sold for $7, and an 1804 cent brought $5.50, among others. The total amount realized for the collection of cents from 1793 through 1858 was $128.68. This was exciting news, picked up by the local papers and soon reprinted throughout the East. Cogan was deluged with letters from people wanting to buy and sell coins. Soon, he decided to become a professional numismatist, which he seems to have done in the year 1860.[5]

Proof coins with deeply mirrored surfaces had been popular with collectors for a long time. In Europe they date back to the 17th century. The first *set* of Proof coins made in England seems to have been the four-piece 1746 silver coins of King George II. In America certain early coins were made with mirrored surfaces that

A Proof 1821 half eagle from the full Proof set of this year in the National Numismatic Collection.

have all the physical characteristics of Proofs, certain silver quarters of 1796 being examples. It is not known when the Mint first specifically made mirror Proofs, called "master coins" in the early days, for collectors. Some scholars have suggested 1817.

The earliest complete U.S. Proof set known is dated 1821 and is in the National Numismatic Collection in the Smithsonian Institution. Scattered earlier coins have been called Proofs in modern times or, alternatively, Specimens— meaning coins especially struck with care. The Philadelphia Mint made Proofs available to interested numismatists, as noted, such as to Robert Gilmor Jr. Widespread sale of Proofs began in 1858 when an estimated 210 silver sets were sold—including the three-cent piece, half dime, dime, quarter, half dollar, and dollar. Proof Flying Eagle cents were sold separately, as were Proof gold coins.

Beginning in the spring of 1859 Mint director James Ross Snowden set in place a secret program to make restrikes from older dies and to issue new rarities such as patterns. These were not entered into official records, but were sold privately by

A token or store card issued by William Idler. As did all other coin dealers of the 1850s and 1860s, Idler traded in many other items of interest to collectors. The obverse of the token is a copy of a copper denarium (penny) made for Maryland in 1658. (Brass, 20.5 mm)

Mint employees to local dealer William K. Idler in particular, but possibly to favored others as well. Dealer Edward D. Cogan was squeezed out and complained.

The pattern 1856 Flying Eagle cent, a popular rarity of which only about a thousand had been made, was restruck in quantity. The market price fell from $2 to $1. From that time until about 1885, tens of thousands of rare patterns, restrikes, and other delicacies were made for the private profit of officials holding positions at the Mint.[6]

In 1859 Director Snowden, an accomplished numismatist, set about forming the Washington Cabinet—a collection within the Mint Cabinet that featured coins, tokens, and medals of our first president. He informed collectors that he would trade restrikes, patterns, and other items for pieces that were needed. This ignited a great interest in Washington pieces, and prices rose sharply. Thus began the first boom-and-bust cycle in American numismatics. For reasons unknown today, the American Numismatic Society disappeared after 1859.

The 1856 Flying Eagle cent.

THE EARLY 1860S

The Washington Cabinet at the Mint was opened in a special ceremony on Washington's birthday, February 22, 1860. In that year a book was published under Director Snowden's name, *A Description of Ancient and Modern Coins in the Cabinet of the Mint of the United States*. It was primarily researched and written by William E. Dubois and George Bull (curator of the Mint Cabinet). This 412-page volume was and still is highly regarded.

After Abraham Lincoln was inaugurated president on March 4, 1860, thousands of political appointees were shown the door, including Snowden. He continued his numismatic activities in the private sector. Snowden had been a member *ex officio* of the Numismatic and Antiquarian Society of Philadelphia when he was Mint director. After spring 1861 he became a dues-paying partici-

A coin collector's coin cabinet, as illustrated in the 1860 edition of Montroville W. Dickeson's book.

pant. In 1861 his book, *A Description of the Medals of Washington*, was published. Later he was the author of *Coins of the Bible*, published in Philadelphia in 1864 and 1870.

Meanwhile, Montroville W. Dickeson's 1859 book was published in an 1860 edition slightly retitled as *American Numismatic Manual*. Another edition was issued in 1864. William C. Prime, perhaps best described as an adventurous writer, was the author of *Coins, Medals and Seals*, copyrighted in 1860 and published by Harper & Brothers in 1861.[7] For reasons not clear today, the books of Dickeson and Prime were not widely cited by numismatists of the era. The Prime book was distinctive in that it gave market prices for many coins. As examples, silver dollars, grades not indicated, were priced as follows: 1794 $7.50; and 1795 to 1803, $1.25 each. For Liberty Seated dollars the following were priced at $1.25 each: 1840, 1841, 1842, 1843, 1844, 1845, and 1846, while 1847 was priced at $1.50, 1848 at $1.75, 1849 and

1850 $1.25 each, 1851 and 1852 at $15.00 each, 1853 at $1.25, the scarce 1854 at $3.00, the 1855 through 1857 at $1.25 each, 1858 $5.00, and 1859 $1.25.

The walls came tumbling down for a number of speculators who had purchased Washington tokens and medals, and the bloom was off the market rose. Pieces worth, say, $5 dropped to $3. Of course, the market was rather small, and the total amount lost was not great. Time seems to heal all such market hiccups, and in later years the values of such items multiplied.

A token issued by Edward Cogan in 1860.
(Copper, 20.6 mm)

A token issued by Ezra Hill in 1860.
(Copper, 28.1 mm)

The American Civil War began in April 1861, and what Yankees perceived as an easy win soon turned into a bloody conflict lasting four years and costing over a million lives. The monetary situation became chaotic. The Charlotte, Dahlonega, and New Orleans mints fell under the control of the Confederacy in early 1861, operated for a while afterward, and then closed. Citizens were uncertain about the future, and starting in late December of that year hoarded gold coins. Banks stopped paying them out at face value.

No prospect of victory was in sight for the Union, and losses in the various military campaigns increased each month. Banks, manufacturers, and merchants became increasingly worried. On January 15, 1862, the *London Post* commented:

> The monetary intelligence from America is of the most important kind. National bankruptcy is not an agreeable prospect, but it is the only one presented by the existing state of American finance. What a strange tale does not the history of the United States for the past twelve months unfold? What a striking moral does it not point? Never before was the world dazzled by a career of more reckless extravagance. Never before did a flourishing and prosperous state make such gigantic strides towards effecting its own ruin.

The United States Treasury was short of money, and in March 1862 it issued Demand Notes. These were not redeemable in specie (gold and silver coins), but only in exchange for other bills. They were nicknamed greenbacks for the color of their back sides. Further concerned about the stability of money, citizens withdrew all silver coins from circulation by early summer 1862. In the second week of July all one-cent pieces disappeared as well. On July 17 the Treasury made ordinary postage stamps legal tender in certain transactions. This engendered the private production of encased postage stamps, copper and brass tokens, and private scrip notes. The Treasury issued Postage Currency notes and, later, Fractional Currency.

The balance in the Treasury was low during the Civil War. Paper money was used to raise money. Legal Tender Notes, first dated March 10, 1862, were issued in denominations from $5 to $1,000, followed by those dated August 1, 1862, of the values of $1 and $2. A $100 note is shown here. These were not exchangeable at par for silver or gold coins. By early August 1862, it took $115.25 in Legal Tender bills to buy $100 in gold coins.

On the West Coast, the State Legislature of California had decreed in 1850 that paper money of any kind was illegal for use in commerce. This would prevent problems with unsound banks, such as many Forty-Niners had experienced back East before heading into the sunset to seek their fortunes. Accordingly, in 1862, when Legal Tender bills were first issued, and continuing for years afterward, they were of no use at face value in commerce in such places as San Francisco and Sacramento. Instead, silver and gold coins were the medium of exchange and were traded at par in commerce. Anyone wanting to spend a Legal Tender bill had to accept a deep discount equal to the premium charged for gold and silver in the East.

In 1863 the National Banking Act provided for banks to have federal charters and operate as national banks. The amount of 90 percent of their capital had to be backed by federal bonds or equivalent. This capitalization raised additional large sums for the war effort. National Bank Notes could be exchanged at par for other National Bank Notes or for Legal Tender Notes, but not for gold or silver coins.

The destruction of Barnum's American Museum by fire on July 15, 1865, was thought to have been at the hand of an incendiary who was a Confederate sympathizer.

When the war ended in April 1865, many citizens felt that gold and silver coins would come out of hiding and return to circulation. The Treasury finances were still uncertain, however, as was the economic outlook. It was not until years later—in April 1876—that silver coins were again circulated at face value, and this did not happen to gold coins until December 17, 1878. In the meantime many of the monetary substitutes such as tokens became collectibles for numismatists, as did the paper money of the Confederate States of America.

In 1877 John Jay Knox, the 1860s Comptroller of the Currency, reported this exchange rates for Legal Tender Notes in terms of gold coins as of July 1 each year, dating back to the Civil War:

1863: 76.6¢ • 1864: 38.7¢ • 1865: 70.4¢ • 1866: 66.0¢ • 1867: 71.7¢ • 1868: 70.1¢ • 1869: 73.5¢ • 1870: 85.6¢ • 1871: 89.0¢ • 1872: 87.5¢ • 1873: 86.4¢ • 1874: 91.0¢ • 1875: 87.2¢ • 1876: 89.2¢ • 1877: 94.5¢ • 1877: 97.3¢.[8]

In other words, in 1864 it took $1,000 in Legal Tender Notes to buy $387 face value of gold coins!

THE NUMISMATIC SCENE IN THE 1860S

In the meantime, beginning in 1860, rare-coin auctions expanded, and regular sales were held. Foremost in the field was W. Elliot Woodward, whose catalogs reflected high scholarship. In 1864 he presented the greatest auction held in America up to that time, featuring the John F. McCoy Collection. It comprised 3,122 numbered lots (actually, there were a few more, as some were numbered twice, as, for example, lot 1811 and lot 1811-2) described in a 160-page (plus covers) catalog. A few coins that arrived after the McCoy catalog was in press were incorporated into a four-page, 45-item addendum. The sale began on May 17 and extended for four days. It was held at the Trade Sales Rooms at 498 Broadway, a venue used by various individuals and firms to sell artifacts, books, paintings, furniture, and other items. (The book trade was especially important. A publisher with a new title would auction the rights of distribution.)

The McCoy sale was posted to begin "precisely at five o'clock" on each day, and no doubt it did. George A. Leavitt as auctioneer was in front of the sale room, which was illuminated with gas lamps. In front of him were several

The cover of the McCoy catalog.

rows of single wooden chairs upon which dealers and collectors sat, catalogs in hand. Those in the trade were apt to sit down front where they could better keep an eye on the auctioneer, on cataloger Woodward as he supervised the event, and on their competitors.

As the sale progressed, the auctioneer would call out the name of the buyer in the audience, such as (presumably) "Sold to Mr. French." The idea of assigning numbers to bidders did not become widespread in the coin trade until nearly a century later. Here is a sample listing from the McCoy auction:

> Lot 338. 1794 [silver dollar]. As regards to impression and condition, this dollar is nearly or quite equal to the one which in my sale of Oct. 21 produced the extraordinary sum of $285.00. This specimen is unfortunately blemished by having the name of "Andrew Spence" pricked into the field of the coin, and some figures on the head, produced by the same process; but it is nevertheless one of the finest and most desirable ever offered. Exceedingly rare. [sold for] $80.00.

For this and other coin sales the payments were either in gold or silver coins or else adjusted to reflect a large amount in bank notes. Some bank drafts were marked to be paid in coin.

As it developed, the American Numismatic Society, which had not met since 1859, was comatose, but not dead. In early 1864 there was a stirring, and on February 5, at the invitation of George H. Perine, M.D., a gathering of collectors was held at his home at 6 East 22nd Street, New York City. In attendance were Mortimer S. Brown, Isaac J. Greenwood, Edward Groh, Frank H. Norton, James Oliver, and Dr. Perine. This included old members plus the new face of Perine. Enthusiasm must have prevailed, for another meeting took place on March 11, at which time the name of the group was changed to the American Numismatic and Archaeological Society, probably in an effort to appeal to a wider population than just the numismatic community.

The front page of the *American Journal of Numismatics*, November 1866, with a discussion of muling (the combination of mismatched dies).

In May 1866 the society launched the *American Journal of Numismatics*, the first such hobby magazine in the country. The first several issues told of the new Shield design five-cent piece and included extensive listings of Civil War tokens, an increasingly popular collecting specialty. Although the journal was filled with current news, research articles, reports of auctions, and much other interesting and valuable information, it lost money.

After publishing the April 1870 issue the society transferred the magazine to the Boston Numismatic Society, which produced it on a quarterly basis into the 20th century.

W. Elliot Woodward was the leading dealer of the era—knowledgeable and highly respected. The *American Journal of Numismatics* called him "the lion of the day." His closest competitor was Edward D. Cogan, who started with a mail-bid sale in 1858 and later moved to New York City. A scholar Cogan was not, but he did handle many important coins. Harvey Strobridge and Ebenezer Locke Mason Jr. also were prominent.

Various coin shops did business in the Eastern cities, and at least two were active in San Francisco. There was no tally, but probably 50 to 100 people dealt in coins on an active basis and several thousand serious collectors acquired coins in many different specialties.

There were no books or other guides to the market value of coins except for the generally ignored and by then obsolete Prime text, and such determinations had to be made by reviewing auction results and consulting dealer lists. There were no grading standards, and commercial policies varied widely. One collector's "Uncirculated" might be another's "Very Fine," and "Proof" applied to just about any coin with a mirror-like surface, including some that had been buffed or polished to make them that way! As the community of collectors and dealers grew increasingly close there was extensive exchange of information, usually by correspondence.

A photographic plate of 1793 cent varieties published in the *American Journal of Numismatics* in 1868. At the time very few photographic illustrations of coins were used in the United States.

A photograph of the first United States Mint (in operation 1792 to 1832) as it appeared in 1854; published in the *AJN* in 1868.

THE LATE 19TH CENTURY

Copper, nickel, and silver Proof coins were popular with collectors in the late 1800s. The lower denominations from the cent to the nickel were sold in sets, silver coins in separate sets, and gold in sets as well. Due to their high face value the mintages of gold coins were small. There was no known interest in collecting mintmarked coins. One of each *date* sufficed for anyone who collected dimes, quarters, or other series. It was not important whether there was no mintmark, or whether such letters as CC, O, or S were present.

In the early 1870s the numismatic scene was fairly quiet. Dealers supplied clients with desired coins, and a steady parade of auctions, mostly in New York City, brought additional pieces into the market. Scholarship advanced. In 1875 Sylvester S. Crosby's *Early Coins of America* was published. It covered colonial and other early issues. Remarkably, today it is still a standard reference! Édouard Frossard published *Numisma*, and J.W. Scott & Co. produced a magazine as well: *The Coin Collector's Journal*. Scott also published catalogs listing the prices of what certain coins would sell for *if* they were in stock. The values were highly irregular and were not widely used.

The first issue of *Numisma*, January 1877. The publisher was dealer Édouard Frossard, one of the leading numismatic scholars of the day.

In 1878 the Chapman brothers—S. Hudson, born in 1857, and Henry Jr., born in 1859—hung out their shingle as numismatists and antiquarians in Philadelphia, after working in the shop of John W. Haseltine. In 1882 they were given the opportunity to sell the Charles I. Bushnell Collection after longtime collector Lorin G. Parmelee extracted coins he wanted. They published a deluxe catalog with photographic plates. Offered for $5, it swept away in appearance any auction catalog ever issued. The sale was a great success, drawing many criticisms from other dealers who were eager to point out errors. The Chapmans went from one success to another and within a decade became the most prominent auction catalogers, succeeding W. Elliot Woodward, who by then was concentrating in developing real estate in Roxbury.

In 1881 and 1882 the Mint explored the possibility of replacing the Shield nickel design in use since 1866 with a Liberty Head design. Many varieties of patterns were made, including some in experimental alloys.

S. Hudson Chapman and brother Henry in their library in May 1890.

In early 1883 the new Liberty Head nickel designed by Chief Engraver Charles E. Barber was released into circulation. The obverse showed Miss Liberty surrounded by 13 stars and the date below. The reverse had UNITED STATES OF AMERICA, E PLURIBUS UNUM, and the value expressed by the Roman numeral V. The latter was logical, as since 1865 the letters III had been used on the nickel three-cent piece, a classical touch. Sharpers realized that the new nickel was the same diameter as a $5 gold coin. It was easy enough to add a reeded edge in a machine shop and to gold-plate a coin. The result was what seemed to be a new design of a $5 gold coin.

1881 pattern Liberty Head nickel by Charles E. Barber, cataloged as Judd-1673.

The multiple perpetrators of this clever go-round tendered a gold-plated nickel, without stating its value, to pay for candy, a cigar, or some other item priced at five cents or less. Shopkeepers, thinking it was a half eagle, returned $4.95 or more in change!

Consternation knew no limits, and the Treasury Department dispensed operatives (agents) across the country to stop the fraud. In the meantime, after 5,474,300 coins had been struck the design was modified to add CENTS below the V. News that the Mint had made an error and was recalling the CENTS-less nickels was printed nationwide. The result was a mad scramble by citizens to find as many as they could of these coins that were sure to become valuable rarities. As it turned out, so many 1883 nickels without CENTS were found and saved that today in Mint State they are far and away the most common of all Liberty Head nickels minted through the year 1912, including dates of which tens of millions were struck.

This treasure hunt resulted in tens of thousands of people becoming interested in rare coins! Many began forming collections by visiting dealers, bidding in auctions, and ordering by mail. Likely, the number of numismatists in the United States tripled or quadrupled. Prices rose sharply, and auctions increased to the pace of about one every week! The hobby had never seen such balmy days.

All of this was very healthy. At least a dozen new hobby publications were born, most of which included stamps and other collectibles in addition to coins.

EVERGREEN.

At his Evergreen mansion in Baltimore, T. Harrison Garrett, of the family that controlled Baltimore & Ohio Railroad, quietly assembled the largest and highest-quality coin collection in America by the time of his passing in a boating accident on Chesapeake Bay in 1886. Today Evergreen House is owned by the Johns Hopkins University and is used for special functions.

C.E. Leal, of Paterson, New Jersey, launched *The American Numismatist* in September 1886, devoted especially to coins.

Dr. George F. Heath, a physician of Monroe, Michigan, and also mayor of that city, introduced his *The American Numismatist* with a cover date of September-October 1888. Heath soon learned of Leal's magazine and dropped *American* from the title of later issues.

Main Street, Wichita, Kansas, a boom town in the 1880s largely financed by bonds and other securities sold to investors in the East. (*Harper's Weekly*, November 29, 1887)

George F. Heath, M.D.

Storm clouds gathered on the economic horizon in 1889 and 1890. Land speculation in the Prairie States such as Kansas and Iowa had resulted in entire cities being laid out in recent years, financed by bonds yielding 8 to 10 percent primarily sold to investors in the East, where normal returns on such securities was often just 5 to 6 percent. By 1889 the excitement had diminished, few new projects were being implemented, and towns as well as other entities had problems paying interest on their bonds. By 1890 many securities were worthless. At the same time the boom in the coin hobby was running out of new faces, prices were dropping, and the market was becoming soft.

In that year Lorin G. Parmelee, who had been collecting since the 1850s and had built the second largest (after T. Harrison Garrett) private holding in America, consigned his coins to the New York Coin & Stamp Company, a leading auction firm of the era, owned by David Proskey and Harlan

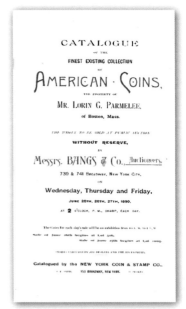

Title page of the Lorin G. Parmelee Collection catalog, New York Coin & Stamp Company, 1890.

Smith. Great rarities were set to cross the block as part of the most extensive auction of United States coins up to that time. Due to prevailing economic uncertainty and the quiet state of the marketplace, the sale laid an egg. Many of the scarcer and rarer pieces failed to meet Parmelee's high reserves, which did not take into consideration that buyer interest was less than would have been the case a few years earlier. Over the next several years Parmelee sold many of the remaining coins privately.

The center of the coin trade in America was New York City, followed by Philadelphia and then Boston. The typical walk-in shop offered coins, stamps, and other collectibles, often including birds' eggs, tobacco tags, fossils, prints, and Indian relics.

Numismatics entered a quiet period that would extend until about 1898.

In the meantime in this uncertain milieu George F. Heath, publisher of *The Numismatist*, envisioned a national organization of coin collectors. A meeting of interested people took place in Chicago in November 1891, and the American Numismatic Association was born. During their stay in Chicago the founders visited the site of the World's Columbian Exposition, then being built, with the anticipation it would open in 1892 (but it did not open until 1893, as discussed in chapter 3).

In 1893 Augustus G. Heaton advertised his *Mint Marks* booklet, a treatise listing 14 points of appeal of mintmarked coins. The presence of a C, CC, D, O, or S mintmark could add a lot of value and interest to certain coins. In time this revolutionized collecting.

Heaton, similar to Heath, was a man of high intellectual pursuits—including being a facile writer. In the same year the ANA held a convention in Chicago that attracted 15 attendees. Another 28 "attended" by sending proxies. Votes were tallied, and the new roster of officers included the following: president, George F. Heath; vice president, Joseph Hooper; secretary, O.W. Page; treasurer, Dr. A.L. Fisher; librarian, William C. Stone; superintendent of exchange, W.J. Luck; and counterfeit detector, S. Hudson Chapman. The proxy system of voting caused no end of problems in later years, with some officers and candidates such as Farran Zerbe using them in devious ways to influence the results.

One of several stores operated at different locations in New York City by the Scott Stamp & Coin Co.

Augustus Goodyear Heaton.

The Carson City mintmark on the reverse of an 1889-CC silver dollar makes it worth many times the value of a Philadelphia coin. Mintmarks were generally ignored prior to Heaton's study published in 1893.

233

The Numismatist was adopted as the official journal of the ANA, although it continued to be edited and published by Heath in Monroe, Michigan. Important articles were published, including descriptions of die varieties, market reports, and histories of coins and their issuers from ancient times to the present.[9] Many anecdotes and amusing incidents were also included, such as the story of a numismatist who preferred coins to love, in the issue of June 1894:

> He hailed from Arizona. He courted a New England school ma'am for two years, two months and 12 days, and then informed her that he could not afford to marry her as he needed all his money to buy old coins with, and even then was owing Ed. Frossard $38.75. The young lady was first surprised, second amazed, and third indignant. She consulted a lawyer, went to court, and got $637.68 damages.

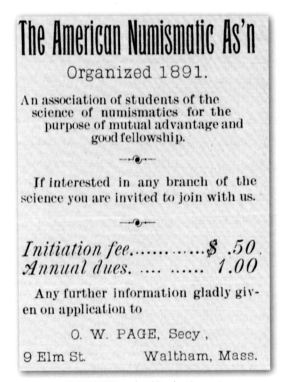

Part of a page from the Friesner catalog with prices inked in the left margin.

The Detroit Museum of Art, where the 1894 ANA convention was held.

An 1894 ANA membership advertisement.

In the same year the W.M. Friesner Collection was sold at auction by Édouard Frossard, the first extensive offering of mintmarked coins in a public sale. Included were many coins that would later be recognized as rarities. In 1894 as in earlier years there were no price guides, and whether a coin was common or rare in a given grade was often a matter of guesswork.

At the time the ANA had about 200 members. In August it held a convention in the Detroit Museum of Art. It was reported that 191 people were in good standing as ANA members.

The dismal national economy of the era, including the financial Panic of 1893, continued to weigh heavily on the coin market. Prices remained low, as did the number of newcomers to numismatics. Heath continually struggled to attract readers and to promote the hobby. In 1896 and 1897 the ANA was comatose. In many instances officers did not respond to letters, and association news was non-existent. Heath withdrew his magazine as its official publication.

Matters brightened in 1898, engendered in part by a growing interest in tokens and medals. The Spanish-American War spurred the economy, as wars usually do. The ANA awoke, and *The Numismatist* became the official journal once again. The future looked bright.

THE EARLY 20TH CENTURY

In 1900 all was well in America, or nearly so. Without question, political matters were more settled. In the presidential contest in 1900 William McKinley aspired for a second term, choosing Theodore Roosevelt as his running mate. The "Hero of San Juan Hill," leader of the Rough Riders contingent in Cuba during the recent war, was considered to be a national hero.

The coin hobby and market continued on an upswing at the turn of the century. It was the dawn of the automobile age, followed a few years later by the development of airplanes. The main method of inter-city travel was by rail, as it had been for many decades. Accommodations on Pullman passenger coaches were luxurious, and business trips could be pleasant excursions. George F. Heath, for one, traveled extensively in this manner and wrote about it in *The Numismatist*. Telephone connections were available in major cities. Most coin dealers were so equipped. Many also had cable addresses to receive telegrams.

Hard Times tokens of the 1832 to 1844 era were hot tickets in the marketplace in the early 1900s.

Advertisement for the 1900 Republican slate. By this time America was on an imperialist streak, good intentions (per the notice) notwithstanding, and had gained control of Cuba, the Philippine Islands, and several other areas.

235

The most famous Confederate States of America rarity, the $1,000 note printed by the National Bank Note Company, New York City, before the Civil War commenced, and issued in Montgomery, Alabama, the first capital of the Confederacy (which was soon moved to Richmond).

The numismatic market strengthened. Most attention was paid to colonial and state coins, encased postage stamps, tokens, and medals. Paper money, a dynamic part of numismatics but outside of the main thrust of the present book, was very popular. Favorites included Confederate and Continental paper money. Federal currency such as Legal Tender Notes, National Bank Notes, and the like was mostly ignored.

Commemorative coins, added to by the 1900 Lafayette silver dollar, were popular. A complete collection included one of these (issue price $2) plus the two half dollars and the Isabella quarter of the World's Columbian Exposition.

Except for minor coins—the Indian Head cent and the Liberty Head nickel—there was not much interest in current federal coins. Collecting by mintmarks was growing as a specialty, but slowly, despite Heaton's book on that subject. Probably not more than a dozen numismatists sought such varieties of Morgan silver dollars, while hundreds specialized in, for example, Hard Times tokens. Back in 1893 Heaton had stated that he had never heard of anyone collecting higher-denomination gold—$5, $10, and $20 pieces—by mintmarks. In bank vaults in the early 20th century American gold coins usually dated back to 1834. Gold dollars and $3 pieces were becoming slightly scarce.

Annual ANA conventions had become a tradition starting in the late 1890s and were continued for nearly every year after that, to the present day. The typical gathering in the early times included up to about 30 or so members, nearly all or completely all men, often accompanied by their wives.

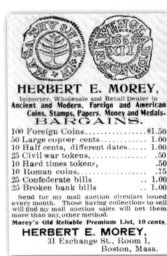

In the early 20th century it was inexpensive to start a coin collection. This advertisement is by Herbert E. Morey in *The Numismatist*, May 1902.

A proposal for an ANA seal created by George F. Heath.

Orders for Proof coins dropped. In 1908 only 545 silver Proof sets were ordered. In the same year the American Numismatic Society moved into its magnificent new building on Audubon Terrace, 155th Street and Broadway, New York City, financed by railroad-fortune heir Archer Huntington. It was later doubled in size by an adjacent building, also paid for by Huntington.

By tradition ever since the Philadelphia Mint began in the 1790s, coin designs were created by engravers on the Mint staff. That changed in the early 20th century, when several well-known sculptors in the private sector were commissioned to design coins.

Official photograph of the attendees at the 1908 ANA convention in Philadelphia. It was customary to have a group photograph taken and to publish it in *The Numismatist*. Most of those shown were well known in their time. At the center is bearded Henry Chapman, host for social events at the gathering. Standing next to him is Farran Zerbe, holding his hat.

The Lamp of Knowledge, as adopted by the ANA and used intermittently to the present day.

In 1908 the American Numismatic Society moved into its beautiful new building on Audubon Terrace in New York City.

Following an organizational meeting in December 1908, the New York Numismatic Club rose to importance in that city and attracted many to its monthly meetings. Clubs in Chicago, Boston, and elsewhere were thriving.

Auction action remained strong across the board, and in the first decade of the 20th century many price records were set. Important in that specialty were Henry Chapman and his brother S. Hudson Chapman (who had dissolved their partnership in the summer of 1906), Thomas L. Elder, who was up and coming strongly, and B. Max Mehl, who conducted mail-bid sales without public attendance.

Representative of the activity, the collection of Captain Andrew C. Zabriskie was auctioned on June 3 and 4, 1909, presented in a catalog by Henry Chapman. A 1787 gold Brasher doubloon slept at $3,650. The buyer was Chapman himself.

The Matthew A. Stickney estate coin had been offered and sold earlier for a world's record price of $6,200. Competition in 1909 was not the same, as the owner of the Stickney coin did not need another, and the underbidder on that was DeWitt S. Smith, who had since died. *Otherwise* the sale did well. *The Numismatist* reported this:

The audience as photographed at the Zabriskie sale by Henry Chapman, June 3, 1909, in the Philadelphia auction-sale room of Davis & Harvey.

> Among the price records were the Ormsby $10, which sold for $1,600, Mr. Chapman announced that the buyer had filed a bid limit of $2,000; $50 Kellogg & Co., $1,250; $50 1851 Humbert, Proof, $1,000; $2½ 1848 U.S. Mint, counterstamped CAL, $85; the unique $1 Bowie in copper, which brought $35 at the Stickney sale, sold for $61; the $2½ Pelican Co. in brass, which sold for a song 10 years ago, brought $105; $20 1860 Pikes Peak, the first to be offered for many years, $645; some of the Georgia and North Carolina pieces made new records; the Mormon $10 made an auction record at $705, and $85 is the new record for a Stella.

A complete set of *The Numismatist*, 21 volumes, was sold for $2.40 per volume. Gold Proof sets from 1897 to 1906 sold for $45 per set. The auction realized the grand total of $26,235.

By 1910 a list of the most active dealers in America included B. Max Mehl of Fort Worth, Texas, who first advertised in *The Numismatist* in 1904; Thomas L. Elder, the most active retailer in New York City; and the Chapman brothers, operating independently of each other.

Year by year most carefully formed collections yielded a profit when sold. In 1912 Wayte Raymond, a rising star in the firmament of coin dealers, published this comment:

> Many harsh words are said about collectors who interest themselves in an actual speculation as to whether or not the coins they are buying today will have appreciated in value 10 years from now. Numismatists of the old school said the true collector is not interested in any such appreciation in the value of his collection but derives his entire profit and pleasure from the coins while in his hands. We feel however that the average American collector, while he greatly enjoys his coins, also feels very pleased if on disposing of his collection he realizes profits. . . .

Edgar H. Adams's first fixed-price catalog. The cover coins were decorative and did not represent the offered items.

Masthead for an Adams column in *The Numismatist*.

The 1915 ANA convention held in San Francisco was a bust, and fewer than 20 members were on hand—despite the attraction of the Panama-Pacific International Exposition in progress. At the left holding his hat is B. Max Mehl, next to his wife and daughter. On the other side of Mehl is Farran Zerbe, who held the concession for selling commemoratives at the fair.

The most accomplished researcher in this era was Edgar H. Adams, author of a groundbreaking work on private and territorial gold coins and, with William H. Woodin, of the standard work on pattern coins. For many years he wrote popular column on coins for the Brooklyn Sun. He also wrote columns for and edited The Numismatist for a time and acted as purchasing agent for a number of collectors and had his own business.

Proof coins continued to be out of widespread favor. There had been more interest in them in 1885 than there was in 1915. In the latter year full sets of Proof coins—from the cent to

B. Max Mehl in his office in 1915 in Fort Worth, Texas. With his back to the camera he is giving dictation to his secretary. On the table are two trays with coins—in an era before albums and holders. At the back wall at the upper left is a Fractional Currency Shield issued by the Treasury Department in the 1860s.

the double eagle—were struck for the last time. In recent years the matte surface on cents, nickels, and gold coins had been unpopular with collectors, and the design of Barber silver coins had never been a favorite. Not until 1936 would Proof sets of current coinage be offered to collectors again.[10]

In 1916 the new designs of the Mercury dime, Standing Liberty quarter, and Liberty Walking half dollar were received with enthusiasm, and many numismatists who had not collected Barber coins began sets of the new issues, including those of branch mints. Interest in mintmarks remained limited, however, and would continue to be until the 1930s when albums were made for date-and-mintmark collecting.

By 1916 the World War in Europe had spurred American industrial output to new highs as factories in the United States supplied munitions to England. The economy had been healthy for a long time, except for a slight downturn in 1908. It was a time of building mansions and driving elegant automobiles. Mintages of most United States coins increased sharply. At the same time the mints spaced dies farther apart in coining presses and turned out a lot of pieces with poor or no details on the higher-relief parts. On the numismatic scene the market was strong, but prices remained steady in most series.

Commemorative coins were in a slump. Many of the 1915-S Panama-Pacific coins went to the melting pot. In 1916 commemorative gold dollars were made for the McKinley Memorial in Niles, Ohio, a classic-style structure designed by the famous New York architects McKim, Mead, and White, but numismatic response was an unstifled yawn.

A 1916 McKinley Memorial commemorative gold dollar. In 1916 10,000 were struck, followed by a lesser quantity in 1917. The issuing commission wholesaled many unsold pieces to dealer B. Max Mehl.

THE 1920S

The years of the Roaring Twenties, so called, were not very roaring for numismatics. In *The Numismatist*, March 1920, Editor Frank Duffield stated:

> In the report of the United States Coin Committee of the American Numismatic Society, at the annual meeting in January, the statement is made that while the price of coins did advance slightly during the war, the advance was not at all in keeping with the increase in the cost of clothing and food. Those who have been buying coins for several years past will corroborate this statement. It does seem that with a doubling of prices for almost every other commodity within the past three or four years the price of coins should also have advanced sharply; but it has remained almost stationary.
>
> The advance in price of the necessities and luxuries of life is attributed to the increased costs under which they are produced. This, of course, cannot be applied to coins. And really there is not good reason why a rare coin should cost more today than it did 10 years ago, except that there are more collectors today, and therefore more competition for it than at that time. The number of pieces has been neither increased

nor decreased by the war. The average line of coins has taken on a fairly standard selling price during the years they have been on the market, and the buyer of today perhaps feels justified in refusing to pay more than that price.

But with our dollar today buying only 50 cents' worth according to the standards of five years ago, the fact remains that with but a slight increase in the price of coins, they are cheaper today than they have been at any time within the past 10 years, and almost anything in the way of a numismatic specimen at prevailing prices is a good investment, with the usual pleasure and enjoyment thrown in. The wise collector will not need to be urged to buy now to the extent of his ability.

In 1921 a financial recession swept across America. Manufacturing slowed, unemployment rose, and prices of many things dropped. For Henry Chapman the sale of the 7,302-lot John Story Jenks Collection (described in a catalog more than 650 pages long) held in Philadelphia from December 7 to 17, was to be the capstone of his career. Instead the auction laid an egg. Not since the Parmelee sale of 1890 had there been such a dud. Many lots were so cheap that dealers, including Chapman himself, rather than collectors, could not resist buying them. In 1922 B. Max Mehl held the rarity-laden mail-bid sale of the James Ten Eyck Collection. Prices were very disappointing. To be sure there were exceptions.

From 1920 to 1922 the Mint issued several varieties of silver and gold commemorative coins. The reception of these varied. Generally, the silver issues found quite few buyers. Many if not most of the two 1922 Grant gold dollar varieties (with and without obverse stars) went begging and were wholesaled to dealers.

In 1923 there was a bright spot when the James W. Ellsworth Collection was sold privately to Wayte Raymond for $100,000, with financing by John Work Garrett, who extracted desired coins for his own collection. However, the details were not disclosed, and it did not affect the market. For the rest of America, or at least much of it, the ensuing years were heady times. With the Florida land boom, the "Roaring Twenties" with cabarets and bootleg gin, skyscrapers rising in many cities, and stock prices increasing to new highs, the era immortalized in fiction by F. Scott Fitzgerald's *Great Gatsby* had no precedent. All crows became swans, deuces became aces, and the sky was the limit. Collectibles had a heyday with record prices for art, autographs, rare books, prints, and more. Several well-heeled buyers competed for autographs and documents, and prices went through the roof. In contrast, Thomas L. Elder rued the fact that most of those who were strong bidders for coins in the 1910s were dead or inactive in the mid-1920s. To be sure, there were some active buyers. John Work Garrett continued to add to his collection, Colonel E.H.R. Green was busy quietly collecting and hoarding (such as owning all five of the known 1913 Liberty Head nickels), and in 1925 Baltimore banker Louis E. Eliasberg bought his first rare coin—the prelude to the greatest collection of United States coins ever formed, complete by date and mintmark from half cents to double eagles by 1950.

Another Baltimore banker, Waldo C. Newcomer, was busy forming an incredible collection that included high-denomination gold by mintmarks. Many new commemorative coins of the 1920s sold well, but nearly always there were remainders that were sent back to the Mint to be melted. The Guttag Brothers, New York securities brokers, entered the coin trade and made it evident that they had unlimited amounts to spend. Overall activity remained measured and rather slow, however. There was no investment excitement. Auctions did not generate gasps of amazement and bold headlines.

Chicago brewer Virgil M. Brand, who had been collecting aggressively since the late 1880s, died in 1926, leaving an estate of 350,000 coins, tokens, and bills. For him, if one rarity was desirable, two were better yet, and even more, such as owning six of the ten known 1884 trade dollars, was even more desirable. By this time Brand was suffering from illness and was not a strong buyer.

THE DEPRESSION ERA—*EXCEPT* FOR COINS!

In early 1929 the Guttag Brothers ran into financial difficulty in face of their expensive new building that had recently been moved into with the expectation that the stock market would continue to rise. They stopped buying coins and began the orderly liquidation of their inventory out of necessity, not from any fear of the future of coin prices. Elsewhere among coin dealers all was in good order—steady, steady.

Common stocks continued to rise. Black Friday in October saw a precipitous fall, but surely this was a temporary situation. The prices of securities kept falling and touched bottom in 1932 and 1933. In Baltimore, Waldo C. Newcomer had severe setbacks with the bank of which he was president. His collection of coins was consigned to B. Max Mehl to sell to clients, and additional coins were consigned to auction.

Many collectors who had a lot of money to spend in the 1920s were now either unemployed or saw the value of their real estate, securities, and other assets decline. There was no optimism. Coin-market prices stayed relatively stable, as they had not risen sharply in the 1920s. Sales were slow, however, and auctions drew fewer participants.

Soon after his inauguration on March 4, 1933, President Franklin D. Roosevelt decreed that gold coins could no longer be released into commerce. Soon afterward, citizens were commanded to turn in gold coins in exchange for paper money, except that collectors and others could retain pieces of numismatic value, and every citizen could keep up to $100 face value. On January 20, 1934, the government raised the price of gold from $20.67 per ounce to $35.00, in effect stealing untold millions of dollars from citizens who had exchanged their gold for paper. In numismatics this had a stimulating effect. All of a sudden, many collectors, Louis E. Eliasberg and Floyd Starr among them, decided to expand their interests and form sets of gold. More attention than ever was paid to scarce issues.

In 1929 in Shippensburg, Pennsylvania, M(artin) L(uther) Beistle, an avid numismatist and a manufacturer of cardboard products, launched his "Unique" brand of coin albums. These were cardboard pages with openings for various coins. On the back and front, clear thin cellulose acetate strips could be slid in and out to permit the insertion or removal of coins. The pages fit conveniently into a ring binder. For the first time, a collection of large copper cents or of another specialty could be conveniently stored and could be examined and enjoyed without touching them. The old standard procedure of storing coins face-up in thin drawers in a wooden cabinet soon became obsolete. Individual coins in dealers' stocks or that were to be sent through the mail or were kept as a collection was being built were usually stored in two-inch by two-inch paper envelopes with information typed or written on the face. The 2x2 standard had been adopted as that was the interior measurement of a box for player-piano rolls, and millions of the instruments were in use in American households.

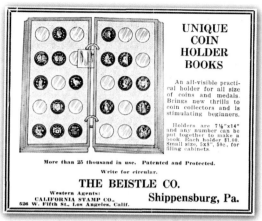

The innovative series of Unique coin albums launched in 1929 changed the course of numismatics and saved the coin hobby from the Depression.

A Scott Stamp & Coin Company advertisement in *The Numismatist*, December 1931. Manager Wayte Raymond vastly expanded the Beistle line and made it possible for a collection of rare coins to be easily stored in a manner in which each coin was visible on both sides through clear acetate windows. Years later the Scott office on the third floor at 1 West 57th Street was occupied by the New Netherlands Coin Company.

Wayte Raymond, who conducted the Scott Stamp & Coin Company in New York City, secured the franchise for Beistle holders, vastly expanded the number of series covered, and marketed pages in two standard sizes—horizontal and small and vertical and large, with ring binders for each. Starting in the early 1930s these were aggressively marketed. These were the right products in the right place at the right time. In the deep Depression times, hobbies came to the forefront. All across America hobby shops opened, specializing in jigsaw puzzles (which were a national fad), board games, and more. During the decade Parker Brothers introduced Monopoly.

243

Whitman Publishing Company took the lead in popularizing coin collecting to the general public, resulting in hundreds of thousands of people joining the hobby.

In 1934 J.K. Post of Neenah, Wisconsin, marketed the penny board—a flat cardboard sheet with openings into which Lincoln cents of different dates and mintmarks could be pressed. Whitman Publishing took notice and bought Post's business. Soon other boards were made available, including for Liberty Head nickels, Buffalo nickels, and, curiously in retrospect, "Morgan" dimes, quarters, and half dollars of 1892 to 1916. (In time the correct *Barber* title, rather than *Morgan*, was used.)

Not many people collected half dollars or silver dollars, but on a low budget or even if unemployed, many could afford the face value needed to fill in the several dozen dates and mintmarks of Lincoln cents from 1909 to date. The Holy Grail was the 1909-S V.D.B. cent, which was worth several dollars. Not many were found, but tens of thousands of penny-board owners had fun trying.

As if the preceding innovations were not enough, Raymond introduced the *Standard Catalogue of United States Coins*. With that, for the first time, one numismatic reference book listed coins from half cents to double eagles, from colonials to commemoratives, and gave mintages (when

Numismatist David M. Sundman and a penny board from the 1930s. These are very collectible today, and much about them has been published in recent times by researcher David W. Lange.

known) and market values. With mintage figures published in that reference and also printed on album pages, all of a sudden collectors realized that certain cents, nickels, and other coins were rare. The 1877 Indian Head and 1909-S V.D.B. cents, the 1885 Liberty Head nickel, and the 1916-D Mercury dime were among such issues that became in great demand.

Almost overnight the coin market changed. In earlier times in the 20th century relatively little attention was paid to mintmarks. Only a few collectors sought them and put them in paper envelopes or trays. Now in the mid-1930s an album or board beckoned, and an empty hole said, in effect, "Fill me!" Within a few years low-mintage coins from the late 19th century onward rose sharply in price, to multiples of what they had sold for in the 1920s. The Depression was anything but for numismatists!

More was to come. In 1935 there were two pivotal events. Lee F. Hewitt, an Illinois publisher, introduced *The Numismatic Scrapbook Magazine*. Unlike *The Numismatist*, which was often filled with authoritative articles on obscure coins, medals, tokens, and bills and which had lengthy reports of club meetings, the *Scrapbook* was chatty, printed letters from lucky finders of 1909-S V.D.B. cents, and concentrated on American coins. Its subscription rolls increased, and soon it had more readers than did the ANA magazine. In Chicago *Hobbies* magazine became very popular and had a section on coins in each issue. Both the *Scrapbook* and *Hobbies* brought thousands of new collectors into the numismatic fold.

The 1935 Hudson Sesquicentennial commemorative half dollar, of which 10,008 were struck.

The Mint had issued commemorative half dollars at intervals since the first Columbian coins of 1892 and 1893. In the 1910s and 1920s many varieties were marketed, usually with unsold leftovers. Coins of the 1928 Hawaiian Sesquicentennial (150th anniversary), of which only 10,000 were offered for sale, were an exception. Offered at $2 each, about half of them were sold to residents of the Hawaiian Islands. The others were snapped up by stateside buyers. Within a short time their market price rose to $5 and $6.

An advertisement for the Hudson half dollars, *Hobbies* magazine, July 1936.

The distributor, the First National Bank & Trust Co. of Hudson, found little local interest in the coins and was perplexed as to what to do with them all.

In 1935 the city of Hudson, New York, decided to celebrate its sesquicentennial with a commemorative half dollar. The Philadelphia Mint struck 10,008 pieces. These were to be sold through the First National Bank & Trust Co. Ten thousand were struck and shipped from the Philadelphia Mint and soon arrived in Hudson, where they were offered at $1 each. There was not much local publicity, and sales were few through the official distributor. Julius Guttag, of the closed Guttag Brothers firm, heard about them, went to Hudson, and offered to buy the unsold remainder for a price said to have been about 85 cents each. The bank was delighted to unload these white elephants.

Not long afterward, announcements and advertisements for the half dollars were published in *Hobbies*, *The Numismatist*, and the *Scrapbook*. Mail orders poured into the bank, but they were all gone. Immediately the market price rose to $5 and more per coin! This engendered a boom that lasted into 1936.

Coinage of mirror-surface Proofs, suspended in 1915, resumed in 1936. Cents, nickels, dimes, quarters, and half dollars could be ordered as a set for $1.91 or individually at various prices. The response was an unstifled yawn, and only 3,837 Proof quarters were ordered, the lowest mintage, which defined the number of full sets that could be assembled.

In 1937 the Treasury Department began melting the gold coins it had on hand. Thomas L. Elder, among others, sent lists of premium prices he would pay to bankers and others who were handling the gold that continued to be surrendered by citizens in exchange for paper money. He was able to save large numbers of coins from the melting pot. In Philadelphia employees of the Mint and the Federal Reserve came in a steady stream to the dealers in New York City, including Stack's, Wayte Raymond, and Abe Kosoff, with rare 1929 to 1933 double eagles that were in storage and slated for melting. They had simply substituted common-date gold coins for them, thus saving even more coins for posterity.[11]

During the Depression years B. Max Mehl advertised his *Star Rare Coin Encyclopedia* in newspapers, in magazines, and even on the radio. Its pages gave buying prices. Anyone lucky enough to find and sell an 1804 dollar could pay for Junior to go to college. Few people found rarities, but a lot of old coins came out of hiding.

All of a sudden in 1944 the Treasury Department declared that 1933 double eagles could not be legally held and set about seizing them. Earlier, such coins had been openly displayed, including at the ANA convention in Washington in 1938, without the slightest problem.

Years later in 1944 the Treasury declared that as 1933 twenties had not been officially released, per their opinion, they were illegal, or almost so. The Smithsonian Institution was allowed to keep the two it had, and one that was purchased by King Farouk of Egypt and sent to him was also held as legal when it is said it resurfaced years later (although not everyone agreed that that coin was the same one once owned by the monarch).

Although the commemorative market was dead or nearly so in the late 1930s, the momentum engendered by the popularity of albums, the *Standard Catalogue*, and hobby magazines continued and expanded. As old dealers died or retired, new faces replaced them.

DYNAMIC CHANGES OF THE 1940S

The Nazi invasions of European countries under dictator Adolf Hitler, the ongoing terrorizing and occupation of China by the Japanese, and the ambitions of Josef Stalin in Russia and Benito Mussolini in Italy and Africa in the late 1930s and early 1940s once again energized the American economy. In 1940 and 1941 factories worked day and night to supply Great Britain, which was suffering greatly, including from devastating air attacks on London. After the Japanese invasion of the American naval base at Pearl Harbor, Hawaii, the United States declared war.

The coin market had been strong since 1940 and became more so. Into the year 1942 commodities such as automobiles, home appliances, and other products were curtailed in their manufacture or discontinued completely in view of the need to make planes, tanks, ships, armored vehicles, and munitions. Home construction nearly stopped in its tracks. Able-bodied workers volunteered for war service or were drafted. Food, gasoline, and other everyday products were rationed.

Consumer goods were scarce. Cash was common. Inflation was everywhere, despite federal efforts to control it.

What to do with the cash? Rare coins offered a store of value and, based on a comparison of *Standard Catalogue* prices in the early 1940s with those in 1934, a seemingly fantastic investment potential. According to dealer Abe Kosoff, the coin

F.C.C. Boyd.

market was turned upside down on September 10 and 11, 1943, when he conducted the auction of the Michael F. Higgy Collection. A bidding frenzy took place, the auction room was up for grabs, and the sky was the limit. Many coins sold for 5 to 10 times their market value of a couple years earlier. Particularly hot were Buffalo nickels.

From that point the market went up and up some more. All dealers did well, and collectors were equally happy as they saw their holdings increase in value. In New York City, Stack's and the Numismatic Gallery (Abe Kosoff and Abner Kreisberg, a partnership formed in 1944) were the leaders in retail sales and also in the conducting of "name" auctions. Robert Friedberg, who operated leased coin outlets in department stores, was another factor. Wayte Raymond was in the twilight of his career and with his wife Olga spent increasing time at their summer home in Montauk at the tip of Long Island. Among collectors F.C.C. Boyd, earlier a rare-coin dealer, later an executive with the Union News Company (with kiosks in railroad stations, airports, and on city streets), was the owner of one of the finest coin collections in America. Mail-order dealers did a land-office business as well. Among these were the Celina Coin Company located in the Ohio city of the same name and the Hollinbeck Coin Company conducted by brothers Arthur and Paul Kagin.

The war in Europe ended with the surrender of Germany in March 1945 and the surrender of Japan in August of the same year. The economic outlook was bright, as pent-up demand for goods and services was soon to be fulfilled.

In November 1946 Whitman Publishing introduced *A Guide Book of United States Coins* with a cover date of 1947 since the new year was so close. Most of the narrative text was done by Stuart Mosher, while Richard S. Yeo, by the nom de plume of *R.S. Yeoman*, was the editor and compiled prices. The book was an instant success. By this time Wayte Raymond was paying less attention to the *Standard Catalogue*. It lost its market dominance quickly, and sales declined. The 17th edition or Raymond's book was published in 1954, and the 18th and final in 1958.[12]

The *Guide Book of United States Coins*, edited by Richard S. Yeo (under the pen name of *R.S. Yeoman*), made its debut in November 1946 with a 1947 cover date. It was an overnight wonder, and a second printing soon followed.

248

Starting in a large way in 1947, consumer goods became available in quantity for the first time since 1941. New houses were built, automobiles were sold, and other elements of peacetime were back in full force. The coin market, which had been in an upswing since the mid-1930s, took a breather. Values, especially for gold and silver coins, dropped, one estimate being that about a 30 percent loss took place over the next several years. Tokens, medals, colonial coins, and other series that had never attracted buyers interested only in investment held their values and even increased. Over the years this has been a steady rule in markets influenced by studious collectors rather than investors.

Prices continued to trend downward into 1948, the depth of the recessive market, continuing into early 1949. In the latter year *Early American Cents*, by William H. Sheldon, was published and immediately attracted a new group of enthusiasts for copper cents.

The Dr. Charles W. Green sale conducted by B. Max Mehl in 1949 was one of the most dynamic and pivotal in the market up to that time. Bids came from all directions, and the prices of many gold coins sold for way over expectations.

In 1949 B. Max Mehl's sale of the Dr. Charles W. Green Collection caused a sensation. Prices set new records! This set the scene for James F. Kelly, a leading dealer with a shop in Dayton, Ohio, to partner with Paul Wittlin to track down American gold coins in the treasuries and bank vaults of foreign countries. These had been shipped to distant places in quantity beginning in the 1870s and continuously after that time, into the early 1930s. When in 1933 President Roosevelt called for American citizens to surrender their gold in exchange for paper money of no equivalent bullion-backed value, foreign owners held on to their gold more strongly than ever!

James F. Kelly in his office, Dayton, Ohio. Kelly was the first person to deal in repatriated gold coins in large quantities.

Switzerland was the first country to be tapped for quantities of gold coins, followed by France. During the Nazi occupation of World War II many gold coins remained underground and it was surprising for me to learn that trading took place on a regular basis.[13] Other countries in Europe, Central America, and South America were explored as well, and many more coins, including former rarities, were located. When starting in the 1960s I called on some banks and government officials in Europe and I learned that they all had copies of the *Guide Book of United States Coins.*

Today, some countries still hold American gold. A representative of Ecuador contacted me early in the present century with information about a large national holding of double eagles. By then they had been picked over by others, and I saw no basis for negotiating a transaction.

After the Dr. Green sale and with an influx of new collectors, the market started on an upward trend.

THE EARLY 1950S

The decade of the 1950s saw the hobby of numismatics evolve in a very dynamic way. In 1950 the market was gaining strength. The Sheldon book on early cents contained philosophies that ranged far beyond that specialty and was an inspiration to explore coins in depth. Copies of Sylvester S. Crosby's 1875 *Early Coins of America* were dusted off, read, and enjoyed. A new order of collectors who enjoyed history was formed. In 1950 Proof coins were minted for the first time since 1942. The price for five coins, cent to half dollar, was $2.10 per set. A total of 51,386 sets was sold in 1950, followed by 57,500 in 1951.

In 1950 Louis E. Eliasberg, a prominent Baltimore banker and financier, did what no one else ever accomplished before and will never do again: he completed his collection of United States coins with every date and mintmark from the 1793 half cent to the 1933 double eagle. Many years later, starting in 1982, I handled this magnificent collection in a series of auction sales.

Louis E. Eliasberg and his collection.

A lot of excitement was injected into the marketplace in 1951 when it was realized that in 1950 only 2,630,030 nickels were made at the Denver Mint. By May 1951 a $2 face value bank-wrapped roll of 1950-D nickels was worth $6. In *The Numismatic Scrapbook Magazine* one dealer advertised: "1950-D Nickels. Hectic! Write for prices."

Perhaps the most exciting single variety in the history of coin investment: the 1950-D nickel.

WANTED FOR IMMEDIATE CASH

THE MOST OVER-RATED U.S. COIN:

1950-D NICKELS IN ROLLS

When the 1946-S was actually selling at $15.00 to $18.00 per roll I said the coin "Will come down," it did, I said the same thing about the 1948-S Nickel, it also came down. This Nickel will do the same way for this reason: 2,630,000 made and at least 75% of those released have gone into the hands of dealers and collectors, That is too many for the collecting public to absorb. Just give it time it will go up and down as the other two have done. I Say "Buy with caution." My customers say BUY FOR ME anywhere from 1 roll to 50 rolls, and we have many customers, trying to please them I will buy from 1 up to 250 rolls of this nickel at $3.00 per roll delivered to me. First come, first served. We have no rolls when this ad is being written.

We do have Mint Sets 1950-P-D-S, also a wonderful buy on Mint Set Holders for Small American Binders. Holds 3 sets 1c, 5c, 10c, 25c, 50c, 30 openings. Price 70c. Order by Number 1461-A.

Paying more than catalogue for many choice Proof Double Eagles. Top prices for all kinds of Rare U.S. Gold and Private Gold Coins. Sold 6 slugs in the past 60 days, also many other Rare Private Issues, including the J.S. Ormsby $10.00; We paid $4500.00 for this coin.

Bargain List No. 41 is out. Did you get your copy? Free for the asking.

R. GREEN

Life Member A.N.A. 118   Tel. HArrison 7-9645

220 South State Street—Suite 1402-04   Chicago 4, Illinois

R. Green had no 1950-D nickels at all in February 1951 and was not sure if they were to be a boom or bust! Ruth Green was the name on the business run by Charles Green, her husband, a World War I veteran. Green sure called the bet wrong! By May, Herbert Feinberg, a dealer in rolls, offered rolls of 1950-D nickels for $6 each and was overwhelmed with orders. Years later in 1964 rolls sold for over $1,200.

This was an easy call for newcomers: Buy some low-mintage rare coins in high grades, and a profit is assured. And, it seemed to be. What else to buy? Bank-wrapped rolls of other coins from cents to half dollars were easily available back to 1935 with some of 1934 being available. Many had been saved in quantity during the exciting mid-1930s when albums became available and many new collectors appeared. In the *Scrapbook* in particular, several dealers specialized in such rolls. Newcomers took a look at Proof sets minted from 1936 onward, and the market warmed up for these and production figures increased. Silver commemoratives made from 1892 onward were nearly always found in Mint State and became hot tickets as well. Exceptions were Booker T. Washington half dollars of 1946 to 1951 and the new Carver-Washington halves made since the latter date. These were not popular at all.

MY EXPERIENCES IN
THE COIN MARKET:
A PERSONAL
SCRAPBOOK

This chapter is more of a personal scrapbook narrative than a view from a distance of what was going on in numismatics and in the marketplace. How I wish that B. Max Mehl, the Stack brothers, and others who spent decades of their lives in as professional numismatists would have recorded their experiences. I once suggested this to B. Max, and he said, "Why don't *you* write it for me?" I suppose that I should have gone down to Fort Worth, note pad in hand, and spent a few days with him. But I never did.

One did—Abe Kosoff—in "Abe Kosoff Remembers," a long-running column in *Coin World* followed by reprinting in book form. Were it not for Abe we would never have known what went on behind the scenes in Cairo when the American contingent attended the sale of deposed King Farouk's vast holdings of rare United States and other coins.

Two others have left a nice trail. In modern times Harvey Stack has shared a lot of his experiences through the Internet via Stack's Bowers Galleries and *The E-Sylum*. Years ago I gathered a tremendous amount of information from John J. Ford Jr., which I assembled in a large narrative file, as yet unpublished. I only knew what he elected to tell me, and that did not include his activities with Paul Franklin in the discovery of hitherto unknown Western gold ingots and privately minted gold coins. After reading the exposé of that scenario in Karl Moulton's book, *John J. Ford, Jr., and the Franklin Hoard*, "privately minted" took on new meaning.

Another who has left a brilliant partial trail on the specialty of collecting large copper cents is John W. Adams, whose adventures in that regard have been chronicled in detail in the pages of *Penny-Wise*, the journal of Early American Coppers, a nonprofit collectors' organization (online at www.EACS.org).

The above said, on to my experiences as a collector, dealer, and researcher, along with other aspects of numismatics, from my early teenage years up to the present time. You are permitted to close this book at this point and go to the next volume on your nightstand. Or, you can follow me and explore some events in my life.

BORN TO BE A COLLECTOR

It was in 1952 that I discovered what many have called the world's greatest hobby. Yes, a hobby. A pastime. A pleasant diversion. At the time I was 13 years old and a student at Forty Fort (Pennsylvania) High School. By then I had been a hobbyist in other fields for quite a few years.

Collecting is a born instinct, not learned, it has been said. I believe that. In rare coins I have found that those immersing themselves in numismatics have a collecting instinct, a born curiosity. In contrast, many have spouses or other family members who are not the slightest bit interested in collecting anything at all. To each his (or her) own.

My first collection was picture postcards. In third grade I was given two cards—one showing Skyline Drive in Virginia and the other depicting the summit of Pikes Peak. How romantic, I thought. I could travel all around the United States by collecting cards. I made my interest known to others, and before long I had several hundred. I looked at and studied each one, and many times I tracked down more information in a Rand McNally atlas. I still love postcards. In 1990 with Mary L. Martin I wrote *The Postcards of Alphonse Mucha*, which in its second edition (2016) is still the standard reference worldwide on the master of Art Nouveau. The new edition was also with Mary L. Martin, but not the "original," who no longer lives. The second time around it was with her identically named daughter, who today conducts what is probably the largest worldwide business in that hobby.

By the time I was 13 I had studied and collected in several different areas. I loved books, and read all of the Hardy Boys and Tom Swift novels, and all 56 Sherlock Holmes short stories and 4 novels. "A Study in Scarlet," the first Holmes story, was pivotal in expanding my thinking—how a collection of words could arouse strong emotions.

I had many books in my library, including the marvelous adventure stories written by Richard Halliburton, texts on astronomy, world travel, and dinosaurs, and a nice selection of books on reptiles. Raymond Ditmars's *The Reptiles of North America* was a favorite. Each snake, lizard, and turtle was described in detail, with its Latin name, habits, and characteristics. I tracked down all of Ditmars's other books, including adventures looking for reptiles in Trinidad and other places. Eager to learn more, I visited the New York Zoological Park (Bronx Zoo) where he had once been in charge of such species. I telephoned his widow and talked with her. I also contacted and talked with Ross Allen, who had a tourist attraction in Silver Springs, Florida, and who had published a book. This was my first entry into widespread research. In the meantime I had a small collection of reptiles including a garter snake, a DeKay's snake, and several baby wood turtles (which I captured as they emerged from their eggs in a sandy spot at Camp Acahela), and snapping turtles.

I enjoyed the unusual and read Robert Ripley's "Believe It or Not" syndicated column in the local Wilkes-Barre *Times Leader* paper. I was also an entrepreneur of sorts. I delivered newspapers, cut grass, sold programs at ball games, pulled weeds, raked leaves, and collected scrap metal to sell. I liked speaking as well. In eighth grade I was captain of our debate team, and in a contest we beat our senior opponents. The subject was North American radar defense against the threat of Russian aircraft coming to America via the Arctic. For George Washington's Birthday in 1952 I gave an oration in the school auditorium to about 300 students—"Things You Didn't Know About Our First President."

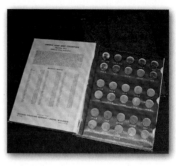

The inside cover and first page of Robert Rusbar's Whitman album for Lincoln cents.

Other interests included fossils, rocks, and minerals, which I often collected with my schoolmate Bob King as we tramped sandpits and hillsides. Someone told me that Robert Rusbar, the town tax collector for Forty Fort, had a nice collection of these. I paid a visit and admired his various specimens. He then asked if I collected coins. I said that I did not, whereupon he showed me a Whitman album with a 1909 penny for which he had paid Gimbel's department store $10. He explained that it was made at the San Francisco Mint, had an S mintmark to prove that, and on the back were the letters V.D.B., for Victor David Brenner, the coin's designer. I became excited as all get-out! He gave me two Whitman folders, and off I went to find a bunch of these valuable coins. Certainly, within a week I would have quite a few!

I never did find a 1909-S V.D.B. cent, but the "coin bug" bit me, and after I learned how to pronounce *numismatist* I became one. The 1953 edition (dated one year in advance) of *A Guide Book of United States Coins* was my passport to a life of numismatic adventure!

I set about building a nice library of coin books, getting every back copy I could of *The Numismatic Scrapbook Magazine* and *The Numismatist*, and reading as much as I could. I learned of George Williams, an insurance agent in the neighboring town of Kingston. He took a liking to me, showed me his collection, and took me to the monthly meetings of the Wilkes-Barre Coin Club held in the next town over. His collection was marvelous, and I spent hours looking at coins the likes of which I had never seen—early half dollars of the Capped Bust design, silver-dollar–size "crowns" of the world, and more. He would have shown me his rare 1895 Proof Morgan dollar, he said apologetically, "but Joe Stack came into town from New York City and offered me two hundred dollars—an offer I had no choice but to accept."

In 1952 the market was very active. I did not know anything about the past so did not know it had been in a slump and now was in a recovery mode.

In that year in Iola, Wisconsin, Chester L. Krause began publishing *Numismatic News*, a monthly trading sheet mostly composed of classified advertisements, although I did not know much about it at the time. A decade later the *News* was published weekly, and with Clifford Mishler as a co-executive Krause Publications grew to become an empire that issued newspapers and magazines in several fields and created a number of important reference books. Among the latter the Krause-Mishler *Standard Catalog of World Coins* became an international standard, a status it still enjoys today.

Members of the Wilkes-Barre Coin Club picked up on my enthusiasm, and before long I was given piles of old auction catalogs, books, and magazines by members who no longer needed them. Such had no commercial value, except that I once paid $3 for a copy of B. Max Mehl's gold-foil-cover 1941 Dunham sale catalog.

Auction catalogs by Stack's and the Numismatic Gallery, the two leaders in the field, typically had brief descriptions of coins—often one line, rarely a paragraph. Many illustrations were "stock" or standard and were repeatedly used, not showing the coins actually sold. Mehl's mail-bid catalogs were similar, although some of his past catalogs devoted a lot of space to rarities. His salesmanship had no equal. The tersest of all were the mail-bid catalogs of the Hollinbeck Coin Co. Auctions and mail-bid sales were held by others as well. At an earlier time Thomas L. Elder, by the 1950s retired, boasted that he could catalog a thousand coins per day!

In reading through old catalogs I learned that brevity in print changed, and dramatically, in 1952 when John J. Ford Jr. of the New Netherlands Coin Company engineered an arrangement of four dealers with different specialties to prepare a catalog for the annual ANA convention held that year in New York City. Working with his employee Walter Breen, Ford created the American coin section of the sale in the form of detailed descriptions, even of relatively common coins of modest value. Whereas a sentence was standard, Ford and Breen used a paragraph. Included were market notes, remarks (often snide or veiled), and more. "Back room boys" secretly scrubbed, cleaned, and improved coins, it was said. Of course, no one at New Netherlands would dream of doing any such thing, as the firm continually reminded readers, touting its high ethical standards. All if this made interesting reading. Collectors loved it!

2195   1840. NA-2. Small date; 8 double struck. MS-65. Mostly red. Lists at $12.00 so, in the Guidebook. ($10.00)
2196   1841. NA-1. Brilliant red Proof. Almost perfect, with slight indications of tarnish upon the obverse. Equal to the Pearl specimen which was sold for $65.00. Ex Hines coll. Plate. ($55.00)
2197   — N-7. Mint State-60. Magnificent iridescent olive; flecked with russet. H.K.D. marked this variety as rare. Ex Hines coll. ($10.00)
2198   1842. NA-1. Small date. Choice iridescent Proof. Minute rim bruise, at the top of reverse. Sharp and perfectly centered. A very pretty and rare coin. Neither Pearl nor Newcomb had a specimen of this date in Proof. Exceedingly rare, in fact equal in actual rarity to that of any cent. The only other Proof example is in the Mint collection. Ex Hines coll. Plate. ($50.00)
2199   — NA-6. Large date. Uncirculated; MS-65. Glittering olive and red, with considerable mint lustre upon the reverse. From a U.S. Coin Co. (W. Raymond) sale of 2/10/15; later, from Hines. ($7.50)

The New Netherlands Coin Company section of the 1952 ANA convention catalog featured information-packed descriptions the likes of which had not been seen before. Shown are several lots cataloged by Walter Breen and edited by John J. Ford Jr.

In time John Ford became a close friend, and we shared a lot of enthusiasm about American numismatic history and tradition, often at his home at 176 Hendrickson Avenue, in Rockville Centre, New York, where he had a magnificent library and collection. Over a period of later years I was given unlimited access to study his collection and make notes. Many coins, medals, and tokens were in original boxes and envelopes acquired when he bought the estate collections of F.C.C. Boyd from widow Helen and the estate collection of Wayte Raymond from widow Olga. John's main interest was in coins and ingots from the California Gold Rush, and he sent his associate Paul Franklin on the earlier-mentioned many trips to the West. In the process many amazing new discoveries were found. I was not involved in that specialty at this early time, so did not play close attention to his activities in that area. Paul Franklin was a familiar figure at coin shows. I remember him as always wearing a blue work shirt.

As the years went by, other auction catalogers gave detailed descriptions as well. Today as you read these words many coin catalogs contain descriptions that lot for lot are multiple times longer than are listings in catalogs for other collectibles of comparable value such as stamps, art, antiques, and prints. (Catalogs for autographs, early books, and historical documents can be exceptions and are often quite detailed.)

In the early and mid-1950s, as knowledge of past profits spread, more collectors were born. The typical newcomer entered with the hope of seeing his (usually) or her coins increase in value, but also became fairly knowledgeable. Collecting only Uncirculated and Proof coins was easy, as no knowledge of grading was needed. As noted earlier, there were no divisions in such as Mint State–60, 61, etc. There were no grading standards, so advanced collectors could argue as to whether a 1794 cent was Very Fine or Extremely Fine, but for Uncirculated and Proof issues that was not necessary. It was standard practice for early copper half cents and cents to use a camel-hair brush on their surfaces every now and then (such hairs being soft and not leaving lines) or to gently rub them with a cloth dipped in mineral oil.

The *Guide Book of United States Coins* remained my main source for market information, but the *Numismatic Scrapbook Magazine* was the place to go for information about rising prices that sometimes left the *Guide Book of United States Coins* values behind. The monthly arrival of the *Scrapbook* was as exciting as all get-out. When it arrived I dropped everything to read it cover-to-cover.

The first coin I ever ordered through the mail was an Indian Head cent—an 1859 Proof from the Copley Coin Company, run by Maurice Gould and Frank Washburn in Boston. The price paid was $11, the full market price. It was a glittering little gem. What a treasure! I liked my beautiful Proof 1859 cent and decided to buy some other Proofs to go along with it. I recall contemplating an 1877 offered for $90, but passed it by in favor of buying most of the later, more common dates from 1879 to 1909 at $2.50 to $3.50 each. My funds were modest, and I needed to make every dollar count. Urban C. Thobe sold me many by mail, and William L. Pukall did likewise. Pukall later provided Proofs in wholesale quantities. He seemed to have an endless supply dated from the 1880s onward, plus Matte Proof Lincoln cents from 1909 to 1916. I also bought some wonderfully strange and esoteric Hard Times tokens from him.

The rest, as they say, is history.

In time I explored just about every American numismatic specialty—every nook and cranny, or at least the majority of them, usually by reading—as my finances were limited for purchases. Learning new things kept my interest intense. I also loved and still love the history of collecting, and today when I learn a new scrap of information it is as exciting as ever. From that time onward my knowledge of coins in the market was not from history but was from first-hand experience.

STARTING AS A DEALER

By 1953 I was a rare-coin dealer—in a small way, part time—at the age of 14. I bought, sold, and traded. Not old enough to have a driver's license, I took the bus or rode my Schwinn bicycle to track down leads that people furnished me. At the Wilkes-Barre Coin Club I bought and sold a lot. At every meeting there was an auction. The rule was that if no collector bid, I as a dealer would be allowed to raise my hand. I remember buying a prooflike Gem 1879 Liberty Seated half dollar. At another time Dr. Albert Thomas brought his Raymond album filled with cents from 1793 to date. He allowed me to hold in my hand his 1799 Draped Bust and 1856 Flying Eagle varieties. How exciting!

Pattern coins became my first major specialty. At the time the most recent reference book was the Adams-Woodin text published in 1913, and few dealers knew about or cared about such coins. I bought all of the patterns I could find for reasonable prices, and soon I had several dozen customers who bought from me regularly. My main sources of supply were dealers Abe Kosoff in California and Sol Kaplan in Cincinnati. Although I never said as much, I gave the impression that I was well financed or my family was. In actuality

In the 1950s few dealers handled pattern coins. The transitional 1859 cent with the shield reverse of 1860, cataloged as Adams-Woodin 336 (today's Judd-228), was one of my favorites. Often these could be found among regular 1859 cents in inventories.

we were of modest circumstances. My father Quentin was a civil engineer and worked in architecture and engineering. The secret to my handling many rare coins was to turn them over quickly. Within two weeks I could usually sell nearly all from an incoming shipment of, say, 100 patterns.

After school hours and on weekends I kept very busy with my growing business. When the impending sale in Egypt of the deposed King Farouk's collection was announced, Abe Kosoff called in December 1953 to ask if he could represent me! In truth, I had little capital to spare. I suggested that if he bought many things he should offer coins to me when he returned from Cairo. Early the next year when the Palace Collections (as they were called) were auctioned, about a dozen American collectors and dealers flew to Egypt to attend. Great rarities were lumped hodge-podge with common coins, such as the 1913 Liberty Head nickel being sold as part of a nickel set; descriptions were sparse and often incomplete; and arrangements with bidders were unusual. Most of the copper and silver coins had been cleaned with silver polish. Many American coins sold for pennies on the dollar.

Ever since 1944 Abner Kreisberg had been a partner with Kosoff in the Numismatic Gallery. In Cairo, Kosoff and Kaplan partnered on purchases, not involving Kreisberg, who seems to have been closed out. Numismatic Gallery was dissolved soon afterward—the end of a dynamic auction house. I bought a lot of the Farouk patterns from both Kosoff and Kaplan. The latter had a background in the stamp business and also dealt in securities. When at a convention I asked if he had a 1915-S Panama-Pacific set of five commemoratives, he replied that he did not, but would sell me one "short." I was to pay an agreed price, and he would find one and deliver it. I declined as I said I wanted to examine each coin carefully first. This was sort of strange for him to hear, as for gold and silver commemorative coins "Uncirculated" was the standard description, and whether a coin had nicks or marks was not important. How curious this seems to relate today!

By 1954 the market was very strong in all sectors. A 1936 Proof set commanded $100. The race for sets was in overdrive, the Mint limited new orders, and the prices of older sets increased sharply. In 1955 a 1936 Proof set cost $300, and many bank-wrapped rolls sold for several times their value of just a few years earlier.

By that time I was going to regional coin shows and meetings, including the Empire State Numismatic Association, whose conventions were staged in the Hotel Syracuse in the city of the same name. I met and enjoyed talking with such veteran collectors as Fiori Pepito, Kenneth J. Santoris, David Nethaway, Jacob Cheris, John J. Pittman, Charles and Arline French, Kenneth Fuller, and Charles Foster. The last was nicknamed "Suitcase Foster," as he carried his inventory in a leather case. He was one of the most friendly and helpful dealers I ever met. In the spring of 1955 I set up as a dealer with my inventory at the first Metropolitan New York Coin Show.

It might have been there that I bought for $200 each two rare Proof half cents of the 1840s from Louis S. Werner, who advertised as "Money Back Werner." When I returned home I sent them on approval to a private client, Lester Merkin, who returned them saying that they were very clever electrotype copies, which could be detected if I took a magnifying glass to see a tiny seam on the edge. I was embarrassed. I mailed them back to Werner, who said that as I had seen them before buying them, there would be no refund! Such were the events that gave me a lot of experience in "survival" in the marketplace.[1]

In 1955 the Philadelphia Mint struck about 40,000 Lincoln cents from an obverse die in which the features were doubled during the die-making process. By the time the offending die was identified, about

The date on a 1955 doubled-die cent.

24,000 coins had been sent off to be shipped, most being sent by the Federal Reserve Bank to the Boston area, to western Massachusetts, and to and around Johnson City and Binghamton, New York. In Johnson City dealer Jim Ruddy was intrigued with bright, new Lincoln cents that had the obverse features doubled, as LLIIBBEERRT-TYY and 11995555, that were brought to his attention. These made news in the local paper, and he announced he would pay 25 cents each for them. Within a short time he had all he wanted, and stopped buying. At the time there was hardly any interest in mint errors, and no references concerning them, and they were usually called "freaks."[2] The 1955 coins, which became listed in the *Guide Book of United States Coins* and were called Doubled Die cents, were the catalyst in changing all of that. Today, mint errors are a vital part of numismatics, and a gem 1955 doubled-die cent is worth thousands of dollars.

THE MID-1950S

In the mid-1950s Uncirculated and Proof coins presented few problems in grading to most collectors and dealers. To be Uncirculated a coin could not have any wear on the higher areas. It could have nicks and bagmarks, however. Sometimes the phrase "cabinet friction" was used if a coin had slight rubbing. However, it was more conservative to call such a piece About Uncirculated. Proofs were also easy to identify—a Philadelphia Mint coin with deeply mirrored fields, exceptions being certain Matte Proofs of the early 20th century.

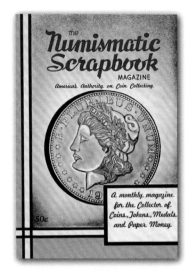

To be About Uncirculated a coin needed to have nearly full original luster and just a small amount of wear. An Extremely Fine coin had little or no luster, but was sharp in all details such as hair strands and leaf veins. Very Fine coins were a step below. Fine coins were noticeably worn but had

In the 1950s *Numismatic Scrapbook Magazine* was the prime source for market news and listings of coins for sale.

all lettering visible, such as LIBERTY in the headband on Indian Head cents and Barber silver coins. Very Good coins were lower, and Good described a coin that was basically identifiable but lacked details.

Although some coins listed as Uncirculated or Proof had problems, I always had an eye for quality. This proved to be very beneficial when buying. I recall visiting the home-office of Arthur Conn in Melrose, Massachusetts. As one of the leading dealers of the time he had the double-spread centerfold in each issue of *The Numismatic Scrapbook Magazine*. Commemorative coins were one of his specialties. During my stay he showed me his inventory. I looked through the coins and cherrypicked those that today would be called gems. All of his dozens of Uncirculated 1900 Lafayette dollars, for example, were priced the same. I picked out the best, for no extra cost.

Lotions, potions, and pastes galore were advertised and promoted to clean and polish coins, as they had been for many years. The August 1955 issue of *The Numismatist* included this:

> BRILLIANTIZE. Makes copper, silver, brass, nickel, and gold coins brilliant instantly and will also clean up the 1943 cents. Its results are truly amazing. Regular size kit $1. . . . Each Brilliantize kit contains a bottle of Brilliantize No. 1 which brilliantizes tarnished coins immediately, and Brilliantize No. 2 which makes old and stained coins brilliant and makes this brilliancy long lasting.

Among coin buyers in the 1950s there were some for whom low cost was the most important consideration. My prices were usually at or close to full market, but my coins were, in my opinion, of above-average quality and always with good eye appeal. I offered no "below wholesale" (whatever that means) coins, although I always gave a courtesy discount to established dealers. Accordingly, I did not attract bargain hunters. I did, however, have nearly all of the advanced and sophisticated collectors as my clients.

Collectors who bought so-called bargains, "bottom feeders" in modern parlance, usually could sell their coins only at low prices when they decide to dispose of their collections. I could tell many stories of unhappy campers with sub-par coins, as could owners of other rare-coin auction houses.

In 1955 the Professional Numismatists Guild (PNG), conceived by Abe Kosoff and his Cincinnati associate Sol Kaplan in 1953, was formally organized. Its first official meeting was held at the annual ANA convention in Omaha. Kosoff, who by that time was one of my best suppliers as well as a great dealer customer, said that when I attained the legal age of 18 I could become a PNG member.

The Professional Numismatists Guild logotype.

Convention badge from the August 1955 show in Omaha.

This was the first ANA show I attended as one of 45 bourse dealers. As I was not of legal age I could not join the ANA either. As a class, young numismatists were perceived by many as a nuisance—they asked a lot of questions, did not buy much, and could not make legal contracts. Despite such stuff, executive secretary Lewis M. Reagan let me set up after getting a letter from my father guaranteeing my transactions and a letter from Lee F. Hewitt stating that he had never had a complaint about me as an advertiser in *The Numismatic Scrapbook Magazine*. The attendance crossed the 500 mark for the first time. None of the other dealers who had tables is still alive today.

The PNG in the early years was more or less an invitation-only private club. Membership applications were not wanted. The meetings held in conjunction with coin shows were always conducted by Abe Kosoff and Sol Kaplan and involved a lot of jokes and hilarity spiced by some profanity, especially in adjectival descriptions of certain non-member dealers and their activities. Earl Parker, a well-known San Francisco dealer, usually spent some time in a bar before attending meetings and often had to be told to sit down, after expounding at length on one usually irrelevant subject or another. Everyone dressed in business suits—not an option—a standard also required at conventions and public auctions of the time.

PNG founder Abe Kosoff and executive director Paul Koppenhaver with PNG president Dave Bowers presenting an award to Kosoff at the Numismatic Association of Southern California Convention, January 27, 1979.

REPUTATION - - -

A good reputation is an enviable honor. It cannot be bought, sold, traded, or otherwise acquired part way through life, or in the midst of a business career. It is elemental, and exists or does not exist at the beginning. A good reputation grows. It starts with the first person to whom you are known or with whom you deal, and expands throughout your career as you come into contact with more people. It must be maintained at all times or it ceases to exist.

•

I enjoy numismatics, and my pleasant dealings with the increasing number of you who write to buy or to sell is a constant inspiration. I buy and sell coins on the basis of fairness and my best judgment of value to both parties. If you have coins to sell, I will be pleased to buy at a price which reflects the true quality and value of your material, and will pay cash immediately. Your correspondence is invited.

•

If you are not already on my mailing list, send me a card and you will receive my periodical bulletins as they are issued, listing choice coins for sale.

•

Q. DAVID BOWERS
203 Second National Bank Bldg.   Wilkes-Barre, Pa.
Tel. VAlley 3-8478

My October 1955 advertisement in The *Numismatist.*

In the early 1960s the gates of the PNG were opened to all qualified dealers who demonstrated experience and subscribed to a code of ethics. I joined in 1958 and years later was president from 1977 to 1979, of which I will say more later.

In the mid- and late 1950s I continued to be a regular advertiser in the *Scrapbook* and *The Numismatist*. In New York City Stack's and the New Netherlands Coin Company held regular auctions, and I usually was in attendance. In autumn 1955 I published my first printed catalog.

In this era the market for Proof sets knew no bounds. Sol Kaplan in particular, and others, posted bid and ask prices. In the spring of 1956 the momentum slowed, many owners of sets decided to take profits, and the market crashed. The 1936 set, which had peaked at $600, collapsed to $300. As was true of all past boom-and-bust cycles, the commemorative craze of 1935 and 1936 being an example, in time the values increased. Today, all U.S. Uncirculated and Proof coins, regular issues and commemoratives, are worth many multiples more than they were in at the height of the market 1956. This demonstrates the general rule that yesterday's peak market price is usually today's bargain. For those who have the rare courage to buy when the market drops, the gains are even greater.

I enjoyed my rare-coin business, was in touch with most dealers and leading collectors, and was still learning. With my Royal typewriter on my desk and a supply of letterheads and envelopes I was an avid correspondent not only with clients, but with those interested in research and study. As a mailing address I used my father's civil-engineering office upstairs in the Second National Bank Building in Wilkes-Barre.

By this time I was well on my way with interviewing old-timers and making notes, as numismatic history continued to be one of my strongest interests. I captured much information that would have otherwise been lost forever. As an example, Abe Kosoff told me that in the 1940s, when King Farouk was his best customer, if the monarch spent $10,000 or more on a collectible (he also bought art, jewelry, pornography, and other things) the payment had to be made through the Egyptian Treasury. To circumvent this, if an invoice for coins ran into the tens of thousands of dollars, his company, the Numismatic Gallery, sent multiple invoices for $9,999 each! I don't know of anyone else who gathered this kind of insider information.

A reporter interviewing me in 1956.

Around this time I was contacted by the Wyoming Historical and Genealogical Society of Wilkes-Barre. Founded in 1858, it had gathered a quantity of miscellaneous coins over the years, mostly through the efforts of Horace E. Hayden, the librarian. The society commissioned me to evaluate and sell them. I did this, and in exchange gave them a type set of federal coins—a selection of various coins, hardly complete, up to the Saint-Gaudens double eagle. Among their holdings was a pasteboard box filled with Canadian coins from 1858 onward—a miscellaneous assortment. Try as I might I could find no dealer interested in Canadian coins. Someone suggested that John J. Pittman, a well-known collector in Rochester, New York, might be interested. I sent them to him and he responded with a nice offer.

In 1957 with Jim Ruddy I conducted the Penn–New York Auction, a mail-bid sale. This was my first such event and was a great success.

In 1957 in Stack's sale of the Empire Collection I paid $4,750 for "one thin dime," an 1894-S. Newspaper stories ran nationwide, and I was invited to be a guest on the NBC *Today Show*. The network put me up for a three-day stay at the Waldorf-Astoria.

By that time I had gone to New York City often, to make the rounds of the dealers and to attend sales. After auctions the standard place to have a late dinner was Mamma Leone's restaurant. It was not uncommon for a dozen or more dealers to go there and sit near each other. The maître d' was a nice fellow who recognized most of us and would tell us stories—such as about the restaurant catering dinners at the Eisenhower farm in Gettysburg. At Stack's auctions I often helped the staff carry boxes of blank invoices and supplies from the gallery at 123 West 57th Street to upstairs in Steinway Hall next door. Harvey and his father Morton were always very nice to me. I did not know Morton's brother Joseph very well, and Norman Stack was usually out of sight in his office cataloging or working on coins. Benjamin Stack was there in the early 1950s, then headed off to Las Vegas where he operated the Imperial Coin Company. Ben had a gambling streak. Once he offered me a high-grade 1855 Wass, Molitor & Company $50 gold coin for $1,500. I was about to write a check when he said, "How about double or nothing?" He flipped the coin (which handed on a soft spot) and lost.

Paying $4,750 for a dime.
Imagine that!

The first issue of *Empire Topics*.

Jim Ruddy and me selling coins
to Arthur M. Kagin (center) at the
1959 ANA convention in Portland,
Oregon. Art selected coins of
interest, he handed them to me for
pricing, and then Jim compiled an
invoice for items sold.

The banquet of the Metropolitan New York Numismatic
Convention on May 3, 1958. I usually attended most of the state
and regional shows in the East in the 1950s.

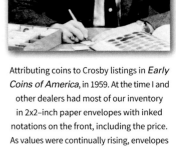

Attributing coins to Crosby listings in *Early
Coins of America*, in 1959. At the time I and
other dealers had most of our inventory
in 2x2-inch paper envelopes with inked
notations on the front, including the price.
As values were continually rising, envelopes
had to be changed regulars—usually in July,
when the latest edition of the *Guide Book
of United States Coins* was released.

In 1958 Jim Ruddy and I formed the Empire
Coin Company, which became well-known
almost overnight, as we both had been active
in the business for several years. Our *Empire
Topics* magazine was very popular and included
research articles by Eric P. Newman, Kenneth Bressett, and Walter Breen,
among others. I wrote most of the issues while a student at Penn State.[3]

The market in 1958 and 1959 was strong in all series, including Proof sets in
a recovery mode. The 1950-D nickel roll was the bellwether by which many judged
the strength of the investment section of the market. The price zipped past $100.
By that time Harry J. Forman, who in Philadelphia began his dealership in 1955,
was the leading seller of rolls and Proof sets. Jonah Shapiro of Syracuse, New York,
was an important dealer as well. Both attended a lot of conventions. Several other
dealers were important as well, as suppliers of coins to investors.

The New York Numismatic Club held monthly meetings in Keen's English Chop House. On occasion I was a guest there, such as in the company of Ambassador R. Henry Norweb. He and his wife, Emery May, took a liking to me. I visited them at their summer home in Boothbay Harbor, Maine, and also in New York City where at the River House they had the entire top floor—with *Time* magazine founder Henry Luce occupying the next floor down. Their other residence was in a mansion on the shore of Lake Erie in the small town of Bratenahl. I recall that a Nike anti-missile installation was put up near that house, and the Norwebs objected, but to no avail. Euclid Beach Park with its rides and attractions was a short drive away. (I always liked amusement parks and visited many over a period of years.)

THE CHANGES OF THE 1960S

In 1960 the old order changed. Traditional numismatics gave way to a market dominated by investors, as it remains today. Warm personal relationships with many others in the dealer community became less frequent. For many it was business and business only, no sentiment needed. To be sure, on the collector side the traditional numismatists who read books, studied their coins, and appreciated their art, history, romance, and other considerations were still a part of the hobby and increased in numbers. Such were the very foundation of my business. However, most newcomers were interested in investment only. Silver and gold coins (never copper and only sometimes nickel) were the objects of desire. "Investment grade" was defined as only Uncirculated (a term that gradually gave way to *Mint State*) and Proof. Any other coins, an Extremely Fine 1793 cent being an example, created no investment interest at all.

The first issue of *Coin World,* April 21, 1960.

Two factors energized the change that year. In Ohio, J. Oliver Amos, owner of the Sidney Printing & Publishing Company, with its *Sidney Daily News*, had been printing *Linn's Stamp News* on contract for many years. Each week thousands of copies were mailed out. Suitably inspired, Amos had a meeting with his staff and also contacted outsiders to develop a related hobby publication that he could own and publish. The winners were A, B, and C: antiques, bowling, and coins. Coins won, and *Coin World* was the result. Launched in early 1960, it was the first numismatic publication to be issued on a weekly basis. Sample copies were sent out, and subscriptions exceeded expectations.

Not long afterward the news was spread that 1960 Lincoln cents made early in the year had a Small Date (capitalized in numismatic usage), a style which was soon changed to the Large Date. The Small Date coins were publicized, and a mad scramble ensued to find them. They proved to be relatively scarce. In several transactions $50 face value bags were sold for $10,000 to $20,000. This was like finding gold in the streets. The story was picked up by broadcast and print media, including a feature in *Time* magazine. Almost overnight rare coins came into national focus. *Coin World* was in the right place at the right time, and within two years the subscription rolls crossed the 150,000 mark.

D. Wayne (Dick) Johnson, founding editor, resigned when his salary increase request was not accepted, and Margo Russell, a reporter for the *Sidney Daily News*, took his place. She had been a helper with *Coin World* since its founding. Margo learned quickly and by the time of her retirement in 1984 was one of the most accomplished figures in numismatics. "Trends," a feature on market activities and prices, was prepared by James F. Kelly, the well-known Dayton dealer.

In the early days before the newspaper had its own experts on staff I was the main consultant for matters involving numismatic history and the authentication of new varieties (such as the 1938-D Over S overmintmark Buffalo nickel and the 1858 Over Inverted Date half dime). In 1961 my weekly "Numismatic Depth Study" column began, later renamed "The Joy of Collecting." It is still popular today, the longest-running column in the worldwide history of numismatics. Upon reflection, this is hard to believe!

IN EUROPE

In the 1960s I was a frequent visitor to Europe, often traveling with Jim Ruddy on behalf of the Empire Coin Company. We would advertise in *The Exchange and Mart* as well as in banking magazines. Our stays in London were usually for two weeks. Jim would be in residence in our hotel suite at the Dorchester or Hilton and receive a steady stream of sellers in our suite. I would hire

I traveled here, there, and all over—a passport page.

a car and driver and go around the countryside. During one of our visits film star Elizabeth Taylor was staying at the Dorchester and created a lot of attention. Across the street was Hyde Park Corner, a grassy area where on weekends various people stood and gave orations on diverse subjects, often political. The rule was not to say anything to offend the queen.

In one of my travels around the British countryside I recall stopping at Stonehenge, the ancient ruins I had read about. The monoliths were in a field, unmarked and with livestock grazing. On another trip I stayed at a small inn in Kirkby Lonsdale and was told by the proprietor that no Americans had been there since World War II. Heat in my room was provided by dropping shillings into the coin slot of an electric fan. Another time I visited the home of a collector who had some American Proof sets from the 1880s and other United States coins, included half cents and large cents. He and his wife served lunch, and we had a nice visit. I admired the hall clock in his living room. He said he was thinking of selling. I expressed interest, and he said he would let me know. Not long afterward I received a notice from an attorney in his town that my friend had passed away, and in his final illness had willed the clock to me. How did I want it shipped? Before I could make arrangements, he wrote again to say that the family refused to honor the request. That was okay, as I had not expected such a gift anyway.

On one trip in mid-December I went to Torquay on the coast and around eight in the evening checked into the Grand Hotel, an imposing Victorian edifice. As I signed in I noticed that there were no other names on the register. I was the only guest that evening, I was told. Only part of the third floor was heated, and I was assigned a room there. I then went to the dining room and was seated. As I was by myself (my driver having made other arrangements), I invited the restaurant manager to sit with me as company. "I am not allowed to do that, sir," he graciously replied. I wondered why the menu had a printed date—as it seemed that a generic one would have done fine when the place was nearly empty. After dinner I went to the lounge. A man seated in a chair stood up and came over to ask, "What can I play for you?" A grand piano was in the offing. I said that he did not have to do that. He insisted, saying, "Our adverts say there is music." Okay with me. "Most Americans like music from 'South Pacific,'" he said, so I had a private concert of those tunes.

In Melksham, Wiltshire, I would usually stop to visit with Fred Jeffery, who ran a tavern and also had a coin dealership. It was he who suggested to the Royal Mint in 1953 that the silver crown for the coronation of Queen Elizabeth II depict the monarch on horseback—a coinage tradition dating back many years. On one occasion I bought his complete collection of British Maundy sets. To this day I find that series to be very interesting.

In and around London I visited many collectors. C. Wilson Peck, a retired druggist, had the largest collection of copper coins of Great Britain ever formed, a subject for which he had written the standard reference book. He invited me to his home, where he said I could browse through his coin cabinets and select any items of interest, after which he intended to sell his collection to a dealer or consign it to auction. I selected a number of things including his unique 1808 penny and unique 1954 penny. I also bought a number of Soho Mint pattern and Proof coppers, a specialty I found especially interesting.

There were four main dealers in London. The old guards were Spink & Son, B.A. Seaby, Ltd., and Baldwin's. I did a lot of business with Douglas Liddell, who was the manager at Spink's. A lot of American tourists came by seeking United States coins. I arranged to ship him Indian Head cents and the like from my office—sort of a turnabout. Unlike the situation in the United States, European dealers who bought American coins, such as commemorative half dollars, to sell to their clients were not particular about the grades. A commemorative in About Uncirculated grade was usually preferred, as such a coin was cheaper than Mint State, and their customers did not care.

I bought and sold a lot of British coins. On one trip I acquired three cased Proof sets of 1826, complete with gold. I sold these to Doug Liddell before I left town. Spink had a drawer filled with dozens of Proof 1935 silver crowns with lettered edges, at £10 each. I asked Mr. Liddell (I always called him Mister) how many I could buy, and the answer was 10 at a 10% trade discount. I then asked if I could buy more at the full listed price. I was allowed 10 more coins. Could I buy even more than that? I was allowed a further 10 at retail plus 10%. Such transactions were a lot of fun. Every now and again I would buy early American rarities, usually copper half cents and cents and colonials that had been acquired by numismatists in England generations earlier.

The B.A. Seaby dealership was up a flight of stairs. They always had a nice supply of Washington tokens, Rosa Americana and Hibernia coins, and other items that had been struck in England, but were listed in the *Guide Book of United States Coins* and were desired by American collectors. Mrs. Bussell, I believe her name was, was the "Copper Lady" to see for coins in that metal. I liked Conder tokens and bought countless pieces with designs that I found interesting—such as depictions of exotic animals and the satirical pieces of Thomas Spence. At Baldwin's I never had much success. "We save our American coins for Mrs. Norweb," I was told. "Any that she does not want we offer to Lester Merkin."

The fourth dealer in London was Michael Stewart Millward, a newcomer to the trade, who ran Stewart Ward, Ltd. We bought a lot of things from him. He was a dealer and trader in the American style—quick decisions, quick turnover.

The theatre in the ancient city of Ephesus.

The Acropolis in Athens.

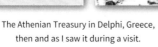

The Athenian Treasury in Delphi, Greece,
then and as I saw it during a visit.

At the Wailing Wall in Jerusalem
with Osnat Zadok.

The castle-home in Rudolstadt, Germany
where Fr. A.D. Richter once lived.

Lenin's Tomb in Red Square, Moscow.

Flying over London.

Downtown in Goteborg, Sweden.

Over a period of years I traveled extensively. This was nearly always in connection with buying for inventory, but I took the time to appreciate the history and tradition of where I was at a given town.

I enjoyed visiting historical sites, museums, art galleries, old buildings, and more, all the while keeping an eye out for rare coins. On the European continent I came to know France, Belgium, Holland, Germany (East and West), and Switzerland like the back of my hand. All of this was very enjoyable.

From the mysterious stone mill in Newport, Rhode Island, to William Randolph Hearst's
San Simeon mansion overlooking the Pacific Ocean.

Bird's-eye view of the historic gold mining
town of Victor, Colorado.

The Gold Coin Mine in Victor
in the early 20th century.

In the United States I spent a lot of time in historical locations in the West. I explored the Gold Country along Route 39 in California, the gold sites in Oregon, and, especially, the mining towns and camps in the Rocky Mountains, especially in and around Cripple Creek and Victor. In the latter city I purchased the home that Joseph Lesher occupied at the turn of the 20th century when he issued octagonal Lesher "dollars" used in local trade. I gifted the building to the American Numismatic Association, which refurbished in and used it as a vacation getaway for employees.

In the East I always enjoyed poking around. Once I took Route 1, the old Boston Post Road, from New York City northward, stopping frequently to photograph and appreciate old buildings and historical sites. I visited old iron furnaces in Pennsylvania as well as the only ones remaining in Vermont (near Bennington) and New Hampshire (in Franconia). In Newport, Rhode Island, I toured the "cottages" that were open to visitors. I even tried, without success, to find the site of the wooden house used in 1785 and 1786 to coin Vermont coppers. In 1875 Crosby wrote that it had long since collapsed in a windstorm.

A Lesher "dollar" of 1900.

A modern commemorative Lesher "dollar" issued by the ANA.

Over a period of time I have gone behind the scenes at the mints in Philadelphia, Denver, San Francisco, and West Point, at the Bureau of Engraving and Printing, and in the Treasury Building in Washington, and in other places key to the making and storage of coins and paper money.[4]

Beginning in 1960 I developed a strong interest in music boxes, coin-operated pianos, and orchestrions (automatic orchestras). Following this hobby I often went around the British Isles and Continental Europe looking for such items.[5] On the Continent my main activity continued to be tracking down American gold coins from banks, mostly in Switzerland, but also in France. Perhaps in another book I will have more to say about my interests and travels involving foreign coins and countries.

THE TREASURY HOARD AND OTHER EVENTS

In November 1962 a vault in the Philadelphia Mint was opened to provide silver dollars as gifts for the holidays. It had been sealed since 1929, when quantities of bagged New Orleans Mint silver dollars had been sent there for storage. Lo and behold, among the coins found were several hundred thousand 1903-O coins! At the time these were legendary rarities that cataloged at $1,500 each in the *Guide Book of United States Coins*, with no Morgan dollar varieties priced higher. Numismatists estimated that fewer than a dozen Mint State coins existed. I had never seen one!

A Gem 1903-O Morgan dollar from the Treasury hoard of November 1962.

After the deluge the price of single 1903-O dollar dropped to as low as $14 or so, and at least one $1,000 bag was sold for $4,000. The silver rush was on! Rare 1898-O and 1904-O dollars were found in even larger quantities. I did a lot of research at the time and kept extensive notes. The only New Orleans Mint Morgan dollar for which I never heard of a quantity being released was the 1895-O. Nationwide a treasure hunt for silver dollars took place. By March 1964 various vaults at the mints, at the Federal Reserve, and in banks had been emptied. Nearly three million Carson City silver dollars in the Treasury Building in Washington were held back and set aside. These were later turned over to the General Services Administration and sold by mail bids to collectors and others.

Amid all of the excitement in late 1962 and early 1963 there was also much uncertainty in the silver dollar market. Would bags of rare 1893-S dollars be found next?

(None were.) No one knew what would turn up. In the early days it was feared that with millions of coins on the market the value of silver dollars would drop and be ruined. The general rule was to buy quickly and then sell as soon as possible.

A tag from a 1,000-coin bag of Mint State 1903-O dollars.

After early 1964, when all vaults were empty, knowledge of the rarity of the different Morgan dollars (and Peace dollars as well) became well established, and buyers became assured. The opposite of the earlier fears happened. Although countless more coins were available, the number of collectors interested in silver dollars multiplied dozens of times over. They became the number one popular series for late 19th and early 20th century coins. Prices *rose* to the point that today, with just the exception of 1903-O, prices of Morgan and Peace dollars are multiples of what they were before November 1962! Just for fun, if you can find a copy of the *Guide Book of the United States* from that era (1963 cover date), look at the prices and compare them with those of today.

The Teletype became popular, and in 1962 and 1963 dozens of dealers were linked nationwide by these noisy chattering machines that spewed out printed information on spooled yellow paper. Several systems were in operation, including one limited only to PNG members. Buying and selling were the main activities, but gossip, opinions, humor, and hobby news were also of interest—punctuated by flashes of national and world news. In our office on the afternoon of November 22, 1963, Ray Merena said that he had just read that President John F. Kennedy had been shot in Dallas and was being rushed to the Parkland Hospital.

In California in 1963 *The Coin Dealer Newsletter* was started, giving weekly bid and ask prices on "investment quality" coins, later expanded to cover many other issues. Prices were often fictitious in the sense that if a dealer posted a bid price he often did so to enhance the price of what he had in inventory. Upon being offered coins he might say, "I have already bought all I needed." As a major buyer of coins for inventory, I often paid "bid less 5%" or "less 10%" when viewing dealers' stocks. Rather than "bid" a better notation would be "guide price" (a term used in England). However, on balance the printed prices added a lot of stability to the market.

The investment market peaked in late 1963 and early 1964 when the demand from incoming buyers fell short of the supply offered for sale by coin owners. By late 1964 the investment market was dead. A roll of 1950-D nickels, which had gone past $1,200, now cost less than $400. Along the way, specialties such as colonial and early American coins, half cents and large cents, Hard Times and Civil War tokens, medals, and various federal silver coins by die varieties and in worn grades, had been ignored by investors. Specialists in such series and the value of their holdings were not affected by the downturn. This has been more or less the rule for all coin cycles fueled by investors compared to markets driven by numismatists.

Once again, however, nearly everyone—and I don't know if there are any exceptions—who bought a diverse selection of "investment quality" coins at the very height of the market in early 1964 would find that they are worth multiples of those prices today! This scenario, which has taken place many times in market history, is rather amazing to contemplate. In summary, investors might not have enjoyed the historical or social side of numismatics, but they nearly always did well financially if they held on to their coins until the next upturn in the market cycle.

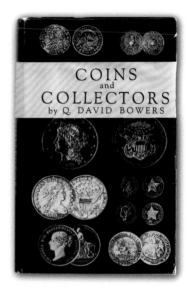

Coins and Collectors.

The decade of the 1960s, continuing into the 1970s, saw the formation of many societies. I have noted earlier that such groups have been essential to the expansion of study and enjoyment in various series. As an example, members of Early American Coppers mix social interface with research and other activities, recorded in the journal *Penny-Wise* (edited by Harry Salyards, M.D., one of the most erudite writers the hobby has ever seen). The typical member of EAC has belonged for many years.

For a long time I had been compiling notes on numismatic history and nostalgia. In 1964 I compiled a selection of this into my first book, *Coins and Collectors*. The first print run of 4,000 copies was quickly followed by 5,000 more, and additional copies after that. Then Crown Publishing requested the privilege of printing and distributing it nationwide, which was done to the extent of 100,000 copies sold. For years afterward I received letters from collectors who said that this book introduced them to numismatics. In 2014 an updated and expanded "Golden Anniversary" edition of *Coins and Collectors* was released by Whitman Publishing.

CHANGES IN COINAGE

The introduction of the Kennedy half dollar in 1964 created nationwide excitement. Nearly all were hoarded, starting in March, when banks paid them out in quantity. The price of silver was rising on international markets. By 1965 silver needed for coins cost more than face value, and clad coins (with an inner core of pure copper sandwiched with alloys of copper and nickel) were introduced. In the next few years nearly all existing silver coins were withdrawn from circulation and melted. No longer was it possible to find or, more likely, hope to find a key coin such as a 1916-D Mercury dime or 1932-D or S Washington quarter in pocket change. This brought about a different direction in collecting. From this point forward, key issues among 20th century coins were no long available in pocket change. Few people had found such treasures anyway, but the possibility was always there.

As speculators rushed to find and save all of the silver coins possible, a nationwide coin shortage developed that illogically included cents and nickels in addition to dimes, quarters, and half dollars. Mint Director Eva Adams, a Kennedy appointee, blamed numismatists for this, although it was the general public doing the hoarding. I don't recall that any collectors started amassing common worn coins. To suitably punish these nasty numismatists Adams discontinued the making of Proof sets, removed mintmarks from Denver coins, and made it clear that henceforth some coins would be struck from dies not corresponding with the calendar year. She was considered to be a villain, so to speak—the first (and last) Mint director in history who deliberately antagonized millions of collectors.

In one of the more curious sidelights of American numismatics, Director Adams later "got religion." Proof coins were again coined in 1968, at the San Francisco Mint and with S mintmarks. She became interested in numismatics and successfully ran for election to the board of governors of the American Numismatic Association. She even performed in skits in the "Bash" (roast) held at the summer ANA conventions. Beyond understanding to me and many other people, the ANA elected her to its Hall of Fame and the Numismatic Literary Guild bestowed upon her its highest honor, the Clemy, although she never wrote anything significant in numismatics! Hmm.[6]

Jefferson nickel designer Felix O. Schlag and Mint Director Eva Adams in 1966, when the artist's FS initials were added to the nickel for the first time. This followed a campaign originated by *Numismatic News*.

The new ANA headquarters in 1967.

The general market was mixed from 1965 to about 1967 or so, as new investors who were attracted to coins became scarce. In time most of the highs of 1964 were again achieved and then surpassed as the building of sets of coins in high grades became more popular than ever before. Many collectors opted to form type sets—one of each major design of copper, nickel, and silver coin from the 1790s to date.

On June 10, 1967, in Colorado Springs a special ceremony was held to open the newly constructed American Numismatic Association Home and Headquarters on the campus of Colorado College. With this, activities of the organization were centered in one place. In succeeding years, under the efforts of Edward C. Rochette in particular, although many others were involved, programs were developed and outreach was expanded. Bill Henderson and Adna Wilde, both local residents, were also important in this growth. The Summer Seminar attracted leading numismatists as instructors and, in time, thousands of participants. Today this remains a dynamic program.

Medals made especially for collectors were released in quantity by the Presidential Art Medal Company, Vandalia, Ohio, in the early 1960s and sold well, inaugurating what became a nationwide passion for collecting such series. The General Numismatics Corporation, formed a few years later by entrepreneur Joseph Segel, changed its name to the Franklin Mint, and made dollar-size tokens for Nevada casinos and a large number of historical and artistic issues for collectors. At one time the Franklin Mint Collectors Society had over 80,000 people on its roster. Listed on the New York Stock Exchange, the Franklin Mint was the star gainer in one year. Many people bought the medals as investments, but there was hardly any aftermarket for them. After a negative program on the CBS *60 Minutes* show in 1978 the interest in such medals collapsed. The Franklin Mint went on to make other types of collectibles.

Although medals faded in popularity, small silver "rounds" usually weighing one ounce and small rectangular silver ingots became very popular and remain so today.

In the late 1960s interest in coins strictly as an investment gained traction once again and drew many new people into numismatics. In 1969 the coin market was strong, but the stock market was weak. Cycles in the coin market have never been in harness with the Dow-Jones Industrial Average.

THE 1970S

Investor interest in gold coins became intense. Emphasis was placed on coins for their bullion value—such as common-date double eagles. American citizens had been forbidden from holding gold bullion since 1933, and modern gold coins of other countries minted after 1933 were not allowed either—unless they were made specifically as numismatic items, such as the four-piece set of 1937 gold coins struck at the Royal Mint in London on occasion of the inauguration of King George VI. Double eagles by the hundreds of thousands were imported by coin dealers and bullion brokers. Several of my clients bought gold in the form of 20 coins by getting one each of as many different dates and mintmarks that were not rarities.

At the time I was a partner with Jim Ruddy in Bowers and Ruddy Galleries at 6922 Hollywood Boulevard, Los Angeles—across the street from the famous Chinese Theatre. We were front row center in the buying and selling of coins and were making our mark in coin auctions, having landed several important collections to sell. It was good news for us when Armand Champa decided to sell his impressive holding of pattern and other coins. He invited dealers to come to his bank in Louisville and make offers. After a month of such appointments he was not satisfied. He consigned his coins to us, and we sold them for more than twice the highest offer he had received. On his own and unsolicited, Armand took out advertisements to thank us! I remember going to Hot Springs National Park to visit and acquire for auction the collection assembled by Robert Marks, that included a rare 1884 trade dollar. I was amazed to see all of the old buildings in that park—actually a city—that were once bathhouses. Lots of memories from a very nice era.

In 1974 there was a great surge of interest in gold after it was announced that after midnight on December 31, gold bullion and modern coins of other countries could be openly bought and sold. After the holding of such pieces became legal, the value of gold dropped for a while. By 1975 there was much less interest in common-date gold coins. That changed, and gold coins increased in popularity and price once again.

By this time General Mills, Inc., had purchased a majority interest in my coin company, Bowers and Ruddy Galleries. General Mills was a far-ranging conglomerate at the time. Its divisions included Parker Brothers games, Foot Joy shoes, H.E. Harris stamps, Eddie Bauer sporting goods, and others. It wanted to get into rare coins. Fletcher Waller Jr., a company executive, commissioned a survey under which people in numismatics were interviewed at conventions and elsewhere. Jim Ruddy and I were told that our company was admired as the best. Runners-up were Superior Galleries (the Goldberg family) and Stack's. We were made a generous offer that we accepted. I immensely enjoyed the General Mills executives—first-class corporate leaders. I visited headquarters in Minneapolis and attended a number of company-wide events to which representatives of all the divisions were invited. In 1976 Jim Ruddy and his wife Nancy (long with the company), left the firm to enjoy retirement and the things that leisure offered.

Per usual, investor interest was fickle—unlike the nearly always steady increase in value of traditional rarities, copper cents of the 1793 to 1857 years, Civil War tokens, colonials, and the like. The unexpected temporary slump in the price of gold in 1975 reverberated to include other series as well, particularly gold and silver issues of the types sought by investors. Many serious collectors became concerned as well and slowed their buying. The slump continued through 1977.

My personal life underwent a change in this era, having divorced in the early 1970s. I was a single person until marrying Christine Valentine in 1978. In the meantime I had a lot of nice social friends. One of them, Cheri Kaye Lemons, was a flight-service director for American Airlines, supervising Boeing 747 flights from Los Angeles to New York and back. Once she helped me collect and pack the Dr. Edward Willing Collection. On another she went on her own to Copenhagen (free travel for employees, you know) to visit the Mekanisk Musik Museum, of which I was co-owner. Cheri remains a fine friend of mine and my wife's today. Bonnie Tekstra was a business partner in American International Galleries, an import-export business that I financed and she managed in a 20,000-square-foot building in Irvine, California. We traveled together on buying trips, included behind the Iron Curtain with special permit. Bonnie, too, remains a fine friend. Another friend from that time, Evelyn King, later known as Evelyn Mishkin, kept in touch in later years, and until her untimely passing in October 2015 was important in several research and writing projects for Stack's Bowers Galleries, the Civil War Token Society, and other entities. Evelyn shared my interest in ghost towns out West, and we would compare notes—although we never visited them at the same time.[7]

In the meantime the new 1776–1976 Bicentennial coin sales fell far short of expectations. Indeed, the entire nationwide celebration of the Bicentennial was rather mild. I recall in the early 1970s discussing the forthcoming event with Philadelphia Mint officials who were hoping that 1976 would see a reiteration of the 1876 Centennial Exhibition held in that city. The matter fell apart when some politicos and others said that the money would be better spent on welfare and other entitlements.[8]

From 1977 to 1979 I served as president of the Professional Numismatists Guild, details of which are not germane to the present comments on the coin market. It was a pleasant experience, but had its challenges. In summation, in particular the American Numismatic Association Certification Service (ANACS), which graded coins for a fee, was very controversial. Some dealers demanded that I as a fellow dealer intercede with ANACS to have their coins receive especially favored treatment. I did not do this. Many dealers and also a number of board of governors members of the ANA felt that PNG was a detriment to the ANA conventions. It was tradition to hold PNG Day next to the opening day for the annual ANA summer show. This siphoned off all of the good deals and took away from the ANA event. Accusations and comments flew left and right. Somehow, all of this worked out fine, or seemingly so.

Today the PNG stands higher than ever and has a code of ethics, but it would be nice if there were some study and licensing requirements all across the hobby to be certified as a professional.

THE LATE 1970S

By 1979 the market changed, and dramatically. The Hunt brothers, Texas oil millionaires, attempted to drive up the price of silver by purchasing large quantities of bullion as well as silver futures. Over a period of time the value of an ounce of silver rose from $1.27, as it had been in 1964 before the international price increase, to several dollars, to $10, $20, $30, and over $40. Citizens brought tons of silverware, coins, art objects, and more to coin dealers and other merchants. Every coin shop had a mechanical counting machine on the counter, yielding large profits that then were often spent in our auction sales, such as by a strong underbidder for the 1804 dollar in our Garrett Collection series of sales, of which more will be said.

Vast quantities of Mint State Franklin and Kennedy half dollars, Roosevelt dimes, Washington quarters, Morgan and Peace dollars, and other coins were sold to be melted, as their bullion value was far more than their numismatic value. Gold bullion increased in value as well. By autumn 1979 silver was over $45 per ounce and gold over $800.

In the meantime under the administration of President Jimmy Carter—not that he was to blame for everything—there was great disruption in the price of oil. Shortages developed, and long lines of automobiles formed at gasoline stations, some of which ran out of fuel. The economy was a mess as well. At one point the inflation rate was over 13 percent. This had been a problem for some time, dating back to the Richard Nixon administration and his unsuccessful W.I.N. (Whip Inflation Now) program.

In the late 1970s dictatorial regime in Iran, a major supplier of oil to the world, was overthrown. On November 4, 1979, the American embassy in Tehran was seized by revolutionaries and 52 members of the diplomatic staff as well as other Americans were taken hostage and confined there.

The coin market was uncertain and confused in 1979 as collectors were selling many gold and silver coins for incredible prices based on their bullion value. Uncertainty slowed down activity in other series not related to bullion. The Johns Hopkins University had consigned the collection formed by the Garrett family, and gifted to the university in 1942, to Bowers and Ruddy Galleries to be auctioned after reviewing proposals from us, Christie's, Sotheby's, and Stack's.[9]

When the board of trustees invited me to meet with them after the award, I asked why my company had been chosen. Steven Muller, president, stated to the effect, "Although your terms were higher than the others, we all felt that you would give the sale some 'P.T. Barnum.'" I was a bit surprised to hear this, but was pleased.

In 1979 I lived at the Evergreen House, so to speak, spending days there with the Garrett Collection.

Appraised at about $8 million, the Garrett collection was stored for security in the basement vault of a Baltimore bank and was no longer used for display or research. Also it was troublesome that a former curator, Carl Carlson, had deaccessioned some coins thought to have been important, although this was under his presumed authority and was not deemed illegal.[10]

It was up to me to study the collection formed by T. Harrison Garrett up to his death in 1886, then continued by sons Robert (who won a gold medal in the 1896 Olympic Games held in Athens) and Ambassador John Work Garrett. My wife Christie and I went to Baltimore and camped there while at Evergreen House and the Johns Hopkins Library looking through thousands of coins and documents. Curator Susan Tripp and her numismatist husband David were of great help. As part of my research I made copies of more than 4,000 letters and invoices. By late summer my book, *The History of United States Coinage as Illustrated by the Garrett Collection*, was ready. I had discussions with the Johns Hopkins University Press about publishing it. After checking their sales records for other books they informed me that they might be interested, but their expectations were that it would take at least 10 years to sell as many as 1,000 books.

I thought that it would be a bit more popular than that. We published it ourselves in an initial press run of 4,000 copies. This was sold out to advance orders! Eventually, about 15,000 copies reached print. Today it remains a favorite classic reference for many people.

In the meantime I and the staff were cataloging the Garrett coins for auction. The first of four sales was held in New York City. With the ongoing silver speculation the market for rare coins was uncertain. What would happen? Would buyers be there in force? Or would they hold back?

It turned out that many records were broken as collectors scrambled to buy coins that had been off the market for many years, some since the 1860s. Abe Kosoff advised his clients that the Garrett prices were so unrealistic that they should not be used as market guides![11]

INTO THE 1980S

Oil prices and inflation continued to be major concerns. Despite the success of the Garrett auction, there were uncertainties galore in the coin market. After all, classic rare coins such as in that sale represented only a tiny fraction of the overall sales volume of the marketplace. Allen Harriman, owner of *The Coin Dealer Newsletter*, published this on January 18, 1980:

> With both silver and gold bullion soaring into new uncharted ranges, trading in many areas of the coin market becomes more uncertain each day—if not each hour! Most strongly affected, of course, is the bullion-related material.... Dealers are deluged with sellers, many of the smelters are either not accepting new shipments or are taking up to three months to reimburse—and, on top of this confusion, many dealers are out of immediate funds with which to buy additional material. This is a totally unprecedented period in history and reactions from both buyers and sellers are entirely without previous experience. It is very strongly urged that care be taken by anyone trading or considering trading in these areas!

Playing it safe, many dealers were paying significantly below bullion prices. Even so, the flood of incoming metal continued. On January 18, the price of silver bullion peaked in London (the main trading center) at $49.50 per ounce, followed a few days later on the 21st by $850 per ounce for gold.

Then, panic! The prices of both metals plummeted. Collectors and dealers put locks on their wallets and checkbooks. The market for coins as an investment dwindled to virtually nothing. Several dealers whose main business was in that category filed for bankruptcy.

In March 1980 the Central States Numismatic Society convention was held in Lincoln, Nebraska. I arrived by plane at a new airport facility and was surprised to see a large number of empty counters. I inquired as to what happened and was told that due to the oil shortage, the vast majority of flights in and out of the city had been discontinued.

In January 1980 a client was offered $15,000 per coin for his set of Proof Barber half dollars, including 24 coins such as the 1907 shown here.

In the meantime inflation continued, and hostages were still held in Tehran. The crash of gold and silver prices plus other uncertainties combined to make activity in most silver and gold coins nearly zero. No one wanted to buy, despite many beautiful coins being offered at prices that were far below their 1979 levels. I had never seen anything like it. To be sure, buying interest in early coins and traditional numismatic items took place, but there were not many dealers on hand who specialized in these.

In early January 1980 Dr. Collier, a long-time client, called me to say that he had received an offer of $15,000 *per coin* for the complete set of gem Proof 1892 to 1915 Barber half dollars he had purchased from me a few years earlier. He asked if he should sell, and I recommended he do so. The market price later dropped to an average of about $3,000 per coin.

Beyond numismatics, the entire nation's mood remained uncertain by January 1981 when the presidential inauguration of Ronald Reagan took place. My wife and I attended that event at the invitation of General Mills, Inc., which hosted a private dinner the evening before with Chief Justice Warren E. Burger and other Supreme Court justices on hand. At dinner we sat with Justice Harry Blackmun and his wife Dorothy. I brought some inaugural medals in my pocket, and these were passed around, one to each table. We all admired and discussed them.

Dorothy Blackmun asked if she could keep the medal at our table, and I said yes. Her husband interjected, "But, I would like to have it."

She responded, "Except that possession is nine points of the law, so it is mine."

"I make the law," the justice replied.

Lots of fun!

At the inauguration on the lawn behind the Capitol we had special seats near the front. It was a bright, sunny morning. Somehow, the incoming Reagan administration had engineered the release of the long-captive Americans in Tehran, and everyone celebrated.

A brass Reagan inaugural medal made by the Medallic Art Company, one of five varieties available in a cased set.

REVIVAL OF THE MARKET

The investment part of the coin market remained in a slump for the next year or so. In the meantime, areas in which collectors were busy collecting did well, Morgan silver dollars being an example. Specialties such as colonials, early half cents and cents, early silver, Charlotte and Dahlonega Mint gold, and the like remained strong.

During the late 1970s and in the 1980s there were many auctions, including the "Apostrophe Sales." These began with Auction '79, an event conducted by a consortium of four dealers: Paramount, Stack's, Superior, and RARCOA. For the next decade catalogs of 2,000 lots per sale (500 for each dealer) played to an enthusiastic audience, with good results. The idea for the Apostrophe Sales was to capture some of the enthusiasm of those planning to attend the summer convention of the ANA by having the sale immediately preceding it. This had two advantages: the sales had exclusive audiences who had no distractions, and no fee had to be paid to the ANA (which the official auctioneer had to do). My company was invited to join this group but did not. In the 1980s these sales created a lot of attention.

Three more Garrett Collection sales were held for the Johns Hopkins University. Not to worry in the slightest about the market for the classic coins, tokens, and medals offered, as I thought all along and as it turned out. Amidst many uncertainties in coin investment, traditional numismatic series remained very strong. The next two sales in 1980 and the final sale in 1981 broke records left and right. The collection, appraised at about $8 million, sold for $25 million!

At the time I remained on the staff of Bowers and Merena Galleries in California. In 1980 I and my family moved to New Hampshire to be in a lakes-and-mountains area. Location is not particularly important in the rare-coin business unless one has a street-floor store. My activities over the years were nearly all by mail and in conducting auctions in major cities.

From the Granite State I continued helping with writing and planning, but was not involved in examining coins for auction. David Sundman and his family, owners of Littleton Coin Company, became fine friends, and in time we did a lot of things together—including going on trips and collaborating in research. In the Granite State at the time, I missed the sale of the Henry Clifford Collection conducted in California and mostly cataloged by John J. Ford Jr. I bid on a number of privately minted California gold rarities, but did not win any. This turned out to be a good thing, as some of the items, including an ingot said to have aboard the SS *Brother Jonathan*, proved to be fakes.[12]

A Diana gambling hall $20 that was proved to be made a bit later than the Gold Rush!

The cover of Karl Moulton's 900-plus page exposé of the fraudulent coins and ingots sold by Ford.

John J. Ford Jr.

Karl Moulton exposed the fraudulent coins and ingots in his magisterial book *John J. Ford, Jr. & the Franklin Hoard*, 2013, with 903 pages and many illustrations. Learning all the details was bittersweet for me, in a way, as I had been a good professional friend of Ford's since my teenage days. Did Ford knowingly participate in the creation of these frauds, or was he duped by an agent, Paul Franklin, whom Ford paid to travel through the West and search for numismatic items?

On my "want list," though I never had the chance to buy one (fortunately), was the Diana gambling hall $20 coin issued in San Francisco. What the perpetrator(s) did was to find the name of an assayer or other establishment in an old Gold Rush directory or other sources and then create fantasy coins alleged to have been made and issued in the 1850s. Oops! In one instance Edgar H. Adams in his 1905 book on the history of assayers and coiners, *Private Gold Coinage of California 1849–1855*, mentioned Blake & Agnell, assayers. Ingots with this name magically appeared on the market in the 1950s. There was a problem: Adams had made a typographical error, and the name should have been Blake and Agrell!

The 1822 half eagle in the Eliasberg Collection.

In 1982 the Louis E. Eliasberg Collection of United States Gold Coins became available. One of Eliasberg's sons, Louis Jr., awarded the auction of these coins to us. I went to Baltimore and spent a number of days carefully examining each coin and making notations on more than 1,000 index cards (no personal computer back then!). I then returned to New Hampshire and wrote the auction catalog as well as a related book, *United States Gold Coins: An Illustrated History*. The sale was conducted in New York City and broke many records, including $787,500 for the unique 1870-S three-dollar coin bought by Harry W. Bass Jr., and the identical amount realized for one of three known 1822 half eagles, the buyers being Mack Pogue and his son Brent. This sale, too, broke all sorts of records.

General Mills was changing its business strategy at this time, and one by one sold off all of its non-food divisions. I purchased the name and assets of the coin company and set up Bowers and Merena Galleries in New Hampshire, inviting Ray Merena, who had worked with me in the 1960s, to be a partner with a substantial equity interest. Although our duties overlapped in some areas, I mainly tended to sales, marketing, auctions, research, and writing, while Ray took care of employees, finances, travel arrangements, contracts, and general operations.

Bowers and Merena Galleries was a success from the beginning. We issued the *Rare Coin Review* magazine, conducted many notable auctions, and were otherwise deeply involved in the heart of American numismatics.

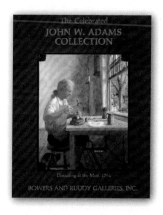

In 1984 Bowers and Merena Galleries offered the incomparable collection of 1794-dated large copper cents formed over a long period of years by John W. Adams.

In the meantime there were many other dealers who enjoyed success. Notably, Jim Halperin was busy in Boston with the New England Rare Coin Co., which had become a big player in the market, while in Dallas, Steve Ivy had a fine business. Years later the two merged to form Heritage, which dealt not only in coins, but also other collectibles ranging from comic books to ladies' purses. This firm, more than any other, became involved in many areas outside of numismatics—including real estate and the licensing of trademark names—a very diversified enterprise, as it remains today.

Stack's in New York City continued its prominence in rare coins, especially in auctions, and sold many great collections. Paramount International Coin Company in Ohio, managed by David Akers, had its fingers in several numismatic pies, including the distribution of modern Proof sets for Panama and other foreign countries. In Beverly Hills, Superior Galleries was owned by Ira and Larry Goldberg, who carved out a large niche in retail sales and auctions and included many entertainment and sports personalities among their clients. A-Mark, conducted by Steve Markoff in California, and its division, Western Numismatics, were major factors in the business, including in large wholesale transactions.

Ed Milas in Chicago ran RARCOA, likewise an important factor. Arthur M. Kagin, long a partner with his brother Paul in the Hollinbeck Coin Company, later known as Hollinbeck-Kagin, dissolved the partnership and formed a new business with his son Don, who, among other areas of expertise, was a specialist in Gold Rush–era coinage.

Many other dealerships prospered, and a list of them would occupy several pages. Tony Terranova in New York City and Julian Leidman in Maryland attended nearly all or possibly even every one of our auction sales. Mike Brownlee, Ron Gillio, Ken Goldman, Bob Hughes, Martin Paul, John Rowe, Laura Sperber, and a dozen or more other "regulars" were often there as well. The former Teletype networks transitioned into electronic coin trading, again with bid and ask prices. For the most part conventions were successful in the 1980s, with the summer ANA show always earning high marks. Other ANA events as well as regional shows had mixed results and ranged from good to disastrous.

I could write a book on coin conventions that I attended. Probably the worst in my career was in the 1950s at a Penn-Ohio show in Akron, Ohio. By the end of three days neither I nor the bourse dealer with a table next to me, William ("Foxy") Steinberg, had a single sale. So, I arranged to spend $300 with

The 1982 Washington half dollar, the first U.S. commemorative coin since 1954.

him and for him to spend the same amount with me. Today that would probably be equal to $5,000 to $10,000 worth of coins—given the dynamic changes in the market since that time. In contrast at the 1957 ANA convention in Philadelphia I had a line of up to a dozen people patiently waiting for their turn to deal with me!

In 1982 the Treasury Department issued the first commemorative coins since the generally ignored Washington-Carver series expired in 1954. A half dollar designed by talented Chief Engraver Elizabeth Jones observed the 250th anniversary of George Washington's birth. Collectors were overjoyed and hoped for more. The adage "Be careful what you wish for as it may come true" turned into reality as beginning in 1983 and continuing to the present era, a large number of commemorative silver and gold coins have been issued to observe obscure people and events, this because various organizations and others influenced Congress. Nearly all of these organizations have profited by getting a surcharge on each coin sold. Some of this was beyond ridiculous, such as the 1991 dollar commemorating the 38th anniversary of the Korean War. This had ample precedent. I need but mention the 1893 Columbian half dollar for the 401st anniversary of the explorer's landing and the 1921 half dollar celebrating the 1919 centennial of Alabama statehood.

The Summer Olympic Games were scheduled to be held in Los Angeles in 1984. Armand Hammer, who headed Occidental Petroleum in California, was a leading financial figure at the time and was frequently mentioned in the *Wall Street Journal* and other news sources. Through his friend Senator Alan Cranston of California, he proposed that Occidental take over from the Mint (with its "sleepy" sales department) the marketing of the Olympic coins and all future commemoratives. Hammer was involved in the art market, and expanding into coins seemed to be attractive.

I got a hurry-up call from the Treasury Department. Would I come to Washington and testify to Congress on behalf of the Mint and Treasury? I did, as did some other hobby leaders including *Coin World* editor Margo Russell and PNG president Ed Milas. This saved the day, and ever since then the U.S. Mint has been in firm control of commemorative sales. After doing this I and some others went to the White House and were welcomed by President Reagan. United States Treasurer "Bay" Buchanan wrote me a warm letter of thanks.

In the meantime the American economy continued to be uncertain—seemingly the rule rather than the exception for this time in history. The shortage of oil continued, to which was added Americans' massive ordering of consumer goods from overseas, resulting in the closing of countless U.S. factories, including for electronics. A few years later in 1987 the American dollar was weak on overseas markets, and huge trade deficits were in place. One of my favorite (in a way, at least in the category of numismatics) memories is of October 19 that year, when the Dow-Jones Industrial Average plummeted 508 points. That evening Bowers and Merena Galleries had a coin sale in New York City that brought record prices!

From 1983 to 1985 I served as president of the American Numismatic Association. I was very familiar with the ANA, having been on the board of governors and having worked with Ed Rochette for many years in the development of programs at their Colorado Springs headquarters. I could devote a chapter on this element of my life, which today brings back many pleasant memories. Someday I will dust off my notes and revisit this era.

THE RISE OF THIRD-PARTY GRADING SERVICES

Although the American Numismatic Association Certification Service had been grading coins for a fee and some others had similar services as well, a great change in the numismatic market took place starting in 1986 when David Hall and a group of dealer associates formed the Professional Coin Grading Service (PCGS) to grade coins and encase them in hard plastic holders soon nicknamed "slabs." Success was immediate. In 1987 John Albanese, one of the best minds in numismatics and earlier associated with PCGS, established the Numismatic Guaranty Corporation of America (NGC), which was well received as well. These are known as *third-party* grading services, because they focus purely on the coins, rather than representing either the buyer or the seller.

An early Professional Coin Grading Service (PCGS) holder or "slab."

PCGS grading in the early days was very controversial. Dealers, including me, were not happy that our professional opinions were being held in less regard than coins certified by this service and, later, NGC.

In time most if not all of us changed our minds, especially when certified coins helped sell tons of coins to buyers who believed numbers were scientific. They did not care about sharpness of strike or eye appeal. Although I always tried to buy coins with good eye appeal, it was common as part of buying entire collections to acquire coins that were as ugly as could be. Usually I and other dealers concerned with high quality would dump these on a wholesale basis. With third-party grading, that changed. If an MS-65 coin listed for, say, $1,000, in the *Coin Dealer Newsletter*, a miserable-looking certified coin of that variety in the same grade, if offered at $900, would find many eager buyers!

Another benefit was psychological. It used to be that if a reputable dealer sold a group of nice coins to a client, and if that client walked into a local coin shop, the shop owner might say, "They are way overgraded. Send them back!" This could damage the warmest of relationships. With certified coins, that no longer happened. If a coin bore a certified label it might as well have been graded by God.

All of the above was very beneficial for coin dealers already in business.

Also, with coins in holders, most were saved from being cleaned and dipped. If only these slabs had been around in the 1890s, now all hairlined Proof Barber silver coins would be superb Gems!

There were some unintended and unfortunate consequences. With a box of PCGS or NGC coins, a price list, and a list of names and telephone numbers to call, any uniformed and clueless sharpie or fraudster could become an instant "professional numismatist." This situation continues today. Many sellers of coins have no clue who designed the Liberty Head double eagle or why MS-65 1884-CC dollars, with a mintage figure of 1,136,000, are very common, while 1901 with a mintage figure of 6,962,000 is a great rarity. All would probably utterly fail the Guide Book Quiz I gave in chapter 4.

Another consequence may be beneficial for collectors but not as much for dealers, although this can be argued. It used to be that most clients were private. If someone were forming a collection of Morgan dollars or Saint-Gaudens double eagles through my company, he or she bought exclusively from us and along the way developed a friendship and close connection. With certified coins the market became homogenized—and collectors are apt to buy from multiple sources. Close professional connections and advice were not deemed to be as important as in years earlier.

In the early days most coins graded by PCGS were usually evaluated as strictly as I would have done. Coins graded by NGC were often assigned slightly higher numbers. Very few early coins were graded by either service as MS-66, and hardly any above that. Today, nearly all coins I have seen in holders from the late 1980s, such as in old-time collections, would certify at a grade or two higher, and some MS-65 coins are now 67 and 68. Of course, the coins have not improved. The labels have changed—as discussed in earlier chapters.

Not long after PCGS and NGC started business, there were questions as to why the same coin could be given different grades at different times by the same service. To answer such criticism PCGS announced in an advertisement in *The Numismatist* in June 1988:

> The reality of coin grading is that perceptions change, but coins don't change. To establish a truly permanent grading standard you need per-

manent physical examples of the grades. You need a set of grading examples. . . . You need a permanent grading set. PCGS is now rapidly expanding its permanent grading set. . . . The goal is to have $500,000 worth of coins by the end of 1987 and $1 million worth (at today's prices) by 1990. . . .

So how does the PCGS permanent grading set benefit you? Quite simply, when you buy a PCGS coin you are buying a coin that has been graded according to a grading standard that will not change . . . EVER! The current standards used by PCGS are the same standards PCGS will use in 1992, 1997 and even 2002 because the coins in the PCGS permanent grading set are the coins that will be the grading standards for PCGS in 1992, 1997 and 2002. The days of changing grading standards are over forever.

A later Numismatic Guaranty Corporation holder.

In the same issue John Albanese advertised:

Numismatic Guaranty Corporation's strict grading standards have brought stability and credibility to the coin industry. Every coin we grade is evaluated by a team of three to five graders, then sonically sealed in a specially developed holder. But with the Numismatic Guaranty Corporation, your investment value remains in the coin itself, not in its plastic holder.

Because we are the most trusted name in coin grading, NGC-graded coins are often bought sight unseen. Market makers and coin services know that NGC-graded coins are not subject to fluctuating grading standards. . . .

By 1988 there were countless thousands of certified coins available with PCGS and NGC labels plus from other third-party grading companies as well. This attracted the attention of many new players ranging from the mentioned fraudsters and telemarketers to respected Wall Street firms. Now, coins could be bought and sold like commodities—one could become a "professional numismatist" with little or no training or expertise at all, as I have noted. Through Phoebe Morse, director of the Federal Trade Commission's Boston office, and attorney Barry Cutler, the FTC took action on tele-marketing abuses, and some perpetrators received jail terms. Others closed up shop.

Several financial firms including Merrill Lynch set up coin funds. "Investment quality" was once again defined as silver and gold coins (not copper) in MS-65 and Proof-65 grades or better. As vast supplies of coins were available for trading in some series, investment focus included Morgan dollars, common-date silver and gold coins of the late 19th and early 20th centuries, Proofs from 1858 onward (many of which were actually rare), and commemoratives. The latter had the wonderful combination of being readily available in Mint State and including many with low mintage figures.

There was trouble in paradise, however: storm clouds gathered on the economic horizon, and in 1989 new "Wall Street money" became scarce, and interest diminished.

INTO THE 1990S

In late 1989 into the 1990s many investors decided to liquidate, and the market for many of their favorite coins crashed. Today as you read these words many MS-65 commemorative coins are less expensive than they were in 1988. However, these were exceptions as most "investment grade" coins recovered, including gold, in step with internationally rising bullion prices. If a clueless investor bought, say, a *diverse selection* of $10,000 worth of Mint State and Proof coins at the high prices of 1988, chances are nearly certain that they would be worth a lot more today.

The investment side of the market was generally quiet in the early 1990s. On the other hand, most if not all *specialties* were very strong, as usual. Buyer activity for Capped Bust silver coins, Liberty Seated coins, colonials, early copper coins, tokens and medals, paper money, and other fields were dynamic, especially in circulated grades (yes, circulated grades). Some coins in higher Mint State and Proof grades that were favored by investors have yet to catch up.

On April 2, 1992, the Mint held its 200th anniversary celebration at the Philadelphia Mint and at the Federal Reserve Bank nearby. I was invited to be the keynote speaker. The attendees included several dozen numismatic figures, a few of whom signed the commemorative envelope pictured.

Computers, once reserved for corporate and government use, became popular nationwide in the 1980s, spurred by Apple, IBM, and others. Personal computers became the rage. My first was a Mac Plus in 1986. The Internet beckoned. Year by year it became more and more important. Harry W. Bass Jr. was probably the leading pioneer in numismatics in this context. He once called to tell me that no longer would I be receiving any written letters from him, but only email messages. He worked to set up a system at the American Numismatic Society, making it probably the first in the world so equipped.

A new craze for sports cards flared into being, and shops were opened all across America.[13] In another area of collectibles, the field of antiques, many stores closed up as their owners saved money on rent, employee salaries, insurance, and other expenses by setting up displays in group shops. Anyone collecting in any field in the 1970s found the marketplace to be vastly different two decades later in the 1990s. The Internet was also front row center, as were personal digital assistants (PDAs) and cellphones. Music storage transitioned from cassettes to CDs, such as used on the Sony Walkman. Many if not most hikers and walkers for exercise on streets and trails had wires attached to their ears. No longer was it necessary to read the morning paper or watch early evening television to learn the news. Internet cable networks were on nonstop.

A few of the hundreds of Bowers & Merena Galleries publications—including catalogs, magazines, and books, many of which won awards.

After it gained traction starting in 1982 Bowers and Merena Galleries did very well in the marketplace. We handled more great collections and achieved a greater volume of sales than did any other rare-coin firm. The collection of Ambassador and Mrs. R. Henry Norweb, the collection of Louis E. Eliasberg, selections from the Virgil Brand estate, magnificent coins from the Harry W. Bass Jr. Collection, the Walter Childs Collection, and many more created a lot of attention.

Pages from the Bowers and Merena Galleries scrapbook.
Part of the B&M Griffins baseball team.

The team poses for a picture.

Picnic time in the summer, one of several family
gatherings each year. The young kids gather for a
scramble to find coins (not rare) hidden in the sand.

In June 1989 the staff was hosted to cruise on a boat
chartered by Harry Norweb (son of Ambassador and
Mrs. Henry Norweb) as a thank-you for our conducting
coin sales for the Norweb estate. Shown is a small
part of the top deck.

Credit for these successes is shared by my staff members, including (alphabetically)
Liz Arlin, John Babalis, Rick Bagg, Mary Lou Barrett, Mark Borckardt, Sigrid Cameron, Annie Clark, Jennifer Douglass, Cathy Dumont, Jane Foran, Roberta French, Karl Hirtzinger, Mike Hodder, Christine Karstedt, Lee Liljedahl, Mary MacIntosh, Jennifer Meers, Rosalie Minnerly, Beth Piper, Doug Plasencia, Andrew Pollock III, Don Snyder, Barbara Thurston, Mary Tocci, Frank Van Valen, Gail Watson, Bill Winter, and dozens of others. Names and in many instances biographical notes can be found in auction catalogs and issues of *The Rare Coin Review* of the 1980s and 1990s.

Among the buyers in these sales was D. Brent Pogue of Dallas, Texas, a connoisseur par excellence who had started his numismatic interest in 1975. With his father Mack he carefully built a collection that emphasized high quality, with each coin being among the finest or the very finest of its kind.

THE NEW CENTURY

In March 2000 Bowers and Merena Galleries became a part of Collectors Universe, a public-stock company based in California. I left that firm in 2003 and signed on as a part of American Numismatic Rarities (ANR) in New Hampshire, under the management of Christine Karstedt.

The company was a gathering of eagles, so to speak, and included a number of former Bowers and Merena Galleries experts. Chris Karstedt, Melissa Karstedt, John Babalis, and I were among our licensed auctioneers.

In the space of a few years ANR became the second-largest rare-coin dealer worldwide (Heritage was first). What I liked to call the "dream team" handled an amazing number of major collections and rarities and had a good time doing it. I have many cherished memories of ANR and its accomplishments. One example from many: Richard A. Eliasberg, the younger of two sons of Louis Eliasberg, consigned the remarkable estate

Greeting bidders at an ANR auction.

collection of foreign coins formed by his father—completing the circle, as we had handled the Eliasberg American and related coins in 1982, 1996, and 1997.

We also published *The Numismatic Sun*, a magazine combining news, research articles, and coin offerings. The coin market was very strong in this era, and consignors as well as collectors enjoyed many successes.

The *Numismatic Sun* magazine covered many diverse subjects including research articles and market news.

Apart from auctions, we were major factors at conventions across the country, including giving educational and other programs. I continued to be deeply involved in numismatic research in addition to my other activities. In the meantime, all across the hobby more and more people became interested in research and writing—a remarkable change from when the Rittenhouse Society was formed in 1957 and I could name the dozen or so active people from memory.

Later, ANR merged with Stack's, then still later became Stack's Bowers Galleries. After that time activities were no longer centered in New Hampshire, which facility was devoted to research, consignor relationships, and graphics.

In 2003 I signed with Whitman Publishing to be their numismatic director, including research editor for the *Guide Book of United States Coins*. My continuing relations with the Joel and Charles Anderson families, Whitman president Mary Counts Burleson, publisher Dennis Tucker, editorial director Diana Plattner, sales guru Dawn Burbank, editors, artists, and others is very pleasurable. I could not ask for finer people as associates.

Although it has been a long time since I've been to foreign countries, I have given more programs at coin conventions than ever before. My "Joy of Collecting" column in *Coin World* has kept me busy ever since 1961! Today, that magazine is slightly different in format. There are weekly issues for which I write a half page, then 12 times a year there are monthly issues for which I write larger features. For *The Numismatist* my "Coins and Collectors" column has been a favorite for many years. In 2016 I was asked to do a separate additional feature each month, January to December—to tell the history of the American Numismatic Association in its 125th anniversary year.

Posing with fellow Whitman authors Bill Fivaz, Dave Sundman, and Ken Bressett in 2006.

Dinners in the evening after auctions and conventions give friends and associates a chance to discuss the day. Shown in a Baltimore restaurant are Evelyn Mishkin, David Sundman, Mary Counts Burleson, and myself. Whitman Publishing sets up a large display at most conventions.

My writing for Whitman Publishing has been a continuing stream of activity—creating or helping with dozens of books, from 96-page monographs to 900-page encyclopedias. The Whitman Web site (www.Whitman.com) has a listing of those in print at any given time.

In the early 21st century, advances in technology have an even greater dynamic effect on numismatics than in the past. Collectors and dealers can now buy and sell through personal computers and "smart" pocket phones. The latter can also take nice pictures of coins, say at a convention, and then send them by email instantly to anywhere in the world.

Elements of the Internet are in the plus column—especially instant communications and convenience.

Years ago it was typical for one of our auctions to have a room filled to standing- room-only, and to have to call for more chairs. Today, it is not unusual for our auctions or those of other auction houses to have only a few bidders attend in person. If anything, prices are *better* in the Internet era, as countless thousands of potential bidders worldwide can participate from the comfort of their homes and offices.

A case in point is our sale of the Dice-Hicks Collection of Hard Times tokens—one of the greatest ever formed. It was a public sale with our staff at the front table and our auctioneer at the podium. A stockholder in our company, who had been in numismatics since the 1950s (and, in fact, went to the Treasury Building in Washington in 1963 to buy silver dollars during the great release), was used to old-time auctions. He called and asked me, "How many people are in the audience?"

"Eight," I replied. "There had been nine, but one is now in the men's room."

"How are prices?" he then asked, in a worried tone.

"Double to triple estimate," I replied.

The number of active bidders online and participating in real time was probably more than could have been fit into a large room!

Today, we have live bidders from China, Switzerland, England, Russia, France, South America, and other distant places that would never have attended stateside auctions, or at least not very often. We have offices in Paris and Hong Kong, the gallery at 123 West 57th Street in New York City (in earlier decades the Stack's emporium), and the main office in Santa Ana, California. In New Hampshire the office is primarily research and writing, which I really enjoy—as much or more than ever.

The younger set, today defined as Millennials reaching the legal age of 18 in 2000 or later years, came into prominence a few years ago. Relatively few of them are interested in collectibles, a negative aspect. No longer is it interesting for a schoolkid to go home and in late afternoon sort through foreign stamps to put into an album. And, it has been a long time since the die-cut openings in Lincoln cent folders can be filled in with pocket change going back to 1909.

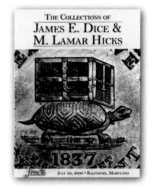

The Dice-Hicks Collection catalog.

Today, most buyers are men, occasionally women as well, who are in their forties or beyond and who enjoy numismatics as pleasing addition to their lives. Speaking of women, it is the distaff set—Kim Kiick and Ute Wartenberg—who are the executive directors of the American Numismatic Association and the American Numismatic Society respectively; Barbara Gregory is the longtime editor of *The Numismatist*; and Mary Burleson has been the president of Whitman Publishing for many years. A nonprofit group called Women In Numismatics (online at www.WomenInNumismatics.com) has members who promote the hobby among women; it was founded in 1991. Here in the New Hampshire office of Stack's Bowers Galleries, men (myself) are in the minority. Youngsters are still here in the hobby, but not in the numbers of a generation ago. Those who are active usually can be seen buzzing around on the Internet, not at coin conventions.

TODAY AS YOU READ THESE WORDS

Today, into the second decade of the second millennium, the basic coin market remains dynamic. With international monetary uncertainty, coins of gold and silver continue to be viewed as an ideal place to store money and to have hard assets. A serious collection or a safe deposit box filled with gold bullion coins does not have to be reported to anyone and can bought or sold without interference. It makes a lot of sense for people living in countries with unstable governments or currencies to buy coins and possibly store them in the United States.

For investors not concerned with the art, history, romance, and other attributes of traditional numismatics, certified coins continue to make it easy to buy and sell. Gradeflation, changing popularity, cherrypicking for quality, and other things discussed in this book are unknown to most such people. This is fine, as they provide a backup in the marketplace.

As for investors, "the higher the numerical grade on a coin, the better" is their philosophy. Modern Mint productions, nearly all of which are made to nearly or absolute perfection, appeal to them. Such coins are commonly sealed in holders marked 69 and 70. These are a delight to investors who know that such grades are the *crème de la crème* of coins, but do not realize that this status creates *rarity* when applied to certain older coins, not to modern ones.

In 2016 I ordered one each of the new Mercury dime, Standing Liberty quarter, and Walking Liberty half dollar struck in gold—a special production of the U.S. Mint. Upon examining each with a strong magnifier I could not find the slightest imperfection in any of them. The Mint calls them circulation strikes. PCGS and NGC call them Specimen Strikes.

Today the market is mixed. In 2017 and as 2018 begins the fields of colonial coins, tokens, and medals are strong. Some federal coins, especially gold and silver issues in higher grades, have been somewhat weak since 2014, although offerings of remarkable quality such as the Pogue coins have been exceptions.

Activity is strong across the board at currently adjusted prices. It takes time for those who bought in 2013 and in the several years before that to become acclimated to market prices as they are now. To paraphrase Herbert Hoover, "High prices are just around the corner." However, seeing around the corner usually involves waiting.

At any given time the future is uncertain across the board—in economics, politics, weather, you name it. Taken in the long term, a fine collection of rare coins, tokens, or medals, if gathered carefully and with knowledge, has always proved to be a fine financial investment. I cannot think of any exceptions! Today might be a good time to buy certain coins. If a coin needed for your collection cost $1,000 in the summer of 2013 but costs $750 today, it seems that now is a better time to buy. Only the future will tell.

The pleasure of reading and learning knows no market season. Today there are more good books in print than ever before. Taking advantage of this costs very little, and the rewards are beyond measure.

Dawn Burbank sells a book at the Whitman display at a coin convention.

A long line down the stairs to the Baltimore Convention Center to the door of a Whitman Coin & Collectibles Expo waiting for the opening bell to the dealer bourse.

On the other hand, books are no longer needed to publish certain information necessary for research. In the 1980s, this included such publications as city directories for New York or San Francisco and back issues of *The Numismatist* or the *American Journal of Numismatics*. It took me time and patience in the 1950s to build an almost complete set of the former and a complete set of the latter. Today the same information is available free on the Internet (or, for example, as a benefit of membership in the American Numismatic Association) and is also searchable.

Similarly, if I want to learn about 19th-century New York City dealer Gaston L. Feuardent I can tap a few keys. Years ago I would have to do a lot of searching. The *Dictionary of American Biography* and the *Encyclopædia Britannica*, which I once consulted constantly, are no longer used in book form. On the Internet the Newman Numismatic Portal (nnp.wustl.edu) offers a huge numismatic library that not only is available for free, but can be accessed on a cell phone—in case you are staying at the Del Coronado Hotel and want to see what a certain medal sold for in the Chapman brothers' sale of the Charles I. Bushnell sale in 1882. When I started in numismatics, such would have been called the wildest of improbable dreams!

Electronic coin images are of a superb quality not seen years ago. I can enjoy my collections of Civil War tokens and New Hampshire paper money, each stored in the bank, more than ever—exquisite high-definition color images are available instantly at the touch of a few keys.

An amazing part of numismatics is that today more people are interested in the art, history, and romance of numismatics than ever before, even though the total number of collectors is not what it was a couple of generations ago. There may not be as many coin buyers as there were then, but the number of specialists who really enjoy the hobby is greater than ever. Who would have thought that?

Beyond the electronic world, there are many other assets that can be tapped today. The American Numismatic Association in Colorado Springs offers not only *The Numismatist* magazine each month—now more information-packed than ever before, and interesting as ever—but also educational courses, a lending library by mail, and conventions. Summer Seminars are going strong and now span two week-long sessions instead of just one. Scholarships are often available for members of the younger set, with several hobby groups and coin dealers volunteering to pay the way for Seminar tuition, meals and lodging, and transportation for deserving candidates.

The ANA Hall of Fame gallery.

The vast bourse floor with hundreds of dealers at an ANA convention.

In modern times *The Numismatist* has contained more information and is more colorful than ever before.

Members of the Rittenhouse Society and guests at their annual breakfast meeting in 1989. Front row from left: "Bert" Bressett, Marilyn Fivaz (wife of Bill, who took this picture), and Walter Breen. Second row: Dave Bowers, Christie Bowers, Kenneth Bressett, and Margo Russell. Back row: Eric P. Newman, Craig Whitford, Bob Julian, Mike Hodder, and Grover Criswell.

Members of the Colonial Coin Collectors Club (www.ColonialCoins.org) at their gathering held in Boston on November 14, 2008.

Members and guests of Nova Nummus, a group of Maryland and Virginia numismatists who meet monthly to share camaraderie and, often, their latest acquisitions. Across America there are 500 or more local and regional clubs. This dinner was held in Baltimore in 2016.

In New York City the American Numismatic Society welcomes new members as well, especially those with a mind-set for traditional numismatic study and appreciation.

In 1955 there was just one specialized group for a specific discipline: the American Vecturist Society, founded in 1948, devoted to transportation tokens. This was followed in 1957 by a group of researchers and writers establishing the earlier-mentioned Rittenhouse Society. At that time and continuing for the next few years there were relatively few numismatists who engaged in writing and research and who regularly attended ANA conventions (so as to be at the annual meetings).

Today there are many societies, most of which issue magazines and hold annual meetings or conventions. These include the Barber Coin Collectors' Society (www.BarberCoins.org), Civil War Token Society (www.CWTSociety.com), Colonial Coin Collectors Club (www.ColonialCoins.org), Early American Coppers (www.EACS.org), John Reich Collectors Society (www.JRCS.org), Liberty Seated Coin Club (www.LSCCweb.org), Medal Collectors of America (www.MedalCollectors.org), Numismatic Bibliomania Society (www.CoinBooks.com), Token and Medal Society (www.TokenAndMedal.org), and the Society of Paper Money Collectors (www.SPMC.org). A few others could be mentioned as well.

It has been my experience that members of the above groups are the essential core of the hobby today. Some of these are dynamic subcultures. Nearly all who belong enjoy numismatics as a significant part of their lives, and most have been collecting or dealing for many years. I dare say, for example, that 90 percent of the members who belonged to the Colonial Coin Collectors Club 10 years ago remain members today. The drop-out rate of these societies is very low.

I would not trade today for the 1950s if it were possible to turn back the clock. Although numismatics has changed dramatically, I believe that today there is more opportunity for enjoyment and to form a great collection than ever before. There is also more opportunity to learn about every item in your collection. Indeed, that is the theme of this book.

Some of this is hardly new. In February 1929 in *The Numismatist* Harvey L. Hansen wrote this:

> A great many collectors simply collect for the pleasure of collecting and possessing. They are not to be criticized so much as they are to be sympathized with. They are losing the best part of collecting, that which comes from connecting their finds and possessions with the knowledge of the world in history, art, heraldry, geography, economics, and so forth. So many of us in our daily rush find time pressing and do not take the trouble to study seriously the pieces that come into our hands.
>
> Let me plead for a relatively small collection, every piece of which the collector is familiar with in a thorough manner. The question then arises, where shall we find out about the coins in our possession? The books you will need are not always available in local libraries. . . .
>
> In order to avail yourself of these offers I would suggest that some of the money you plan to spend for coins be spent for reference books. In other words, budget your spendable resources and follow a definite program. Not so romantic, perhaps, but productive of results. Books are necessary in order to make you a numismatist instead of a collector. *Research* is the word every collector should become familiar with and practice.

The above is déjà vu all over again, as Yogi Berra said.

There many fine people in numismatics today, as many if not more than in the past. At the most recent ANA convention I spent nearly all of my time talking with friends and clients, and not a single conversation was negative. As the Whitman Publishing display we had two sessions of "Spend an Hour with Ken and Dave," in which Ken Bressett and I interfaced with hundreds of happy people and signed books for them.

There is a lot in numismatics to look forward to. God willing, I hope to be a part of it for many years to come.

NOTES

CHAPTER 1

1. His collection passed to John H. Clapp in 1906, whose estate collection was sold to Louis E. Eliasberg in 1942. In a series of sales from 1982 to 1997 I had the honor, with staff, of cataloging the Eliasberg Collection and presenting it at auction.
2. The fact that toned coins could be desirable was emphasized by the New Netherlands Coin Company beginning in the early 1950s. Still, most buyers wanted bright coins, and dipping and polishing continued to be widespread. This changed in 1979 when my firm sold the Garrett Collection at auction, with many coins that had been kept intact since the 1870s and 1880s and never brightened. Across the board these beautiful, naturally toned coins sold for record prices.
3. This was the 1909 American Numismatic Association convention, held in Montreal. Henry Chapman was one of the most knowledgeable and respected dealers of his era.
4. Although the term Mint State had been used in the 19th century, it fell out of popularity, and by 1949 Uncirculated was nearly universally used.
5. Certain information is from Q. David Bowers's book, *The Expert's Guide to Collecting and Investing in Rare Coins*, Whitman Publishing,
6. Abe Kosoff and Kenneth Bressett wrote the description for the standards, based on input from extensive surveys and correspondence with dealers and collectors. I wrote the introductory material.
7. I must insert, however, that wines are now graded on a scale up to 100, but not without great criticism.
8. See the *Numismatist*, September 1990, for details.

CHAPTER 3

1. The Newcomb book published in 1944 dismissed the overdate feature as a die crack. In the early 1950s I studied an example and reported it, along with the belief that as it had plain hair cords the die had to have been made prior to 1838, when beaded hair cords were implemented. I was supported in this belief by experts of the era. Today the overdate feature is standard information.
2. Prices compiled by Whitman Publishing in January 2016; the *Guide Book of United States Coins* has a cover date one year ahead of the calendar date.
3. Today the most popular classic series is Morgan silver dollars, following the widespread availability of these at low cost after the great Treasury hoard release of 1962 and 1963.
4. Or mostly all. At the New England Numismatic Association convention on November 11, 2016, John Frost told me of a just-discovered new variety of 1876 circulation strike.
5. Daniel Carr, the operator of a private mint in Colorado, created some fantasy "1964-D" dollars by overstriking this date on some Peace dollars from decades earlier. He also made fantasy "1964" Franklin half dollars.
6. First illustrated and described by Robert Ezerman in *Errorscope*, November–December 1999.
7. From an e-mail to Whitman Publishing, December 4, 2013.
8. Correspondence between Garn Smith and Q. David Bowers, October 6, 1992.

9. In February 2005 this special variety was recognized by numismatists when one was sent by California collector Pat Braddick to NGC.

10. Today the unique 1870-S is on view as part of the loan Harry W. Bass Jr. Collection at the American Numismatic Association headquarters in Colorado Springs.

11. Other pattern strikings exist in copper and aluminum. See *United States Pattern Coins*, by Dr. J. Hewitt Judd, for more information.

12. Today the Saint-Gaudens home is a National Historical Site. Certain displays relate to coinage.

CHAPTER 4

1. Brother Jonathan was a popular term for America as part of the "family" of lands in the British empire, an early-day counterpart of Uncle Sam (England was sometimes known as John Bull).

2. Concerning the weight of the ship, William M. Lytle states 1,359 tons. Erik Heyl, *Early* pp. 63–64, gives an excellent account of the *Brother Jonathan*.

3. An excellent account and a passenger list of the *Brother Jonathan* are found in Don B. Marshall, 1978, pp. 157–167. Harry Rieseberg and A.A. Mikalow, *Fell's Guide to Sunken Treasure Ships of the World*, 1965 pp. 138–139, "The Deep-Fathomed Tomb of the *Brother Jonathan*," includes useful information.

4. A.k.a. St. George Point. A crag known as Jonathan's Rock is said to have administered the fatal hull puncture.

5. From Dudley L. McClure's, "$250,000 Face Value Now Worth Millions: Shipwreck Deposited Legal Tender Notes with Davy Jones, Recovery Still Possible?" *Numismatic News*, April 17, 1976. This writer suggested: "Probably because the *Brother Jonathan* losses in paper currency seemed to lack impact, the dollar totals consistently reached the public prints in terms of gold and silver coins." The same account mentioned "a few ingots which somehow were recovered, possibly having come ashore in trunks, boxes, crates, and other such flotsam from the wreck." The last had been publicized by John J. Ford Jr., and were later found to be modern fakes.

6. Beth Deisher, *Coin World*, September 14, 1992.

7. Detailed inventories of the shipwreck coins and ingots mentioned in this book may be found in *Lost And Found Coin Hoards and Treasures: Illustrated Stories of the Greatest American Troves And Their Discoveries*, Whitman Publishing.

8. *Lost and Found Coin Hoards and Treasures*, also gives details of other coin-laden ships for which I was not closely involved in the distribution of the coins.

9. Cited by W. Elliot Woodward in the sale of his collection of catalogs, October 13–18, 1884, lot 3317: "Coins and Medals, Friday, Oct. 14, 1856, by Bangs & Co., 13 Park Row, large sheet. The coins are known as the Crystal Palace Collection. Sheet of prices."

10. I purchased it from Mark Yaffe who found it in the possession of a Florida family. Dwight Porter did the restoration.

11. A popular 2016 book, *The Curse of Beauty: The Scandalous & Tragic Life of Audrey Munson, America's First Supermodel* by James Bone, tells her life story, which ended in tragedy. Two of her films were directed by Edwin Thanhouser, one of the most accomplished directors of the early 1900s.

12. Letter to the author, April 29, 1998.

13. Two other useful references include a brief listing (without much narrative and with no history) in *A Guide Book of U.S. Paper Money* (Friedberg EP numbers, which are widely used), and L. Fred Reed III's *Civil War Encased Stamps* (1995, S numbers).

14. A comprehensive reference book on these medals by David T. Alexander is available from the American Numismatic Society.

15. Betts acknowledged a debt to Joseph Addison's *Dialogues Upon the Usefulness of Ancient Medals*.

16. A listing of medal books for sale will be found on its website.

17. In July 1947 in *The Numismatist* Gould's article on counterstamped large cents was the first ever on this specialty and denomination.

CHAPTER 5

1. George Parish Jr., *American Journal of Numismatics*, August 1866; also, Attinelli, *Numisgraphics*, 1876, pp. 5, 85. In 1876, when Attinelli compiled his work, this was the earliest American coin sale he could find.

2. Attinelli, *Numisgraphics*, 1876, p. 82; later editions were also published.

3. See *American Journal of Numismatics*, May 1867.

4. The "clock excitement" to which he referred was the failure of the Jerome Clock Company and the great financial difficulty Barnum, as co-signer of the company's notes, had in 1856 (not 1860). Barnum garnered widespread public support for endeavoring to honor his obligations when many others would have filed for bankruptcy. In Bridgeport a mass meeting was held in his honor. Barnum was truly loved by the people of his time.

5. In later years some called him the "father of coin dealers." In reality he was a latecomer.

6. Years later, in 1887, when a new Mint director sought to learn details, he was amazed to find that the only records on hand were for a few 1868 Proof sets struck in aluminum. Everything else was "off the books."

7. Prime traveled widely in Europe and Africa. He maintained a summer home in Franconia, New Hampshire, where he wrote about angling, the scenic White Mountains, and other topics. His sister-in-law, Annie Trumbull Slosson, who was often on hand, was a well known entomologist and author.

8. Executive Documents, 2d Session 45th Congress, 1877-'78, Vol. 12. *Reports of the Comptroller of the Currency and Commissioner of Internal Revenue, John Knox*, December 3, 1877.

9. All issues of the *Numismatist* are available free online to ANA members. Reading through the earlier years of the magazine is a unique and informative experience.

10. In 1916 Matte Proof cents and nickels were offered as a pair and did not attract much interest.

11. I interviewed the Stack brothers and Abe Kosoff in depth in the 1950s and learned much about the flood of gold coins that the dealers bought. It was a win-win situation, it was thought at the time: bankers and government employees who sold coins earned money, dealers earned money on reselling them, and untold numbers of rare coins were preserved.

12. At that time John J. Ford Jr. had the rights to the Raymond work. He asked me if I wanted to edit the 19th edition, but as I was busy with my coin dealership I declined. No later editions were ever produced.

13. Information from interviews with James F. Kelly, Paul Wittlin, and French and Swiss bank officials.

CHAPTER 6

1. Lester Merkin, then a professional clarinetist, soon became a coin dealer and for a number of years conducted a store and held auctions in New York City, and was widely admired. Some years later when discussing numismatics, Joel J. Orosz said "Try to Get Your Money Back Werner" would have been a more appropriate slogan. As exposed by Eric P. Newman and Kenneth Bressett in their 1962 book on the 1804 dollar, Werner knowingly sold counterfeit rarities to A.J. Ostheimer III and refused to make a refund.

2. Later, mint errors became an important sector to the hobby. Leaders in this respect were Michael Kolman Jr., of the Federal Coin Exchange in Cleveland and Frank Spadone in New Jersey.

3. One day a close friend, Darlene A. Andersen, a journalism major, was reading an issue and admired my writing style. After some discussion she influenced me to learn a lot more about research and writing and pointed me in the direction of some sources she had found useful—one of many enlightenment points in my career.

4. Mint information is included in my *Guide Book of the United States Mint*, Whitman Publishing, 2016. Tom Jurkowsky and Dennis Tucker were of essential help in certain of my modern visits.

5. As another part of my life story I could say a lot about such instruments. I wrote several books on the subject, including *The Encyclopedia of Automatic Musical Instruments* (1972), and for a number of years was co-owner with Claes O. Friberg of the Mekanisk Musik Museum, a popular attraction we set up in a mansion at Vesterbrogade 150 in Copenhagen. I had special passes from the East German government to travel unrestricted behind the Iron Curtain to do research in music boxes and other instruments once made in quantity in Leipzig, Zeulenroda, Rudolstadt, and other cities there.

6. On the other hand the Pulitzer Prize is named for Joseph Pulitzer, the father of "yellow journalism" that was in its time a discredit to the writing profession.

7. For Stack's, Evelyn Mishkin helped edit the first two books and first two catalogs of the D. Brent Pogue Collection; for Whitman Publishing, she assisted on research trips to the Philadelphia Mint, the Bureau of Engraving and Printing, and the Treasury Department; for the Civil War Token Society, she edited and did the graphics for *Civil War Store Cards*, third edition; on my behalf, she did research at several historical sites in the East and much of the graphics for *The Postcards of Alphonse Mucha*.

8. On a trip to Moscow to visit with the USSR Ministry of Finance, which was soliciting ideas for the marketing of coins for the forthcoming 1980 Summer Olympic Games, I took a supply of 1776–1976 Proof sets to pass out. American participation in the games was later canceled by the U.S. government. Accompanying me on that trip were David Selby and Fletcher Waller Jr., executives of General Mills.

9. Bill Hawfield and I represented Bowers and Ruddy Galleries, John J. Ford Jr., acted for Christie's, David Tripp for Sotheby's, and Norman Stack for Stack's. The four of us greeted each other in the lobby of Garland Hall. This was alarming to Dr. Zdanis, provost of Hopkins and in charge of the presentations, who was super helpful to me later and I even had dinner at his home.

10. Carlson's offer of some choice 1794 copper cents to John W. Adams alarmed him, and Adams contacted the University, which told him that whatever Carlson was doing was okay.

11. This was printed in the next edition of the Judd book on pattern coins, of which Kosoff was editor at the time.

12. Some years later it was learned that many Gold Rush and related coins and ingots sold to dealers and collectors by Ford were modern fakes. I had been suspicious of some, but was surprised at the extent of the deception.

13. In one meeting with executives at the Smithsonian Institution I was told that the large section devoted to the National Numismatic Collection might be downsized so as to use the space for audio-animatronic action figures of baseball heroes, and that discussions with Walt Disney Enterprises were planned. That change never happened.

BIBLIOGRAPHY

Adams, John W. *United States Numismatic Literature. Volume I. Nineteenth Century Auction Catalogs.* Mission Viejo, CA: George Frederick Kolbe Publications, 1982.

— *United States Numismatic Literature. Volume II. Twentieth Century Auction Catalogues.* Crestline, CA: George Frederick Kolbe Publications, 1990.

Adelson, Howard. *The American Numismatic Society 1858–1958.* New York City, NY: American Numismatic Society, 1958.

American Journal of Numismatics. New York, NY, and Boston, MA: Various issues 1866 to 1912.

Attinelli, Emmanuel J. *Numisgraphics, or A List of Catalogues, Which Have Been Sold by Auction in the United States. . .* New York, NY: Published by the author, 1876.

Augsburger, Leonard D., and Joel J. Orosz. *The Secret History of the First U.S. Mint.* Atlanta, GA: Whitman Publishing, 2011.

Bowers, Q. David. Various titles in the Bowers Series. See www.whitman.com for selected titles.

Breen, Walter H. *Walter Breen's Complete Encyclopedia of U.S. and Colonial Coins.* New York, NY: Doubleday & Co., 1988.

Bressett, Kenneth E. (editor). *A Guide Book of United States Coins.* Racine, WI: Various modern editions. Earlier editions edited by Richard S. Yeoman.

— *A Guide Book of United States Coins, Mega Red,* 2015–2017. Pelham, AL: Whitman Publishing.

Bressett, Kenneth (editor). Narrative by Q. David Bowers. *The Official American Numismatic Association Grading Standards for United States Coins.* 7th ed. Atlanta, GA: Whitman Publishing, 2013.

C4 Newsletter. Journal of the Colonial Coin Collectors Club.

Carothers, Neil. *Fractional Money.* New York, NY: John Wiley & Sons, Inc., 1930.

Civil War Token Journal; earlier titles: *Journal of the Civil War Token Society* and *Copperhead Journal.* Published by the Civil War Token Society.

Coin World. Sidney, OH: Amos Press, *et al.*, 1960 to date.

Coin World Almanac. 7th edition. Sidney, OH: Amos Press, 2000.

Coinage Laws of the United States 1792–1894. Modern foreword to reprint by David L. Ganz. Wolfeboro, NH: Bowers and Merena Galleries, Inc., 1991.

COINage magazine. 1964 to date.

Colonial Newsletter. Published by the American Numismatic Society, New York, NY.

Crosby, Sylvester S. *The Early Coins of America.* Boston, MA: 1875.

Davis, Charles E. *American Numismatic Literature: An Annotated Survey of Auction Sales 1980–1991.* Lincoln, MA: Quarterman Publications, Inc., 1992.

Dickeson, Montroville W. *American Numismatical Manual.* Philadelphia, PA: J.B. Lippincott & Co., 1859. Also slightly retitled to *American Numismatic Manual* editions of 1860 and 1865.

Dictionary Catalogue of the Library of the American Numismatic Society. Boston, MA: G.K. Hall & Co., 1962.

Doty, Richard. *America's Money, America's Story.* Atlanta, GA: Whitman Publishing.

Dubois, William E. *Pledges of History: A Brief Account of the Collection of Coins Belonging to the Mint of the United States, More Particularly of the Antique Specimens.* Philadelphia, PA: C. Sherman, Printer, 1st ed, 1846: New York, NY: George P. Putnam, 2nd ed., 1851.

Eckfeldt, Jacob Reese, and William E. Dubois. *A Manual of Gold and Silver Coins of All Nations, Struck Within the Past Century.* Philadelphia, PA: Assay Office of the Mint, 1842.

— *New Varieties of Gold and Silver Coins, Counterfeit Coins, Bullion with Mint Values.* New York, NY: George P. Putnam, 1850 and 1851.

E-Sylum. The Internet publication of the Numismatic Bibliomania Society. Various issues.

Evans, George G. *Illustrated History of the United States Mint.* Philadelphia, PA: published by the author, editions of 1883, 1885, 1889, 1893.

Fivaz, Bill, and J.T. Stanton. *Cherrypickers' Guide to Rare Die Varieties,* 6th ed. Atlanta, GA: Whitman Publishing, 2015.

Garrett, Jeff, and Ron Guth. *100 Greatest U.S. Coins,* 4th ed. Atlanta, GA: Whitman Publishing, 2017.

Gobrecht Journal. Journal of the Liberty Seated Coin Club.

Historical Magazine, The. Morrisania, NY. Issues in Series 1, 2, and 3, 1850s and 1860s.

John Reich Journal. Journal of the John Reich Collectors Society.

Johnston, Elizabeth B. *A Visit to the Cabinet of the United States Mint, at Philadelphia.* Philadelphia, PA: J.B. Lippincott & Co., 1876.

Julian, R.W. *Medals of the United States Mint. The First Century 1792–1892.* El Cajon, CA: Token and Medal Society, 1977.

Longacre's Notebook. Journal of the Flying Eagle and Indian Head Cent Club (Fly-In Club).

Lupia, John N., III, www.numismaticmall.com.

Newman Numismatic Portal.

Numismatic News. Krause Publications, Iola, WI. Various issues 1950s to date.

Numismatic Scrapbook Magazine. Lee F. Hewitt, Chicago

Norton's Literary Letter. New York, NY: 1857–1860.

Numisma. House organ published by Édouard Frossard, 1877–1891.

Numismatic News. Iola, WI: Krause Publications, 1952 to date.

Numismatist, The. George F. Heath, Monroe, MI: American Numismatic Association.

Colorado Springs, CO (and other addresses), various issues 1888 to date.

Orosz, Joel J. *The Eagle That Is Forgotten: Pierre Eugène Du Simitière, Founding Father of American Numismatics.* Wolfeboro, NH: Bowers and Merena Galleries, 1988.

—"Robert Gilmor, Jr. and the Cradle Age of American Numismatics." *The Numismatist,* May 1990 (expansion of 1985 article in the *Rare Coin Review*).

Penny-Wise. Journal of Early American Coppers.

Raymond, Wayte. *Standard Catalogue of U.S. Coins and Tokens.* New York, NY: Wayte Raymond, 1942 to 1958.

Ruddy, James F. *Photograde.* Los Angeles, CA: Published by the author, 1970.

Shippee, Robert W. *Pleasure & Profit: 100 Lessons for the Building and Selling of a Collection of Rare Coins.* Atlanta, GA: Whitman Publishing, 2015.

Smith, A.M. *Illustrated History of the U.S. Mint.* Philadelphia, PA: A.M. Smith, 1881.

— *Coins and Coinage: The United States Mint, Philadelphia, History, Biography, Statistics, Work, Machinery, Products, Officials. . .* Also issued as *Visitor's Guide and History.* Philadelphia, PA: A.M. Smith, 1885.

Snowden, James Ross. *A Description of Ancient and Modern Coins in the Cabinet of the Mint of the United States.* Philadelphia, PA: J.B. Lippincott, 1860.

Stewart, Frank H. *History of the First United States Mint, Its People and Its Operations.* Philadelphia, PA: Frank H. Stewart Electric Co., 1924.

Taxay, Don. *Counterfeit, Mis-Struck, and Unofficial U.S. Coins.* New York, NY: Arco Publishing, 1963.

— *U.S. Mint and Coinage.* New York, NY: Arco Publishing, 1966.

Token and Medal Society Journal. Various addresses: 1960s to date.

Vermeule, Cornelius. *Numismatic Art in America,* 2nd ed. Atlanta, GA: Whitman Publishing, 2007.

Young, James Rankin. *The United States Mint at Philadelphia.* Philadelphia, PA: "For sale by Capt. A.J. Andrews," 1903.

CREDITS AND ACKNOWLEDGMENTS

Images are from many sources including John W. Adams, American Numismatic Association, American Numismatic Society, Richard August, Bancroft Library, Mary Counts Burleson, *Coin World*, Richard Doty, David Fanning, Jeff Garrett, Helen Gerth, Ira and Larry Goldberg, Heritage Auctions (www.ha.com), Wayne Homren, Christine Karstedt, George F. Kolbe, John Lupia and the Numismatic Mall, Syd Martin, Jennifer Meers, Clifford Mishler, Tom Mulvaney (photographs of National Numismatic Collection coins), New York Public Library, Joel J. Orosz, Donn Pearlman, Brent Pogue, Michael Printz, Roger Siboni, Robert Simpson, Pete Smith, Stack's Bowers Galleries and its antecedents, David M. Sundman, the U.S. Mint, and Whitman Publishing.

ABOUT THE AUTHOR

 **Q. David Bowers** has been in the rare-coin business since 1953, when he was a teenager. He is also a founder of Stack's Bowers Galleries. He has been central in showcasing at auction the greatest collections ever sold, including those of T. Harrison Garrett (for the Johns Hopkins University), Ambassador and Mrs. R. Henry Norweb, Virgil M. Brand, Louis E. Eliasberg, Harry W. Bass Jr., and D. Brent Pogue—accomplishments unmatched in professional numismatics. The author is a recipient of the Pennsylvania State University College of Business Administration's Alumni Achievement Award (1976); he has served as president of the American Numismatic Association (1983–1985) and president of the Professional Numismatists Guild (1977–1979); he is a recipient of the highest honor bestowed by the ANA (the Farran Zerbe Award); he was the first ANA member to be named Numismatist of the Year (1995); and one of only a few living people enshrined the Numismatic Hall of Fame (at ANA Headquarters in Colorado Springs).

Bowers is a recipient of the highest honor given by the Professional Numismatists Guild and has received more "Book of the Year Award" and "Best Columnist" honors given by the Numismatic Literary Guild than has any other writer. In July 1999, in a poll published in *COINage*, "Numismatists of the Century," Dave was recognized as one of six living people in this list of just 18 names.

He is the author of more than 50 books, hundreds of auction and other catalogs, and several-thousand articles including columns in *Coin World* (since 1961, the longest-running column in numismatic history) and the *Numismatist*.

Dave is a trustee of the New Hampshire Historical Society and a fellow of the American Antiquarian Society, the American Numismatic Society, and the Massachusetts Historical Society. He has been a key consultant for the Smithsonian Institution for decades, beginning with the curatorship of Dr. Vladimir Clain-Stefanelli, the Treasury Department, and the U.S. Mint, and is research editor of *A Guide Book of United States Coins*. For 18 years he was a guest lecturer at Harvard University. This is a short list of his honors and accomplishments. In Wolfeboro, New Hampshire, he is on the Board of Selectmen and is the town historian.

Kenneth Bressett, writer of the foreword, is a candidate for the one of the most accomplished numismatists of all time. He has carefully studied and enjoyed coins since the 1940s. Today he is well-known as the author of many books and articles, as a past president of the American Numismatic Association, is enshrined in the ANA Hall of Fame and is the recipient of its highest awards, and is the long-time editor of *A Guide Book of United States Coins*—a short list of what could be said. He and the author have been friends for many years and in 1957 were both co-founders of the Rittenhouse Society.

Index